Emma Raymond Pitman

Heroines of the Mission Field

Biographical sketches of female missionaries who have laboured in various lands

among the heathen

Emma Raymond Pitman

Heroines of the Mission Field

Biographical sketches of female missionaries who have laboured in various lands among the heathen

ISBN/EAN: 9783337195298

Printed in Europe, USA, Canada, Australia, Japan

Cover: Foto ©Lupo / pixelio.de

More available books at **www.hansebooks.com**

"THE WOMEN OF ALL LANDS FOR JESUS."

HEROINES

OF THE

MISSION FIELD.

BIOGRAPHICAL SKETCHES

OF

FEMALE MISSIONARIES WHO HAVE LABOURED IN VARIOUS
LANDS AMONG THE HEATHEN.

BY

MRS. EMMA RAYMOND PITMAN,

Authoress of "Vestina's Martyrdom," "Profit and Loss," "Margaret Mervyn's Cross," &c.

LONDON MISSIONARY SOCIETY'S EDITION.

CASSELL, PETTER, GALPIN & CO.:

LONDON, PARIS & NEW YORK.

TO

ROBERT ARTHINGTON, Esq.,

WHOSE PROMPT AND MUNIFICENT EFFORTS FOR THE EVANGELISATION OF THE

"DARK CONTINENT,"

ESPECIALLY IN THE REGIONS AROUND LAKE TANGANYIKA,

HAVE SO LARGELY CONTRIBUTED TO THE ESTABLISHMENT AND SUPPORT OF

MISSIONS IN CENTRAL AFRICA,

THIS VOLUME

Is respectfully Dedicated,

BY PERMISSION.

CONTENTS.

	PAGE
Women's Work in the Mission Field	1
Story of the Zenana Mission	21
Mrs. Mary Moffat, of the Kuruman, South Africa	42
Mrs. Maria Regina Christina Gobat, of Jerusalem	67
Mrs. Hannah Catherine Mullens, of Calcutta	81
Mrs. Emily C. Judson, of Burmah	96
Mrs. Mary Williams, of the South Seas	121
Miss Fidelia Fiske, of Persia	140
Mrs. Mary M. Ellis, of the South Seas	160
Mrs. Dorothy Jones, of the West Indies	175
Mrs. Jane Chalmers, of Rarotonga and New Guinea	186
Mrs. Anna Hinderer, of Ibadan, West Africa	198
Mrs. Sarah Smith, of Madras	215
Mrs. Rebecca Wakefield, of Ribé, East Africa	221
Miss Susan B. Higgins, of Yokohama, Japan	241
Mrs. Hannah Kilham, of Sierra Leone	252
Mrs. Mary Hope, of Kunnunkulum, India	267

WOMAN'S WORK IN THE MISSION FIELD;

OR, THE SPECIAL MINISTRY OF CHRISTIAN WOMEN
TO THE HEATHEN.

"The rights of woman! what are they?
The right to labour and to pray;
The right to comfort in distress;
The right, when others curse, to bless;
The right to love whom others scorn;
The right to comfort all who mourn;
The right to shed new joy on earth;
The right to feel the soul's high worth;
The right to lead the soul to God,
Along the path the Saviour trod:
Such, woman's rights! and God will bless,
And grant support, and give success."

THE Mission-field demands various instrumentalities, and different classes of workers. Preachers, teachers, catechists, native pastors, translators, printers, handicraftsmen, and last, but not least, female missionaries, are all needed to teach the way of salvation to those who sit in heathen darkness. Each class of workers finds its own peculiar mission; but rarely can it succeed in doing the work of another class. Devoted men, who counted not their lives dear unto them, have laboured for over eighty years among the savage and heathen people of the earth, but only in a few countries have they been able to reach the women. The men and youths have listened to the Word of Life attentively,

B

and often lovingly, but in too many instances the *female* population has been prevented from listening to the preacher's words. It is true that in those cases where the missionary was accompanied by his wife, *she* has laboured among the females, conveying to them the precious, soul-transforming truths, and this with so much success that numbers of heathen wives and mothers have cast in their lot with the Christians. Especially is this true with regard to India, China, Turkey, Egypt, Palestine, Japan, and Persia. In all these countries it has been found by actual experience that the evangelisation of the women must depend upon womanly agency to a very large extent. Male missionaries are denied access to the zenanas, harems, seraglios, and inner apartments, among all Eastern homes. They must not, in the majority of instances, even refer to the *existence* of the female members of the family; as, for instance, in India, where it would be resented as a studied insult, were a male visitor, while chatting with the gentlemen of the family, to inquire after the health of the wife and mother. These dwellers in the zenanas and harems only hear the far-off echoes of the Gospel; and not then, unless the men of the family judge it proper or wise that they should do so. But *ladies* bearing the Gospel message are always welcomed, listened to attentively, and besought to come again. This work of teaching *heathen women* to come to Jesus, is emphatically one which belongs to *Christian women*. It is a high and holy part of women's ministry, and wherever tried has been found eminently successful.

To see the *necessity* of woman's work in missions, we need only consider the lot and labours of an ordinary missionary preacher. He must give himself chiefly to the work of preaching the Gospel, because that is the principal agency, as well as his first duty. But suppose that the work of conversion goes on, and that converts are brought into the fold. Their first demand is for education; then for the civilisation of themselves and their homes; then for instruction in various trades; then for literature. Who is capable of meeting all these varied demands? On a well-filled mission-station where three or four missionaries are maintained, a division of labour is carried out; but in all these labours the exertions of the *wives* of the missionaries are counted upon, and arranged for. But the share which falls to the lot of the "weaker vessel" is often such that bode health and life are sacrificed under the strain. Especially does this result follow where a missionary and his wife are alone on a station. An American writer, treating of this matter, says : " A missionary and his wife together can do great things, but they cannot do everything. Try it at home. Lay out here such work as is done there. Let a man be pastor of the church, whether in village or city, and let the minister's wife, with her home, her children, her uncounted cares, and her imperfect health, be the chief teacher in the day-school of the neighbourhood. Let that school be kept on the minister's ground, and let his wife have the personal care of a great part of the pupils. Let the minister's house, too, be the apothecary's shop for the country round. Let the minister's wife help her husband in teaching on the Sabbath, and let her travel with him sometimes in the travelling season, making, not pastoral calls, but visitations to churches far remote ; or, if she cannot go with him, let her have the charge of affairs while he is away. Try such an experiment. Call a minister, with the understanding that such work shall devolve on his wife. Conceive, if you can, that such an arrangement is fairly entered into, and common humanity will quickly ask whether some one else could not be provided to do part of the work. The experiment is being tried again and again in Asia; and that same question is the one that is before us now. The missionaries' wives do as much of the work as they can, but they do it often at the expense of health, if not of life."

Then, not only Oriental customs, but the overwhelming nature of the work itself, renders it necessary that female labourers should be set apart to do it. If they be not forthcoming, who shall fill the gap? Alas! no men can fill this gap. The women and children form in these heathen lands, as with ourselves, two-thirds of the population; and while free, open, confiding conversation is forbidden with men, *women* will always win their confidence. But these women must be single—free from the cares and toils of home and family duties, consecrated wholly to the work of teaching, visiting, and ministering.

A further argument for the *necessity* for such an agency, lies in the fact that Roman Catholicism largely employs the aid of women, even among the recently-converted adherents of Protestant churches, and sets them to neutralise the work done by European missionaries, by winning over the women and children. This course was recently adopted in Madagascar. Catholic Sisters of Mercy caught hold of the mothers, wives, sisters, and daughters of the Christian converts, and made much mischief. Their success was mainly due to the fact that the natives *preferred* to have *female* teachers for their wives and daughters; and while the missionaries' wives did all they could, they could not cope with the full need which prevailed. But the London Missionary Society resolved to fight the foe with their own weapons, and appointed Miss Bliss to labour in the capital, dealing especially, of course, with the women and girls. And this instance is only one out of many that could be quoted.

The *channels* into which woman's work in the mission-field should be directed are these:—(1) Zenana visiting; (2) teaching the children; (3) instructing the females in womanly arts, as well as in religious matters; (4) affording medical advice and assistance; (5) teaching singing, and using generally the ministry of song. These are the especial ways in which woman can deal with those of her own sex in heathen lands; and such work is most womanly. No one who engages in it steps out of her proper sphere in the slightest degree. It is not unwomanly to do such work as this among the heathen; the memories of the sainted women whose lives are given in this volume, negative such an idea. It *would* be unwomanly to stand idle in Christ's kingdom, to refuse to help our perishing sisters, but to obey the great command is most Christ-like. Says a lady-worker who is engaged in the mission field: "Never has the old, old story seemed so sweet to me as when I have told it to those dark-faced and darker-minded heathen women to whom it was not 'old.' As I have watched the lighting up of those dull faces, when first their hearts took in the wonderful news of a Saviour *even for them*, as I have listened to their eager questionings, I have realised the blessedness of the work. Not many months ago I stood beside the bedside of one who had heard of Jesus, and had come to Him; and as the shadows of death were gathering, and I bent to catch the faintly-whispered words, she said, 'It is all peace, peace. I have nothing to do now, only to wait for Jesus to come and take me home.' Was it not worth a sacrifice to have taught one poor helpless heart so to rest upon Jesus, to have helped one soul to stand at the gateway of eternity without fear?"

Female medical missionaries are most urgently needed among heathen women. In India, and other Eastern countries, the numbers of sick women and children are enormous—a percentage in proportion to the population which is frightfully great. Statistics prove that thousands of the women die yearly, from neglect or ignorant treatment, during illness, and from the confinement in the dull, close, unhealthy zenanas. Female medical missionaries can enter where no medical *man* may venture, and convey life, health, and comfort, by enjoining those simple rules of hygiene which are so well known to educated Englishwomen, in conjunction with the required medical treatment. A medical missionary, writing home from India, says: "If an epidemic is raging, the women are left to the ignorance and barbarity of the native servants. Too often, alas! they are forsaken by all, and simply left alone to die." Another writes: "The death-rate among women and children is enormous; and constant sickness is one of the greatest hindrances to the zenana missionary." Another writes: "Among the many zenanas which I have been allowed to visit, I have never entered one where they did not bring a sick child or woman entreating my assistance, and what would I not have given to have had the requisite knowledge to have prescribed medicine for them, or to have been able to have sent to them a medical lady, who would indeed have been 'a friend in need.'" Miss Beilby, who is carrying on a successful medical mission at Lucknow, writes: "I am thankful for the additional knowledge I gained while at home, because I am of greater power for good than I was before; and if I have more medical knowledge to distinguish case from case, and to give to each its proper treatment, surely this will tell in a deeper, higher sense." Others have borne similar testimony, which might be quoted were it not for lack of space. But without question, it is abundantly clear that this medical mission agency is destined to play an important part in the christianising of Eastern females. And it is encouraging to know that the various female missionary societies are providing this agency. They are sending out, as funds and opportunities permit, young ladies who have received a medical education, in order that they may work in this great cause. A recent missionary journal stated that there were, during 1879, as many as twelve ladies studying medicine at the London medical schools, in order to go out to the heathen.*

The various missionary societies interested specially in providing for heathen women are as follow:—The Society for Promoting Female Education in the East, founded in 1834; Ladies' Association (of Scotland) for Heathen Women, founded in 1843; Ladies' Committee for Ameliorating the Condition of Heathen Women, formed in connection with the Wesleyan

---

* A Zenana Medical Mission Hospital and Training School for Ladies has lately been opened in London, and five pupils are already preparing themselves to labour as female medical missionaries in the East.

Missionary Society in 1859; Indian Female Normal School and Instruction Society, founded in 1861; Ladies' Committee for Female Missions in India, Africa, China, and the East, in connection with the London Missionary Society, formed in 1875; Association of Ladies, connected with the Baptist Missionary Society for the support of Zenana Work in India, formed in 1867; Ladies' Association, connected with the Society for the Propagation of the Gospel, founded in 1866; Women's Missionary Association of the Presbyterian Church of England; various Women's Foreign Missionary Societies of America, formed at different dates; the Berlin Ladies' Society; and other Continental Societies.

It is somewhat difficult to calculate the number of female labourers now in the missionary field, sent out and equipped by these various societies. Nevertheless, we can give some approximate idea of the number by quoting the statistics of those societies with which we are acquainted. The London Missionary Society, during 1879, employed twelve English ladies; the Indian Female Normal School and Instruction Society had fifty-two English ladies, besides thirty-one trained native teachers, and about seventy native Bible women; the China Inland Mission employed ten ladies, besides ten native Bible-women; the Society for Promoting Female Education in the East had thirty-five English ladies, besides about two hundred native trained teachers; the Ladies' Association in connection with the Society for the Propagation of the Gospel had thirty-four ladies in the work, besides forty-three native teachers; the Association of Ladies connected with the Baptist Missionary Society had nine European ladies engaged, besides about thirty-three native Bible-women and teachers; while the various American missionary societies had about two hundred ladies engaged in the different fields of labour. Of this large number, it may be interesting to know that quite fifty were labouring in the Turkish Empire. We cannot speak certainly of the numbers employed by the other societies, but enough has been said to prove that, all over Christendom, Christian women are waking up to the sense of their responsibilities, as far as missionary work is concerned; and not they alone, but others who are known to occupy foremost positions in the ranks of philanthropy and thought. Professor Monier Williams says: "The missionary band must carry their ark persistently around the Indian home, till its walls are made to fall, and its inner life exposed to the fresh air of God's day, and all its surroundings moulded after the pattern of a pure, healthy, well-ordered Christian household, whose influences leaven the life of the family and the nation from the cradle to the grave. My belief is that until a way is opened for the free intercourse of the educated mothers and women of Europe who understand the Indian vernaculars, with the mothers and women of India, in their own homes, Christianity—at least in its purer forms—will make little progress, either among Hindoos or Mohammedans."

Of the *success* of this new missionary agency there can be no doubt. Cases, testimonies, and proofs can be adduced by the score to show that the Lord of the vineyard is abundantly owning and blessing the labours of His servants. These lady missionaries, together with their trained native helpers, penetrate where male missionaries would be rudely and resolutely denied admittance. They are also untrammelled with the cares and labours incidental to the household and family, health and time being free from the strain which these duties bring. They also live, as far as possible, with the married missionaries of various societies, and thus enjoy all the protection, comfort, and help which comes from a united social life. As the result of the sending forth of this class of labourers, many thousands of degraded, down-trodden, uncared-for heathen women have been brought into our Christian sisterhood, have been lifted out of the mire of heathen serfdom, and have recognised with grateful emotion the truth that they, *even they*, are "one in Christ Jesus" with the good and blest of other lands. What may not be expected when the wives and mothers of heathendom rise from their thraldom, and embrace the pure faith of Christ? Napoleon once sadly said, "France wants mothers;" and the educated, Christianised Hindoo thoughtfully echoes the cry. It has been found next to useless to deal with the sons and daughters while the mothers retain all their old heathen proclivities and superstitions; and the husband is unconsciously influenced by his heathen wife, far more, sometimes, than he would like to own. So, amid all the agencies brought to bear in converting the world to Christ, this one has arisen as a helpmeet to all the rest.

Mrs. S. A. Wheeler, American missionary in Armenia, says: "It was quite hard to get at the women at first; they did not come to see us; they were afraid of us. They said we were wicked women. 'Do you not know that these women that read are leather-faces? See their uncovered, shameless faces. Do you wish to be like them?' their priests would say, to keep them from coming to us. And when we went into the streets they would call to one another, 'The women who wear washbowls on their heads are coming.' Then the boys would gather at the corners, and sometimes a stone would go whistling by us. Sometimes a stream of dirty water would come down from a high roof, and we would just escape an unpleasant shower-bath." But after a little while, on gaining access to these women, Mrs. Wheeler's intelligence, Christian courtesy, and refinement began to tell, and the poor creatures came to acknowledge their own ignorance in terms such as these. "We are only donkeys; we do not know how to read and write, as these women do." "Why are these women honoured so much more than we are? Why, even our own husbands honour them! We will learn to read, and then we, too, shall have a place as equals with our husbands." Then came a sowing-time, which was, as all sowing-times are, a season of trial, hardship, and partial darkness. But soon the joyous harvest-time came too. One after another, these dirty, repulsive, ignorant, prejudiced

Armenian women were drawn by the attractive power of the cross of Christ. Mrs. Wheeler gives the following beautiful instance: "Among these strange ones comes a poor woman, who seizes your hands, and with tears flowing fast down her withered cheeks says, 'Teach me how to pray.' She has been to Jerusalem on a long pilgrimage. She will tell you that she has looked into the Saviour's sepulchre, and wept as Mary did; that she has stood on Calvary's mountain, and seen the cross upon which her Saviour died, and has taken her hard-earned money to the priest to have a ticket to heaven printed with indelible ink upon her arm. The image of Christ upon the cross has been pricked into her quivering flesh, to teach her that her Redeemer has suffered for her. What more could this heroic woman do? Is she not safe? She thought so. Her neighbours looked upon her as holy—as one to be honoured. But the Bible has been read in her home, and old Hadji Anna has heard, 'Blessed are the pure in heart, for they shall see God.' She had not found Him who could purify the heart. So the missionary has the golden privilege of leading her to the fountain where she may wash and be clean; and now she is casting her crown at His feet, who redeemed her with His own precious blood."

Another missionary collected five or six little girls together on the housetop of an Armenian house, and taught them until they were all converted and trained to go out as teachers into the surrounding villages. This solitary, humble little housetop school was the nucleus and beginning of the Female Department of the Armenia College, from which nearly *two hundred* trained teachers have gone out to labour for their dark, uncared-for sisters. Since then, in this part of the great mission-field, about 1,000 girls were at one time receiving instruction, and, out of 1,200 members of Christian churches, over 400 were women.

Mrs. Alcock, who is labouring in Ceylon in connection with the Society for Promoting Female Education in the East, writes: "The girls' school at Telekada is doing well. Two of the children are anxious about salvation, and we trust to see them bright Christians. We had a very interesting baptism last month, at Baddagama; a mother and her two daughters came out on the Lord's side, and promised to serve Him. The mother is very earnest, and gives great promise of future usefulness. Perhaps she will become a Bible-woman to the degraded mothers and daughters of this village."

Miss Challis, of the same society, writing from Syria, says: "When we come to consider that there are thirty girls under our care, hourly to be taught and trained, not only for this life, but for eternity, and that one hasty word or rash action on our part may do more harm than years of toil may undo, it makes the responsibility too great. Then it is so sweet to hear these comforting words, 'My grace is sufficient for thee.' What should we do without that all-sustaining grace? Many of the girls have left school, mostly to become teachers elsewhere."

Mrs. Soondrum, of the London Missionary Society, reports thus: "Those girls to whom I teach singing and needlework influence their mothers and relatives to meet them at a certain place, when I teach them to read and write, as well as speak to them about the salvation of their souls. I have met with much opposition from heathen priests, who have visited the houses which I visit, and have said many things against my coming, and injurious to my work. I am glad, however, they have not prevented people from receiving my visits."

Miss Heward, of the same society, writes from Calcutta: "My work has been particularly interesting of late. One of my pupils has become very anxious to be baptised, but at present she has not sufficient courage to speak to her husband on the subject. He is an uneducated man and irreligious, and he beats her if he finds her reading."

Miss Bear, also of the same society, writes of her work at the hospital, Shanghai, China: "My work in the hospital, like the country visiting, is a sowing of the seed broadcast, with little apparent result hitherto. I go in sometimes and find from one to twenty women already there, the majority perfect strangers, and knowing nothing whatever of Gospel truth. I sit down and quietly converse with those nearest to me, and, after mutual friendly inquiries, I speak to them as simply as possible of the merciful and loving Father."

Miss Rowe, of this society, writes from Hong-Kong thus: "We had a most interesting baptism last month—an elderly woman, with her husband, two daughters, daughter-in-law, and grandchild. I have been going to the house occasionally to teach the women ever since I came to Hong-Kong, and latterly the younger women walked every day to my school to read the Gospels, and in the evening went home and taught their mother what they had heard in the Scripture class. The old father was ready for baptism some months ago, but he preferred waiting for his wife and daughters—a new feeling in a Chinaman."

Miss Condon, in connection with the Indian Female Normal School and Instruction Society, writes from Calcutta: "The native training class, which constitutes an important part of our work, consists of ten pupils, native Christian women, mostly new converts, all of whom are very intelligent, and some show considerable ability. They are taught daily in the Bible, and secular subjects; and they take part in the teaching in the central school."

Mrs. Blackett, of the same society, writes from Barrackpore: "Though the sound of the Gospel has gone into all the earth, there are hundreds and thousands of the women of India who have not yet heard its faintest echo, and are at present altogether out of the way of doing so unless taken by *women* into their homes; and it has come before me very forcibly that it is now no longer because the women are hard to get at, but just from *the simple want of some one to go to them.* When I go and talk to them and assure them that I am *a woman* like themselves—which many of them have great doubts about, never having seen an English lady before—they throng around me and listen to my words. They are always interested in hearing that English ladies think about them and pray for them; but how often have I been saddened, after coming to the end of my story, to hear them say, 'We are only poor, ignorant women; we know nothing; how can we? we have never been taught.' Just as we were leaving a village the other day a Hindoo gentleman came and begged me to go and visit his ladies. I went, and found about thirty-three women assembled together from the neighbouring houses. . . . Has not the time come when evangelisation among the women of India may be begun?"

Miss Blandford, of this society, writing from Trevandrum, says: "We have between us 162 houses open for visitation and Bible reading; this includes the palaces, and other places to which I go alone. Go where we will, we find open doors and willing listeners. I am so sure that though the bread is cast as it were upon the waters, it will be found to our great joy after many days."

The Society for the Propagation of the Gospel has four good girls' schools in Burmah, and one in Japan, beside a large number of others in mission-fields more occupied. Mrs. Wright, in a communication from Japan, says: "Hitherto the work has been almost entirely limited to the men, as the missionaries, unless they are married, have no opportunity of getting the women around them; but we have such a good opening that we feel every day more and more the golden time we are losing. I am engaged every day in the school from nine till half-past three o'clock, and am so tired when I return that I can do but very little. It requires some one to give their whole time to it, and to studying the language."

Miss L. Mitchell, of the China Inland Mission, writes thus:—"If some of our dear friends in England could have seen the crowds of poor Chinese to-day, as they for the first time heard the story of the Cross, they would have been constrained to leave all to follow Jesus, and to say, 'Here am I! send me.' Think of the millions who die in sin; no joy here, no heaven there; think of the great harvest-field of famishing souls who almost ask you to come."

A lady in connection with the American Women's Foreign Missionary Society has opened a mission-school in Cyprus under encouraging auspices. A Bible-woman visits among the Druses and Maronites near Mount Lebanon. The poor women visited say: "We fear that we are nothing but sinners; and we are thirsting to hear the Word of God: we wish you would come often and teach us." Other ladies are labouring in Italy, Mexico, Burmah, South Africa, and the Mauritius, with abundant and cheering results. We might quote page after page of reports from their letters home, but forbear for lack of space. We will just add that the heathen women of Central Africa are, like the rest of their sisters all over heathendom, now looking for, and expecting the Gospel. A little story, which comes to us from Lake Nyassa, proves how implicitly they trust the white man, and how willingly they work for the benefit of those who bring to them the new Evangel: "When the missionary steamer owned by the mission of the Free Church of Scotland was to be placed on Lake Nyassa, the leader of the expedition applied to the chief of the tribe for reliable help to carry the craft round the Murchison Cataracts. The chief responded by sending 800 *women*—a compliment, certainly, to the trustworthiness of the sex. Some of them came fifty miles, bringing their provisions with them. These women were entrusted with the whole, when if a single portion of the steamer had been lost, the whole scheme would have failed. They carried it in 250 loads in five days, under a tropical sun, seventy-five miles, to an elevation of 1,800 feet, and not a nail or a screw was lost. They trusted the Englishman, asking no question of wages, and received each six yards of calico, and, for the sake of being liberal, each was given an extra yard."

Does this work pay? The question has often been asked, and answered to the full satisfaction of all who ask sincerely. Still, it may not be unwise to adduce a few testimonies by way of answer now.

Dr. Eitel, of the London Missionary Society, writing of the missionary labourers and agencies in Hong-Kong, China, says: "To sum up then, we find that the Protestant missions of Hong-Kong have brought together 2,200 native Christians, formed in permanent churches, with regular administration of the ordinances, besides which they are maintaining 563 native children, under daily instruction in the Word of God. As all these schools have voluntarily placed themselves under Government inspection, I can refer you to the impartial testimony of the Government School Inspector, as published in last year's *Gazette,* where full credit is given to the regularity and thoughtfulness of the teaching given in these schools. As to the native Christians, with all their weakness of Christian character, I confidently believe that every one of these native churches will stand a comparison with an average Christian church of Europe or America in Christian earnestness and Christian life." Mrs. Williamson, of the United Presbyterian Church, writing from Chefoo, China, says: "At intervals, all during the day, I spoke to different crowds of women of our Heavenly Father and His Son our Lord and Saviour Jesus Christ. I never spoke to more interested audiences of women, who for the first time heard the Word of Life. Often the women got so interested that they sent out some crying child, who disturbed them in hearing far more than it did me in speaking. Sometimes the men are averse to the women taking our drugs, because they say in that way we get their hearts to go after us. In one district, where a great many have lately become Christians, they said it was entirely done through our giving medicines. Under the sense of my own nothingness, I felt my whole being roused in prayer that God would send out more women to teach these millions of immortal beings; and under that sense of need I would implore you, O ye Christian women of Scotland, to think of the claims of your sisters in heathen lands. Women are one half of the human race; there ought therefore to be as many women as men in the field, especially in such countries as China, where only women can properly and powerfully teach women. At Tei-nan-foo I examined and prescribed for 342 women and girls during our stay; at Wei-Hein I prescribed for 254 women and children; I pray you, therefore, to commend this matter to my fellow-countrywomen at home." To take the whole of China, we find it stated by competent judges that, as the result of all missionary effort, there are now 15,000 communicants and 50,000 native Christians. Of these, seventy-three are native ordained pastors, seventy-seven are colporteurs, and ninety-two are Bible-women. During 1876 the contributions of these native Christians averaged about 14s. 6d. per head, as proofs of their sincerity and sacrifice.

Statistics are sometimes looked upon by doubters as uncertain and unreliable, but unless we do quote statistics it will be impossible fully to answer the question as to whether mission-work *pays*. We will quote the statistics of only one society—the London Missionary Society—which is very catholic in its spirit, its fundamental principle being, "not to send Presbyterianism, Independency, Episcopacy, or any other form of church order, but the glorious Gospel of the blessed God to the heathen." And we think it will be seen that, after making all deductions which prejudice or criticism may dictate, there still remain great and glorious paying results. This society was founded in the year 1796; it has therefore been in existence eighty-six years. As the results of the missionary operations of its agents among the different heathen nations to which they had been sent, they report in 1879 the following grand totals:—Native ordained missionaries, 357; native preachers, 4,195; church members, 100,578; native adherents, 367,170; boys under instruction, 69,467; girls at school, 15,280; while the contributions of these native churches towards the support of the missions among themselves amounted in 1878 to the magnificent sum of £14,868. And these are the results following only the labours of *one* society! Surely, then, *the vast aggregate of all the results, following the labours of all the missionary societies,* will furnish an abundant and overwhelming answer to the question, *Does mission-work pay?* More than all that can be put into statistics, "in ten thousand forms the missionary's influence shows itself—in the physical aspect of the people, in the birth-rate and death-rate, in dress, houses, public buildings, domestic life, employments, education and literature, law and social order, peace between rival factions and tribes, commercial intercourse with other nations, interest in and acquaintance with the history and proceedings of people of other lands, but above all in character and life, in Christian tone of whole communities, and in unfaltering trust in Him who conquered death."

Who will go to engage in this noble, blessed work? Not every one can. This high privilege cannot belong to all, nor even to many who long and pray to be engaged in it. Many have glowed with the desire to work for Christ in the foreign mission field, but have by unavoidable circumstances been kept back. Such look sadly at the work of others, and regret that they too are not summoned into the vineyard. Let such remember God's message to David, when he was not permitted to build the temple: "Thou didst well in that it was in thine heart." Remember also the words of our own Milton, that while

"Thousands at His bidding speed,
And post o'er land and ocean without rest,
They also serve who only stand and wait."

But such as these—denied active service in the missionary field—can give money, effort, and prayer to speed those who do go forth. How many ladies are there who, although they cannot resign all and go to the heathen, yet are blessed with material wealth. *These* could *maintain* a lady missionary in some approved field of

c

labour, and kindly sustain the hands of the active worker by prayer, correspondence, and friendly help. Such could labour in the field *by proxy*, thus constituting themselves joint stewards of the gifts of Providence. And when earth fades away, and creation melts before the eye of Him who will sit on "the great white throne," will it not be better to have the benediction of the Judge than His frown? Will it not then be more comforting to reflect that, instead of hoarding up wealth and increasing investments here and there, the wealth has been *conscientiously taxed* for the support of God's servants who are labouring among the far-off heathen? God's heroes and heroines "in that day" will be, not the magnates of banking establishments, nor the millionaires of commerce, nor "the dwellers in ceiled houses," nor the titled ones of this life, *but those who have laboured, spent, suffered, and witnessed for Him*. What a wonderful revolution of public opinion will come to pass in that day when the "King's sons and daughters" shall stand revealed! He, or she, who was only a missionary " will shine forth as the sun in the kingdom of the Father;" the unlettered and unknown child of God who laboured as a tract-distributor or village preacher; the painstaking but sorely-tried Sunday-school teacher who sowed beside all waters, scarcely daring to hope for a blessing, so unpromising was the soil; the much-taxed pastor and minister who had often to echo despairingly the cry, "Who hath believed our report?"—all these will have a glorious recognition and coronation, while those who laboured for earth, grubbed for gold, worshipped mammon, and despised Christ, will wake up to a bitter sense that they have, by serving and gaining the world, *lost all*.

One question remains, and then we have done. When we came to Christ, helpless, sinful, clinging and trusting to Him alone for salvation, did we not in return *surrender* ourselves to Him? Did we not echo the words—

"Were the whole realm of nature mine,
That were a present far too small;
Love so amazing, so divine,
Demands *my soul, my life, my all*."

And did not that surrender involve everything which we possessed—money, health, time, service, talents, opportunities, yea, even life itself? It is, however, enough to know that "the Master hath need" of us, and that he *permits* us to be co-workers with Him. Will not the ladies of Christian Britain respond to the appeal rising from millions of their sisters in heathendom, and go forth "without the camp," bearing, if necessary, the reproach, but bearing also the lamp of life?

> "Shall we, whose souls are lighted
>   With wisdom from on high,
> Shall we to those benighted
>   The lamp of life deny?
> Salvation, O salvation!
>   The joyful sound proclaim,
> Till each remotest nation
>   Has learned Messiah's name."

When God's church shall arise in the fulness of her might to the conception of her duties, responsibilities, and high privileges, we shall see the dawning of that day to which prophets, bards, and saints of all ages looked forward with exultant joy.

> "The Saviour comes, by ancient bards foretold:
> Hear Him, ye deaf, and all ye blind, behold;
> He from thick films shall purge the visual ray,
> And on the sightless eyeball pour the day.
> 'Tis He the obstructed paths of sound shall clear,
> And bid new music charm the unfolding ear;
> The dumb shall sing, the lame his crutch forego,
> And leap exulting, like a bounding roe.
> No sigh, no murmur, shall the wide world hear;
> From every face He wipes off every tear.
> No more shall nation against nation rise,
> Nor ardent warriors meet with hateful eyes;
> But useless lances into scythes shall bend,
> And the broad faulchion in a ploughshare end.
> See a long race thy spacious courts adorn;
> See future sons and daughters, yet unborn,
> In crowding ranks on every side arise,
> Demanding life, impatient for the skies;
> See barbarous nations at thy gate attend,
> Walk in thy light, and in thy temples bend.
> The seas shall waste, the skies in smoke decay,
> Rocks fall to dust, and mountains melt away;
> But fixed His word, His saving power remains,
> Thy realm for ever lasts, thy own Messiah reigns."—POPE.

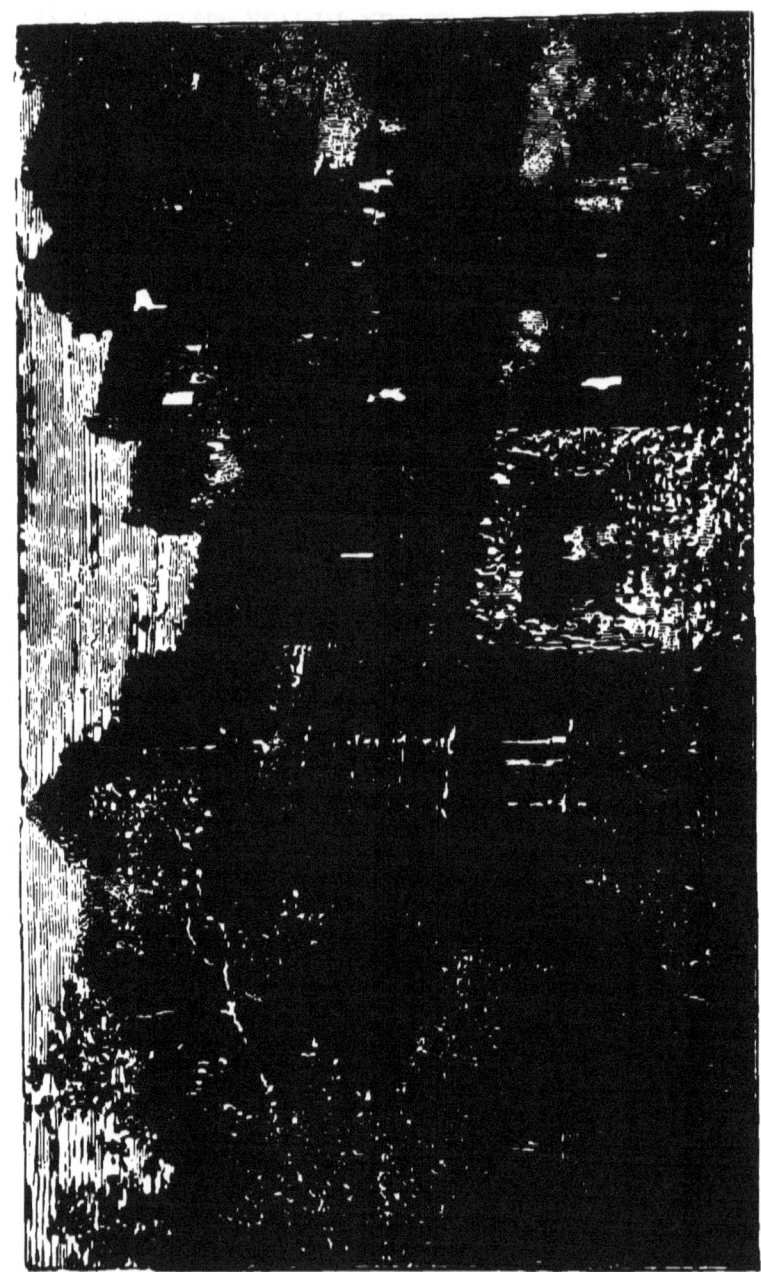

THE ZENANA IN THE PALACE OF RANA KHOUMBHOW, CHITTORE.

ZENANA MISSION WORK IN INDIA.

THE STORY OF WHAT CHRISTIAN WOMEN ARE DOING FOR THEIR HINDOO SISTERS.

"Rise, and take the Gospel message,
 Bear its tidings far away—
Far away to India's daughters;
Tell them of the living waters,
 Flowing, flowing, day by day,
That they, too, may drink and live;
Freely have ye, freely give;
Go, disperse the shades of night
With the glorious Gospel light."

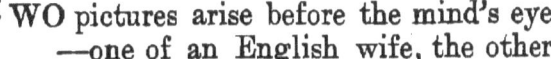WO pictures arise before the mind's eye —one of an English wife, the other of a Hindoo wife. The English wife sits in the bright, warm, cosy sitting-room, bright with pictures, books, furniture, fire-light, and the gambols of merry children—herself the centre of all the household joy. The Hindoo wife is shut up in her apartments like a prisoner, or waits upon her lord and master like a slave—sometimes only one out of three or four slaves —and after waiting in silence and submission until he has appeased his hunger, she withdraws to her own apartments, there to feed on the remnants of his repast. The meal would have been contaminated had she shared it with him. Her Shaster

says: "She must never eat until her husband is satisfied. If he fasts, so must she; and she must abstain from all food that her husband dislikes."

Two more pictures arise—the one of an English bride, the other of a Hindoo bride. The one wooed and wedded for her own sake, goes with the husband of her affections and of her choice to a *home* sanctified by love, esteeming that spot the dearest on earth. The other, a poor, timid, crying, terrified child, whose age varies between five and twelve years, is bought and sold for money, carried off forcibly from her childish home to dwell among strangers, who may or may not be kind to her—the child-wife of a man who esteems women as a polluted, worthless race, expiating in their sex the sins of a former life.

Two more pictures pass before our mental vision—an English mother, in the first warm flush of motherhood, surrounded by comforts, warmth, luxurious appliances, with ministering friends, whose loving voices and hushed footfalls testify to their respect for her, while she clasps her child to her bosom, rich in the possession of a new tie. A Hindoo mother is literally "cast out" at such times. In the courtyard, under a rough shed, a mere lean-to, upon the mud floor she wrestles with her weakness, and counts it all joy if her child be only a boy, for then her husband will love and respect her for her boy's sake. But if she have the misfortune to be the mother of a girl, then is her grief intense. For the birth of a girl is a calamity in a household; and as the poor mother, sitting in the hopeless night of heathenism, contemplates the future of the child, she regrets that it was ever born. And then, frequently, after hugging her baby to her bosom with convulsive sobs, she gives it to the Ganges, that it may at least secure heaven, and avoid the hard, bitter lot of women in India. Her heart breaks—but she makes the sacrifice for her infant's salvation. Poor mother!

Yet two more pictures pass before us, those of two widows. The one an English widow, although crushed and heart-broken, has the sympathy of friends and the ministrations of Christian kindness to assist her in bearing her heavy load of sorrow. Especially if she be

HINDOO MOTHER CONSIGNING HER CHILD TO THE GANGES.

young, do loving hearts ache for the desolation of her recently-blessed life. But the Hindoo widow is, by her very bereav... nt, made the object of scorn, ill-treatment, and barbarous 1. glect. As soon as her husband died—

before British rule abolished the suttee—she was prepared for death, and burnt on the funeral pile beside her husband's dead body, her own son, supposing she were a mother, applying the torch; for she was taught that in order to secure a passport to heaven she must go there to be her husband's slave. Since the suttee has been abolished, her life has been spared, but that life is made as bitter as heathenish cruelty can devise. All her jewels are taken away, and she is attired in the coarsest garments, she performs the most menial duties, and eats the poorest food, being avoided and despised as a criminal who has forfeited the rights of a human being. What wonder that many widows wish for death, and that some childless ones seek in suicide relief from their heavy woes. The Shaster says: "A woman has no other god than her husband." So she is his slave, both in life and death.

But this condition of women, from the cradle to the grave, is the outcome of the teachings of their Shasters, or holy books, and their teachers. Manu, the great lawgiver, says: "We may trust deadly poisons, a swollen river, a hurricane, beasts of prey, a thief, a savage, a murderer, *but women, never.* She has no business with the Vedas, or holy writings, and having no knowledge of expiatory texts, all women must be as foul as falsehood itself." Again: "The husband gives bliss to his wife here below, and he will give her happiness in the next world." Again: "Every man shall give his daughter in marriage to an excellent and handsome youth of the same caste, even though she has not attained her age, *i.e.*, eight years." Again: "A man, both day and night, must keep his wife so much in subjection, that she by no means shall be mistress of her own actions; she must never stand at the door, never look out of the window; she must never presume to eat till she has served her husband and his guests with victuals." Again: "In the absence or sickness of her lord, a good wife renounces every gratification, and at his death dies with him."

Immured in a zenana for life, what is a lady of high rank to do? She cannot pass away her time in cooking, and in attending to the wants of her family, as do her poorer sisters; she cannot read; she must receive no visitors. In what, then, can the poor prisoner engage? A little fancy work, tapestry or the like, but little even of that; playing with the dolls and toys of her childhood, arraying herself in gaudy finery and jewels, braiding her hair, fondling her children, and listening to the gossip retailed by the zenana servants—these things make up the sum of her occupations. It is well for her if her husband does not espouse another, and another child-wife, as her charms fade; for whatever he may do in this respect, he is held blameless by his Shasters. Indeed, it is known that some men espouse wives merely for the sake of getting the marriage portions of the brides; and cases have been known in which priests have married as many as fifty different wives, on purpose to obtain the dowry given with each one, while the fathers of these girls have eagerly given them to the so-called holy man, thinking that thereby they have secured their daughters' happiness in this life, and salvation in the next. Bought, bartered, and sold, like so many sheep, esteemed unfit for instruction, looked upon as polluted, vile creatures, to be saved only by their marriage to a husband, despised in life, and condemned to share the husband's death, what wonder is it that women are sunk in the depths of ignorance, sorrow, and suffering? A Hindoo lady bitterly exclaimed one day to a kindly missionary visitor, "Ignorance is the ornament of women in our land." And another Hindoo woman, on hearing of the grace and love of Christ to women, said wonderingly, "Your Shaster must have been written by a woman; it speaks so kindly of us."

Before passing on, I would say that it is in the thickly-populated presidency of Bengal that this strict seclusion of women is most maintained. It is not so rigidly practised in the other presidencies; and, indeed, in Bengal, the poorer Hindoo women have more liberty

THE SUTTEE.

necessarily so, because they must prepare the food, fetch the water, and perform all household duties for their families. Still, in these cases, the ignorance and ill-treatment are the same : it is only in the one particular of possessing more *liberty*, that there is any difference; and the first use a Hindoo makes of increased means or of improved social position, is to seclude his women in a zenana.

The word " zenana" is derived from two Mohammedan words signifying " the place of the women." A Hindoo writer says : " The zenana is that part of the house of a native gentleman in which the women live, entirely distinct from that occupied by the men, and usually presenting to the eye of the European the appearance of a prison ; for the windows, if any, on the outside, are very small, and high up, so as to effectually preclude the possibility of the women looking out, or of any one from the outside looking in. Sons, when they marry, do not set up a house of their own, as in England, but bring their wives to their father's house, in which they all live together, and the younger woman becomes subject to the elder, and all to the mother-in-law. Often three or four generations are living in the same house." Into such a place Hindoo customs consign a young child of five, six, seven, or eight years, to the wholly unsympathetic companionship of a man of thirty, forty, fifty, or sixty years. In this case she becomes his toy, or shares that honour with other girls, while all are subject to the mother-in-law, who mostly rules them with a rod of iron. But although Hindoo girls have become habituated to the idea of these early marriages, they are beginning to rebel against them. The light of the Gospel has penetrated even into the heathen zenanas, and parents as well as girls are beginning to see that such customs are not good. " A. L. O. E.," a well-known English authoress, who has given up her high prospects of literary success, to enter on zenana work in India, writes as follows : " I was to-day in a Hindoo zenana, where the husband, having embraced Christianity, was telling Bible stories to his wife and her sweet, bright-eyed little child of five years. One may smile at her childish exclamation, ' I don't want to be married, mother; I want to go to school;' for that mother had secretly planned uniting her to a Brahmin a few weeks before; and her infantile speech expressed a sense of *real danger*, from which her father's conversion happily delivered her. But the girl, still bound in the shackles of Hindooism, has never seen the man who is to govern her destiny for life, nor his mother, with whom she is to reside. If allowed to remain a while, as she usually is, with her own mother, yet the dreadful moment must come at last, when that mother, for the only time that she is permitted to look her son-in-law in the face, takes his hand, and joining it with that of her daughter, pronounces a benediction on the young couple. Perhaps of the most important controversies of the day in India at the present time is this one of child-marriage. A rising native Christian barrister has repeatedly declared that he will devote his life and all his influence and energy to its abolition. May God bless and speed his efforts."

After the poor girl has passed into the zenana of her husband she is closely veiled, and if belonging to the upper classes must not so much as *look* at a male relative other than her husband. An accidental glance at a man has been known to be punished with torture so as to cause death. Sometimes the poor child finds a kind motherly heart there who will shelter and protect her; in such cases her life by degrees becomes more bearable; in other cases the cruelty and unkindness she experiences induce her to escape back to her parents again, but this offence is only to be atoned for by severe penances, which sometimes cost the child-victim her life. Her life only becomes at all endurable when she becomes the mother of a boy, for *then* her husband and his relatives respect her for the sake of her boy. From that time she lives, as it were, in her son. She trains him up in the worship of his gods, recounts to him the idolatrous legends, fasts, prays, and makes offerings that her boy may be spared, and by every means in her power trains up her child for idolatry. Her influence over him is unbounded, and if she has more sons, that influence grows every year, until the secluded, ignorant, idolatrous mother becomes indeed the ruling power, although unseen in the family. This power it is which forms a strong counter-influence, preventing the spread of Christianity. A son can give a heathen mother no greater sorrow than by espousing the Christian religion. His mother then looks upon him as lost, while her own salvation is imperilled by having no son to perform the funeral rites.

Says another zenana visitor: "Six weeks ago I was told by a bright girl of twelve, a child of deep feeling and much intelligence, that in a month she was to go home to her husband. At my next visit she was a widow, the picture of grief and disappointment, actually dumb with sorrow as she sat in the dust mourning. At length the pent-up feelings of the little girl's mother, who sat beside her, found vent in a flood of tears, as she bewailed the sad fate of her beloved child, so bright and clever, yet doomed to widowhood. Her husband had given her beautiful dresses and jewels she would never wear, 'unless,' said her mother, '*you*, Mem Sahib, will persuade her to put them on once, so as to assuage her grief.' I entreated her not to allow her to keep the cruel fasts, and she answered, 'While with me I will not let her starve, but when she goes to her husband's mother, by-and-by, she must fast, according to the custom.' Another mother, less feeling, complained of the naughtiness of her little widowed girl of five years, saying, 'She actually cried for food on the very day her husband died.'"

Not only is the zenana a place of close confinement, but it is also a place *destitute of comfort*. A zenana visitor writes: "I had often wondered why one had such a dim impression of what a zenana was like, and wished for a minute description. I now wonder no longer, for a zenana is simply indescribable. A collection of dirty courtyards, dark corners, break-neck staircases, filthy outhouses and entries, overlaid with rubbish or occupied by half-clad native servants, narrow verandahs, and half-furnished small rooms. Such is a zenana and its surroundings. Once inside the zenana, you are struck, as a rule, by the entire absence of all that constitutes, to our ideas, the complement of a room—its furniture. Tables and chairs are not to be thought of, except when brought in from the gentleman's own apartments, for the teacher's use for the time being." Sometimes a sheet is spread on the floor, with a number of small pillows; at other times there is the *tuktaposh*, a kind of bedstead or large square wooden stool, and these, with a few mats, constitute the furniture of the women's apartment. The gentlemen of the family may furnish their rooms according to modern ideas, and enjoy every comfort, but the women must never know anything of this enjoyment. Is it any wonder that at times they take to opium-eating, or grow so depressed that their life, poor and miserable as it is, becomes a weariness to them? It is testified by zenana visitors that as a rule Hindoo women are " so oppressed and depressed that one rarely sees a merry woman among them." The misery of their own lives weighs them down continually; they would prefer death for their little daughters rather than life; and they pass through this world destitute of any hope for another. "Oh," said one of these poor creatures the other day, "if you only knew the lives of us poor Hindoo women, and all we have to suffer, you could not help weeping for us." And as English missionary ladies—for male missionaries *never* see them—behold their apathy and despair, their hearts bleed. Poor girls of about fourteen or fifteen look twenty-five or more, while at the age when English-women are in their prime, these poor creatures are old and wrinkled. Says another zenana visitor: "I entered the enclosure of a poor labourer's dwelling, and squatted beside his wife, who had been ill for a month. Barbarous treatment had done its work. I could only place my hand soothingly on her forehead, commend her to the care of the Great Physician, and leave her to die. I then visited a rich lady, who was lying on a rotten bedstead without even a mat beneath her or a clean covering above her. She could count her jewels and splendid dresses by hundreds, but on this bare cot in an empty room she lay dying, for we soon saw that all hope of life was gone. She died next day."

The state that I have been describing is the state of millions of women—all subjects of our Queen. They are closely imprisoned for life in their zenanas, and are assiduously prevented from *knowing anything*. The term "zenana" may not be used in all the districts of India, but it is well understood, because everywhere the *system* is the same; although in some parts of the country other words, such as "purdah," "gosha," or "anthakar" are used. They all signify "curtained women," or the place where they are kept. Some writers have stated that there are about one hundred millions of Hindoo women kept in this degradation and bondage. Suppose we say that fifty millions are belonging to the poorest classes—then they have some little modification of their lot in the fact that they are free to fetch water, cook the food, and do the work of their households, *but not to obtain knowledge*, or mix in society. Then there remains the startling number of fifty millions, whose lives are passed in the zenanas we have been describing.

Missionary zeal and womanly Christian piety have endeavoured to cope with this great mass of ignorance, suffering, sorrow, and dense, dark superstition. Male missionaries and reverend gentlemen, although learned, clever, respectful, and gentle, would never be allowed to instruct Hindoo women. The zenana doors were closely shut against all such; and the men of a Hindoo family became acquainted with, and amenable to, Christian influences, while their mothers, wives, sisters, and daughters were still buried in the night of heathenism, and exerting an influence favourable to the old idolatry. Very slowly Hindoo gentlemen themselves have grown to recognise this state of ignorance among their female relatives, and to admit that it must be altered before the country will be Christianised. At a recent meeting of the Bengal Literary Club the question was eagerly discussed, and all the more eagerly because the gentlemen who composed the club had requested Dr. Thoburn, an American missionary, to take the chair. The subject for discussion that night was "Young Men," and most of the members were educated native gentlemen, although not Christians. One of them, a professor in a Bengal college, got up and spoke on the question, which he did with much earnestness, concluding in the following words, "You must accept truth and live religious lives, for this is your only hope, either in this life or in the world to come. If any of you are moral it is by accident, for everything connected with your lives tends to pull you down to destruction. You will never amount to much until you respect your women, and educate them." Another spoke to the following effect : " We will never make much progress as a nation until we have happy homes, where we will receive proper instruction. You cannot expect us to be good and useful men until we have good mothers, good wives, and good sisters." Hindoos themselves are beginning to see and express the truth that " the salvation of India depends upon Christian women"—a truth that has been recognised, more or less, for the last forty or fifty years, by European and American missionaries.

Fifty years ago, Miss Bird gained access to some of the zenanas in Calcutta, but so secretly, that it was never spoken of; still, she had a few converts as the fruits of her work. Thirty years ago, the Calcutta Normal School was founded, in order to provide *native* female teachers for these secluded women; and more than 100 young women, born in India, have been trained there for the work. After coming out, they have laboured here and there, wherever openings have occurred, in schools and zenanas, and not without large success. Lady missionaries have made zenana mission-work what it is to-day, by the persistent labours of the last thirty years. They have gained access alike to Hindoo, and

Mahommedan ladies, and have instilled a desire and created a demand for Christian instruction. These lady-missionaries have been sent out from Europe and America, they have been connected with all churches, and have laboured mostly unknown to fame. But the field is so

STREET SCENE IN DELHI.

large, and the growing desire for instruction so wide and intense, that many, many more lady-missionaries are called for. This "harvest truly is great, but the labourers are few," compared with India's need. India needs *Christian* women—*medical* Christian women, to deal with her vast female population, for male doctors, whether European or native, are denied all access to the
D

zenanas, and so the poor women perish like rotten sheep. A Christian zenana missionary lady, knowing something of medical science, will be eagerly welcomed among the native women, and as she cures their bodily ailments she paves the way for Gospel instruction. In view of this need it is most gladdening to know that several of the most prominent missionary societies of England and America have trained, and are still training, young ladies for service in India, China, Burmah, and Africa, as medical missionaries to their own down-trodden suffering sisters.

And they do not labour without encouragement. Very early in the progress of this work, souls were gathered into the Lord's garner. Mrs. Weitbrecht gives two beautiful instances of success in those early days. One case was that of a child-wife, who died at the age of fourteen, of fever, after giving birth to a son. She had heard of salvation through Christ by the lips of the zenana visitor, and had silently learnt to trust in Christ for salvation. When she came to die, they took her down to the banks of the Ganges, according to their faith, in order to fill her mouth with the mud, and so suffocate her before being consumed on the funeral pile. They went through the horrid rites, and the poor girl's teacher stood near, powerless to prevent, witnessing the scene; but before the dying girl saw the last of earth, she gave to that teacher a testimony that her heart was fixed upon Jesus. Did not this poor young Hindoo mother go forth "from night to light?"

The second instance was that of another dying girl-mother, who, having resigned her recently-given babe, asked for water. When it was brought she placed her open Bible upon her head, and *baptised herself* in the name of her lately-found Saviour. Then she passed away, as her failing lips uttered her fervent petitions to Him upon whom she trusted. Yes, even at that early date, God blessed this zenana mission, gathering His jewels, one here, and another there, from out idolatrous superstitious Indian harems, to shine with glorious beauty in the Redeemer's crown.

There are four particular agencies for the evangelisation of the women of India—1st, strict zenana work; 2nd, Bible women; 3rd, girls' schools of three kinds, zenana, bazaar, and boarding; 4th, medical missions. We will briefly look at each agency as it exists at the present day, and quote from the workers' reports:—

1st. ZENANA WORK.—In all directions, as we have said before, there is a growing desire to receive instruction in the seclusion of the zenanas. But when we consider the vast number of Hindoo women—one hundred millions—and the small number of missionary women in India—not much above one hundred—we shall see the disparity between the demand and the supply. What are these few women among so many? This number of workers allows about one lady-missionary to one million of Hindoo women; but if we consider, and deduct the number of ladies engaged in purely educational work in schools, we shall find the strength of the zenana agents sensibly diminished. Yet, India's daughters—and sons, too—are stretching out their hands unto God and begging for teachers. A native gentleman in one part of India recently said to one missionary lady, "The work your society does is very good. It must tell on the next generation. You are influencing the young mothers of to-day, and they will influence their children. You have no idea how hard it is for a native of the old school to give up his superstitions. When he is quite a tiny child his mother shows him a stone, and says, "There is Krishna, make a deep salaam to it." Then she shows him an image, and says, "That is another God; salaam to it," and she makes her child bow until his forehead touches the ground. I was brought up like that, and it has taken much time and much learning to make me see that such things are wrong, and to make me willing to have my daughter sent to school. But my children will not have those superstitions to struggle with; they will not be taught to think that contact with Europeans defiles them." Says an American lady missionary: "We find the inmates of the zenanā always prepared for religious conversation by what they have heard from the inmates of the household of our wonderful Book and beautiful hymns. I generally go with one or two of our Bible-women, to help in the singing, and the hymns are eagerly listened to. At my last visit to one zenana one young woman listened with such eagerness that I was compelled to keep on. When any one begun to talk she would say, 'Hush! why will you talk such talk now? Let her speak to us; who knows when we shall get such instruction again? We can talk idle talk every day.' I agreed to go again the next day."

But these zenana visitors work also among the humble homes, where the confinement is not so strict. Among the lower classes the women not only do their own cooking, washing, &c., but also endeavour to earn something by means of their art in needlework, in order to add to the family income. Some take in plain sewing from the tailors; others do embroidery, herringbone stitch, and darning patterns; others make up ornaments; others weave ribbons. And the mission ladies sit and talk with these busy women, finding in them a readiness to receive information. They are delighted to look at pictures, especially of foreign lands, and ask multitudes of questions about their more highly-favoured sisters in these lands. Very often the entrance of a few new ideas concerning other countries wakes up the dormant faculties, and induces a desire for learning the religion of far-off blessed Christian lands. Then these women like singing, and almost regularly ask for *bhajans*, or hymns. So the visitor sits down on a straw mat, if no raised seat is to be had, and sings some of our old familiar hymns, "There is a better world, they say," or "There is a happy land," or others like these, and soon all the women and girls within hearing crowd around to listen to the tunes, and ask questions about the Great Master who did not disdain to talk to the woman by Samaria's well. So singing leads to reading, and reading leads to conversation, until the women are quite in love with the good news they hear, and promise to send their children to the schools, while they themselves are eager to hear more. Then when the time is gone, and the visitor must return home, comes once and again the earnest request, " Sing another *bhajan!* The words are good! They are true!" A large amount of good was accomplished during the late famine by the distribution of relief and employment to the starving women. The *spirit* of the Gospel was seen and appreciated by those who received aid, so that at the present day a large number of women are looking for Christian instruction, and asking for it, from those who ministered to their bodily need. Prejudice thus lost its power.

2nd. BIBLE-WOMEN.—Mrs. Weitbrecht says: "Native Christian Bible-women, superintended by lady missionaries, are the crying want of India at the present moment. I would fain allude to some of them, and tell how, after passing through most harrowing ordeals, even seas of sorrow, at the time of their conversion, when all had to be forsaken for Jesus' sake, they were carrying rays of sunshine into dark dwellings by reading that Word whose entrance giveth light." These Bible-women are always native females, whose Christian character and attainments have been tried and proved. They work under the direction and superintendence of European or American lady missionaries, and do a work which is similar to that of the London Bible-women, in places, and under circumstances, where European ladies could never go. Being accustomed to the climate they bear the toil much better, and experience more freedom from disease; and being one with the women in birth and habits, they obtain a large influence over the lower-middle and lower classes. The Bible-woman is an institution of modern date, but she may now be found in other countries besides India; China, Syria, and Turkey, enjoy the blessings of her ministrations, for it has been found that in order to evangelise the female population who do not, as a rule, go to hear the Word preached publicly in those countries, the Word must be taken to them by those of their own sex who have experienced its converting power. These women work in private homes, and among such of their country-women as they may meet with, in markets, hospitals, or gaols. The Indian Female Normal School and Instruction Society has about seventy of these Bible-women labouring in "the highways and hedges," among the fields and lanes, and from house to house, among their poorer sisters. The reports of their superintendents show abundantly how blessed an agency this has been for Hindoo women, especially for the pariah classes. The Society for Promoting Female Education in the East also employs this agency with marked success. An extract from the report of "Susan," a Bible-woman employed by the first-named society in India, will illustrate, in simple yet forceful language, the work of all. "I greet you with much love in the name of Jesus, and since you are interested in the poor Bible-woman's work, I will try and give a little account of it. I visit among the people every day. I read to them from the Bible, and have many talks about the things of the unseen world. I have learned some sweet hymns which I sing, and which are always very acceptable. As a rule, when I first begin my visits, there is a good deal of discussion regarding the religious creeds of the country; questions of how old customs and usages so strong can be overcome. The Hindoos marvel at the idea of *one* Divine and Living Intercessor between God and man. They tell me of how they mean to make their peace with God by pilgrimages to different shrines, bathing at holy places, offering sacrifices, and giving alms. Female enlightenment and elevation are subjects of no small interest to those who feel the degradation of their own position more and more as they realise better things; with great joy do they receive the promise made to woman, that her seed should bruise the serpent's head, and that through her, redemption should come into the world. Twice I have been to my native place, called Ramkote, near Cashmere; there also my Bible went with me, and I read to my people the wondrous words of life. On each of these occasions I was put in prison for this reason; nevertheless, those who heard received the message with eagerness. I will just tell you the names of those who have professed Christ since I have been reading to them. Prairnie, with her husband, son, and brother; Daku, with her two daughters; Look Dai, and Esar Dai, Rupa, and Rupa's sister, who in dying took hold of the precious hope in Christ, and one woman more, who now decides to be a Christian. I have been reading to her for fifteen years."

3rd. ZENANA SCHOOLS, BAZAAR SCHOOLS, and BOARDING SCHOOLS.—These schools, as our readers may infer from their several designations, are intended for different classes of the community. Zenana schools are for the upper classes, and are taught within the privacy of the zenana. Bazaar schools are for the children of the lower classes, and have been found extensively useful. Boarding schools are of two kinds: one kind, purely benevolent, such as orphan schools; while the other kind receives only pupils who can pay good fees, and are mostly self-supporting. Indeed, as the women get Christianised it becomes one aim on the part of the missionaries to instil into their minds the lesson that education must be paid for. And wherever this has been carried into action it has been found that the education which is paid for is more valued. The late famine has greatly increased the numbers in orphan boarding schools. It will be remembered that Mrs. Mullens and Mrs. Porter engaged prominently in Girls' Boarding Schools. A report from one lady worker of the present day may be given. Mrs. Lewis, from Bellary, thus writes: " The particular school of which I have charge is the orphan and day school. In the day school we have two paid teachers, and two monitors taken from the elder girls; all the orphan girls attend, and about twenty day scholars, the daughters of our Christian people. We have thirty-five little orphan children to clothe and feed, most of them, poor little things, left destitute by this dreadful famine. We have long had a Girls' Boarding School at Bellary, and of late years I have had a rule that none but orphan girls were to be admitted unless the parents paid at least half the cost of their maintenance." Thus, these schools are laying hold of the *girls* in various ranks of life, and training them up for usefulness and Christian work in their after-womanhood. As these girls grow up into life they will be free of the shackles which superstition and oppression have fastened upon their mothers.

4th. MEDICAL MISSIONS.—The success attained by missionaries, who, to a desire to teach Christ unite a knowledge of medicine, is most remarkable. While ministering to the sickness of the body, the grandest opportunities occur for speaking to the natives of Jesus. The missionary who has received a medical training is armed twofold for the fight. Acting on the knowledge gained of this success some of the largest women's missionary societies have sent out properly qualified ladies to engage in medical work. Among these societies the Society for Promoting Female Education in the East, the Indian Female Normal School and Instruction Society of England, and the Women's Foreign Missionary Union of America, are most distinguished for their employment of medical missionaries. The same experience is repeated in their case also. Everywhere the poor women crowd around the lady missionary who possesses healing power, and almost worship the hem of her garment. In the peculiar seclusion of the higher class women of India and China, she is doubly welcome; and many a bigoted Hindoo, or lordly Chinese husband, will come pleading to the "Mem Sahib" to save his wife's life. She goes and grapples with the disease, her womanly sympathy, handiness, and skill, earning golden opinions from the older bigoted relatives. Then, as the lady explains the nature of the disease, or gives a few simple directions for the nursing of the patient, she gradually leads the hearers' minds up to that God who alone can bless the means used. On these occasions the voice of prayer has, for the first time, ascended to God, the other women kneeling or standing around, awe-stricken, and, as the ultimate issue, whole households have become Christianised. In the regeneration of the women of India, medical missions are destined to occupy a large and growing position, and the best Missionary Societies are laying hold of this agency very eagerly. Shall we not, by giving money, our prayers, and *ourselves*, sustain their hands?

So the great work goes on, and as "knowledge is increased," and many willing servants of Christ "run to and fro," Satan's kingdom is getting smaller, and Christ's kingdom growing larger. From east, west, north, and south, our sometime heathen sisters are rising up, shaking off their bonds, and becoming in deed and in truth the Lord's free-women. And in years to come they, too, shall in their turn minister to others who now sit in darkness and in the shadow of death.

MRS. MARY MOFFAT,
Wife of the Rev. Dr. Moffat,

MISSIONARY TO SOUTH AFRICA; OF THE LONDON
MISSIONARY SOCIETY.

"Take my life, and let it be
Consecrated, Lord, to Thee!
Take my feet, and let them be
Swift, and beautiful for Thee!
Take my voice, and let me sing,
Always, only for my King.
Take my lips, and let them be
Filled with messages for Thee.
Take my intellect, and use
Every power as thou shalt choose.
Take myself, and I will be
Ever, only, *all* for Thee."   F. R. HAVERGAL.

MISS MARY SMITH was born of respectable and educated parentage, on May 24th, 1795, at New Windsor, near Manchester. Mr. Smith was a Scotchman who came south and settled in Yorkshire. Her own education was completed at the Moravian School at Fairfield, near Manchester; and it was here that Miss Smith's mind was first powerfully attracted towards the mission cause. It was the custom in that institution, to read among the young ladies the short monthly reports of what God was doing in the dark places of the earth, principally by means of Moravian missionary workers; and Miss Smith not only listened with interest to these accounts, but gave in her adhesion to the missionary principle, there and then, in her girlhood's days. After really entering upon mission work, Mrs. Moffat never ceased to feel lively gratitude to the gracious providence which had caused her to be placed at Fairfield; because, in tracing all the way which that providence had led her, she could distinctly discern the guiding hand which even then was fitting her, although in this retired position, and unconsciously, to become a "vessel meet for the Master's use" among the far-distant Africans.

Miss Smith was the eldest child, and only daughter of a family of four. Mr. Moffat was a few months younger than herself, having been born on December 21, 1795; and circumstances having thrown the young couple together, a kindred spirit was soon developed. Young Moffat had prospects of advancement and honour, had he followed secular pursuits; but his mind was providentially turned to the mission cause, and as he determined to yield up himself a living sacrifice for the work, Miss Smith cheered and upheld him in the resolve. Finally, after some acquaintance and friendly interchange of sentiment, the two young people were betrothed, resolving together to devote themselves to the work of the Lord, in whatever position should offer in the great missionary field. So great an impression did Miss Smith's noble self-renunciation make upon her brother John, that he was led carefully to examine the *motives* and the *spirit* which caused such a sacrifice. He knew that his sister was giving up a happy home, a life of comfort, plenty, and intellectual luxury, as well as the prospect of ease and riches in England, to go out to Africa; and the thought of all this at first staggered him. His reflections ended in conversion. Although he was just preparing to enter into a lucrative business, he renounced everything, and giving himself up to mission work also, he entered Blackburn Academy, under Dr. Joseph Fletcher, to prepare. Finally, in 1828, he went to Madras, South India, where he laboured among the heathen with great success. Returning by ship, in 1843, from Vizagapatam to Madras, after an ordination service, he perished in a storm, the vessel being lost at sea.* After his dedication to the missionary work, Mrs. Moffat very earnestly desired that her brother might join herself and husband in South Africa, but this was not to be. He was not only to labour on another continent, but to perish at last, far away at sea, in the howling storm. We cannot wonder that his death proved a great trial to his bereaved sister.

Mr. Moffat sailed for South Africa in October, 1816, and after some delay, joined Mr. Ebner, a missionary who had been settled there a little time, at Africaner's Kraal. Doubtless there were seasons when the mission work to which Miss Smith had dedicated herself appeared full of difficulty and trial, for the young man was settled in the midst of a savage and barbarous people, upon a salary of £25 per annum. The prospect was anything but inviting: the people were so uncivilised that they laughed to scorn the idea of the sacredness of human life; so greedy that they stole his food at all opportunities; and so dark and imbruted in mind, that it was with the greatest difficulty they could be made to understand the meaning or purpose of the letters of the alphabet. In habits, practices, bloodthirstiness, and lack of feeling, they were more like the beasts that perish, than aught else. Indeed, travellers who had mingled with them doubted whether they possessed souls at all; while the conditions of life in that sterile and drought-stricken country, were sufficient to frighten away all who valued existence at all, from the bare contemplation of the self-immolation necessary to dwell among those so needing the Gospel.

But none of these things moved Miss Smith from her purpose. In 1819 she went out to Cape Town, whither Mr. Moffat had travelled to meet her. They

---

* A memoir of the Rev. John Smith's first wife is given in this volume.

VIEW OF CAPE TOWN.

were married there, and in January, 1820, started for the interior. They arrived at New Lattakoo, afterwards called Kuruman, in March, but returned to Griqua Town, where they laboured for a few months. In May, 1821, at the desire of Mothibi, the chief, they settled at Kuruman station, and took up regular work among the people. Here Mr. Moffat had to be his own gardener, blacksmith, carpenter, and tailor, while Mrs. Moffat was compelled to do all her own domestic work, as well as to instil, by degrees, ideas of modesty and honesty, into the females who flocked around her, and viewed her as a curiosity, to be teased, robbed, or let alone, as it pleased them. She had to be her own cook, and to be thankful when she got anything to cook, for the natives would watch the hut, and in the absence of the young couple would break in and steal all the food, so that many times Mr. and Mrs. Moffat returned home to an empty cupboard, after being out for hours, trying to instruct the natives. She was compelled to do her own washing, or send it for distances of from fifty to a hundred miles to be done, on a hired bullock, for no woman was industrious enough to help her, or well-disposed enough to commence learning the art of washing. To get a girl even to nurse the baby for an hour or two was a feat attended with danger. The girl's body, according to the native custom, was smeared all over with grease and red ochre, and it was only as an act of great condescension that she would consent to put on a loose cotton dress, which Mrs. Moffat had made, in order to prevent the baby from being discoloured like her own skin. Occasionally, when the nurse was ill-tempered or offended at any reproof, she would hurl the poor infant across the hut at Mrs. Moffat's head, and then dart away, with words of impudent defiance. Missionary life in South Africa was no bed of roses at that time.

To begin with, the houses were as unlike English ideas of comfort as they were possible to be. These huts were invariably built by the women—who did all the drudgery—and were composed of a number of poles placed in a circular form, and covered with mats. When the sun shone it was unbearably hot; when it rained the water poured in; while it was not unusual for dogs and serpents to force their way into some quiet corner. The cleanliness practised by the missionaries in regard to their food or clothing was a constant source of amusement to the Bechuanas, who would say, if pleased to speak favourably, "Ra-Mary, your customs may be good enough for you, but I never see that they fill the stomach." They had no single idea of God, or of a Creator; there was literally no remnant even of a false faith, or of a dark superstition, on which to lay hold of in order to commence preaching or teaching. They knew nothing of idol-worship; they lived the lives of oxen, enjoying only ravenous meals of flesh, and sensuality of life. What could a missionary and his wife do with such a people? Nothing can better describe their situation than Mr. Moffat's own graphic words: "The site of the station was a light sandy soil, where no kind of vegetables would grow without irrigation. Our water ditch, which was some miles in length, had been led out of the Kuruman river, and passed in its course through the gardens of the natives. As irrigation was to them entirely unknown, fountains and streams had been suffered to run to waste. The native women, seeing the fertilising effect of the water in our gardens, thought very naturally that they had an equal right to it in their own, and took the liberty of opening our water-ditch, and allowing it, on some occasions, to flood their own gardens. This mode of proceeding left us at times without a drop of water, even for culinary purposes. It was in vain that we pleaded and remonstrated with the chiefs, the women were the masters in this matter. Mr. Hamilton and I were daily compelled to go alternately three miles, with a spade, about three p.m., the hottest time in the day, and turn in the many outlets into native gardens, that we might have a little moisture to refresh our burnt-up vegetables during the night. Many night-watches were spent in this way, and after we had raised with great labour, vegetables, so necessary to our constitutions, the natives would steal them by night, as well as day; and after a year's toil and care we scarcely reaped anything to reward us for our labour. Our situation might be better conceived than described; not one believed our report among the

BUILDING A HOUSE, SOUTH AFRICA.

thousands by whom we were surrounded. Native aid, especially to the wife of a missionary, though not to be dispensed with, was a source of anxiety, and an addition to our cares, for any individual may not only threaten but carry a rash purpose into effect. For instance, Mrs. Moffat, with a babe in her arms, begged, and that very humbly, of a woman, just to be kind enough to move out of a temporary kitchen, that she might shut it as usual before going to the place of worship. The woman seized a piece of wood to hurl it at Mrs. Moffat, who, of course, immediately escaped to the house of God, leaving the woman the undisturbed occupant of the kitchen, any of the contents of which she would not hesitate to appropriate to her own use. It required no little fortitude and forbearance in the wife of a missionary who had to keep at home and attend to the cares and duties of a family, to have the house crowded with those who would seize a stone and dare interference on her part. As many men and women as pleased might come into our hut, leaving us not room enough even to turn ourselves, and making everything they touched the colour of their own greasy red attire; while some were talking, others would be sleeping, and some pilfering whatever they could lay their hands upon. This would keep the housewife a perfect prisoner, in a suffocating atmosphere, almost intolerable. As it was not pleasant to take our meals among such filth, our dinner was often delayed for hours, hoping for their departure. On some occasions an opportunity would be watched to rob when the missionary was engaged in public service. The thief would put his head just within the door, discover who was in the pulpit, and, knowing he could not leave the rostrum before a certain time had expired, would go to his house and take whatever he could lay his hands upon. Knives were always eagerly coveted; our metal spoons they melted, and when we were supplied with plated iron ones, which they found not so pliable, they supposed them bewitched. Very often when employed in working at a distance from the house, if there was no one in whom he could confide, the missionary would be compelled to carry all the kitchen utensils with him, well knowing that if they were left they would take wings before his return."

Among the perils to which missionaries situated among those savages tribes are exposed is that of invasion by other tribes. On one occasion the Mantatees made an incursion into Mothibi's country, and produced great terror. Many of the natives were killed, while the mission party experienced great anxiety. Mr.

E

Moffat was compelled to be absent on a visit to Makaba, and his wife was left alone at the station with two infants, and a young Hottentot woman. In the night she was aroused by a loud knocking at the door of the hut; and on inquiring, Mrs. Moffat found that it was the chief Mothibi come to tell her that the Mantatees were indeed coming quickly. He and his warriors crowded into the hut, and after stating the position of affairs to Mrs. Moffat, took counsel with her as to what should be done. She immediately wrote to Mr. Hamilton, their fellow-missionary, to come to the rescue. This gentleman came by eight o'clock, in obedience to the summons, and packed up and secreted as many articles of property as he could, preparatory to flight; but by noon the intelligence arrived that the dreaded invaders had directed their course *from* the station, instead of to it. This intelligence was the unwitting source of much sorrow to Mrs. Moffat; because, although she herself was safe, her husband's journey lay right in the track of the Mantatees; and, knowing that they would rejoice to kill such a distinguished victim, the poor wife endured, for three weeks, agonies of suspense and trial. During that time her sorrow was increased by the garrulous reports of the natives, who, to gain some measure of popularity and consequence for themselves, reported all sorts of unlikely things. One had seen portions of Mr. Moffat's clothes stained with blood; another had tracked pieces of the wagon; while a third had found the saddle, hacked to pieces. But, after three weeks of terrible alarms and long-drawn agony, the husband and wife were once more re-united. We may fancy the joyful thanksgivings which ascended from their little hut that day!

It is impossible to imagine the difficulty of bringing up children amid such surroundings. Mr. and Mrs. Moffat did all in their power to neutralise the gross influences of heathenism by the careful training of their little ones, and, finally, by sending away their girls to different schools in Cape Colony. Fancy pictures how tenderly and prayerfully Mrs. Moffat would draw her little ones around her, like many an English mother in far more favourable circumstances, and tell them the elevating story of the Cross. Amid all the dense darkness of heathenism, and the demoralising influences of savage

SOUTH AFRICAN BULLOCK WAGON.

life, she would do her best to instil into their little minds both by deed and word, some echoes of English civilisation; but chief among all the instrumentalities relied upon by her to bring them up as Christian children should be, is the religion of Christ. Was the mother's heart never despondent? Was her soul never sick with fear? Was her spirit never heavy within her, as she contemplated her children's life—as she remembered the manifold advantages of the poorest English peasant child? O yes! This trial is one of the keenest which missionaries have to endure, and allied to it is the separation between parents and children. The missionary received more salary than of old, and with his increased means, though far from rich, they resolved to send away their daughters to school. So Mary (afterwards Mrs. Livingstone) and her sister were sent away to Cape Town.

To show the dangers of travelling, we will transcribe a lion story which concerns these two sisters, though not at the time of their education. Mary had been married to Dr. Livingstone, and Ann had gone to visit her during a time of illness. As the station at which Mrs. Livingstone was settled was 230 miles away, it was not often that the sisters could visit. Accordingly, Miss Moffat spent a few weeks with her married sister, and nursed her back again into strength and health. The journey to Mabotsa took a fortnight, but nothing was seen of any lions, only occasionally a loud roar, though distant, was heard; and the young lady set out on the return journey in good spirits, accompanied by an old woman and three native drivers. On the afternoon of the second day this old woman discovered that her kaross had fallen out of the wagon, though nobody knew when or where. She insisted on two of the men going back to look for it, which they did, taking the only gun among the party for defence, leaving the solitary wagon in the midst of a howling wilderness infested with lions, with only two trembling women, one man, and no gun. It would have been wiser to have lost the kaross, than to have dared other and worse dangers, as the event proved. Mrs. Moffat, writing a letter to a friend, gives an account of these dangers in the following words:—" At length they were benighted. They unyoked the oxen, but neglected to fasten them properly. They prepared a meal, and drank a little tea; when, all on a sudden, came down the shaggy monster—an enormous lion—and levelled an ox in a moment, not ten yards away from the wagon. They were soon all huddled together in their vehicle, and sat, with horrified feelings, watching the movements of the lion. Having sufficiently regaled himself, he came close up to the wagon, and roared. The man in the wagon had a stick, which he lighted by the candle, and which he stretched out to scare the animal. He turned on his heels, and marched off somewhere; but he returned before sunrise, and made another meal off the ox. The man then took his long whip, and tried to frighten the lion by cracking it as close to his ears as he could reach. At length, much to the satisfaction of the party, the unwelcome visitor turned to the right-about, and skulked away among the bushes. But yet there they were, far from water during the hottest season of the year; the oxen had all scampered back from whence they came; they had no weapon of defence; and the two men had not yet returned with the kaross. So they resolved on setting off on foot, back again to Mabotsa, and to leave the wagon—a poor little cat being the only live thing in it—to the mercy of the lion. They started before sunrise, and soon met the men. This was some comfort, for their number was now augmented, and they had got the gun. On they went, through the burning desert, and beneath the scorching sun—imagining that every bush they saw had a lion behind it—sitting down now and then to taste a drop of the last bottle of water they had with them. At last they reached a native village, and a house was provided for Miss Moffat; and there, with a single ox-hide for a bed, she and the woman stretched their weary limbs, but were far too excited, and too fatigued, and too hungry, to obtain sleep. Next morning the march was resumed, and in the afternoon they reached Mabotsa. The family had, however, left the day before, and a man was left in charge of the premises. Very soon some coffee was roasted, and some bread baked; the chief of the village also sent a fowl, and so a meal was obtained. Five days were spent in this solitude. The wagon was then brought back, and another commencement of the homeward journey made. This occupied eight days, travelling almost incessantly, day and night. They neither saw nor heard any lion this time, and they reached home about one o'clock in the morning."

The Miss Ann Moffat who was the heroine of the foregoing adventure was accustomed to teach in the infant and Sunday schools at the Kuruman. But, before the children could be instructed or Christianised, the *mothers* had to be dealt with, and this work fell largely, if not entirely, to Mrs. Moffat's share. But this was a work of faith, and most assuredly a labour of love—a labour, too, in which success seemed almost hopeless. Many long weary years were passed in labouring to keep the mission in the country, surrounded by many thousands who, instead of feeling any interest in the mission, displayed the most vehement opposition to it. There was no interest in the object of the mission; no aid in any department of missionary work; and no appeal in case of injury, except to a barbarian. The women were the most conservative, and the most difficult to manage. In no domestic emergency would they lift a hand to help, for many years; and a poor old refugee slave woman, who lived about fifty miles away, was the only one to whom Mrs. Moffat could apply for domestic help at this period. Fancy what it must have been to have brought up a family of nine children amid these savage wilds and yet more savage people! The world has been told of both "the madness" and "the romance" of the missionary enterprise; but the two phases are pathetically mingled in Mrs. Moffat's life-story. Nothing but a God-like charity, which endured all things, suffered all things, and hoped all things, united to the faith which removeth mountains, could ever have sustained the heroic woman through these long, terrible years. Although the Bechuana women were so unpromising, Mrs. Moffat unceasingly endeavoured to benefit them. She commenced with those who appeared willing to learn, and endeavoured to impress on them the necessity for abandoning their heathen dress. But this was a difficult task; for the women were neither the manufacturers of the raw materials, nor the dressmakers. The materials were the skins of goats, sheep, and gazelles; while the *men* formed the skins into garments, no woman being ever known to attempt such a feat. However, in time, the prejudice of the women against European clothing began to wear away, and the first converts, who were chiefly women, adopted some articles of light attire more in consonance with womanly modesty and their Christian views. These first converts became the special objects of Mrs. Moffat's care as well as instruction; and the barriers to trade in European produce being broken down, a demand was made for dressmaking and dress materials. This naturally led to a sewing school being set up for all the women who were willing to learn. This school, as well as classes for spiritual instruction for the women, became particularly Mrs. Moffat's charge, so that she entered into "labours more abundant." In addition to these classes, public schools for general instruction were opened, as opportunities grew, until, in time, the whole Bechuana people were prepared to receive the translation of the Bible which Dr. Moffat had made. One fact may be mentioned, which will afford some idea of the progress of the people. In the earlier years of the mission a few traders possessing courage penetrated so far beyond the boundaries of civilisation as to reach the Kuruman. They exhibited all that they thought attractive in the way of fine dress, &c., but could not obtain a single purchaser. The clothing was looked at with laughter and scorn, and the traders had to return sorely mortified. But since the conversion and civilisation of the Bechuana females, who numbered some thousands, as well as those of the neighbouring tribes, the demand for European produce is so great, that Dr. Moffat states that the latest accounts show an amount of something like three hundred thousand pounds' worth of goods annually passing through the missionary stations into the interior. So thoroughly did a reformation take place, and especially in female attire, after the influence of Divine grace was spread abroad, and after the art of reading became common, that the community around the Kuruman presented an entirely different appearance from what it had in bygone years. The contrast was remarkable and complete.

Referring to the commencement of this part of their civilisation, Mr. Moffat writes: "Those who were baptised had previously procured decent raiment and prepared it for the occasion, with Mrs. Moffat's assistance, who had to supply two of the women with gowns from her own wardrobe. Hitherto a sewing-school had been uncalled for, the women's work being that of building houses and raising fences; and it was a novel sight to observe women and young girls handling the little bright instrument, which was scarcely perceptible to the touch of fingers accustomed to grasp the handle of a pickaxe, or to use them to supply the absence of trowels. But they were willing, and Mrs. Moffat, in order to encourage them, engaged to meet them as often as her strength would permit. She had soon a motley group of pupils, very few of the whole party possessing either a frock or a gown. The scarcity of materials was a serious impediment to progress, and living as we did, far beyond the reach of traders, and six hundred miles from a market town, it was next to impossible to obtain them just when wanted. The same Gospel which had taught them that they were spiritually miserable, and blind, and naked, discovered to them also that they needed reform externally, and thus prepared their minds to adopt those modes of comfort and cleanliness which they had been accustomed to view only as the peculiarities of a strange people."

The first converts were baptised in June, 1829. The following interesting extract from a letter written by Mrs. Moffat in Oct., 1829, to a friend in England will show her joy over the "first fruits" of their labours: "You will doubtless have anticipated our feelings in the events of the past year and a half, in observing the progress of the natives in divine knowledge, their regular attendance on the means of grace, the solemn and devout attention in the house of God, and at length the general commotion in the minds of almost all on the place inquiring with the greatest possible earnestness what they must do to be saved; and after that had subsided, the decided profession of a number who have been judged fit subjects for the Christian ordinances of Baptism and the Lord's Supper. We must have been truly insensible not to have felt—tears of joy and gratitude often flowed to give vent to those feelings which could not be expressed; we were frequently overpowered with a sense of the goodness of God, that He had not suffered any of us to descend to the grave without the sight—a sight which we sometimes thought was reserved for those who should follow after us. The day on which they were baptised was a solemn season, and that part of it especially on which we surrounded the table of the Lord, where we could not but weep together at the recollection of the days and years that were past as contrasted with the present scene. It was not a little singular that the Communion vessels should arrive only the Friday night before, just when they were needed, and we could not but regard even that incident as a condescending mark of the Divine approbation of the measure of faith exercised both by the donors and the applicant; for sure to some they would have appeared very superfluous at the time they were sent from Sheffield. I am happy to be able to inform you that the converts are going on well, walking consistently with their profession, and we hope soon to have some addition to their numbers, as there are several on the station who appear to have abiding impressions. The standard of morality is considerably raised, so that those who are no way particularly serious abstain from those sins which were formerly committed with impunity. They are becoming generally more civilised. The station affording great facilities for agriculture, it is carried on to a considerable extent. The missionaries have now fine gardens, vineyards, orchards, and corn-fields, so that they have our example, which they follow very well; they are chiefly poor people of different tribes. The head of each family has a garden on the mission-ground, and all who have that privilege are bound to work (*for wages*) whenever their services are required for building, agriculture, or any public work. Their industry enables them to barter very profitably. The place is much frequented by strangers from different parts of the interior; for this purpose they bring their karosses, ivory, &c., which they exchange chiefly for tobacco grown on the place, so that it forms a kind of mart, and keeps up a friendly intercourse with the natives in general. The females are beginning to be ashamed of their heathenish dress, of which they are naturally very tenacious; and all who feel the importance of a change of life and manners, cast it off as soon as they are able to procure skins for a petticoat. They are now, many of them, learning to sew, and make tolerable progress. Many of the young people can both read and write; but, as may easily be conceived, those who are older are but dull. Mr. Moffat has now nothing to do with the school; Mr. Hamilton has it to himself, Mr. Moffat's engagements in the way of translation are so numerous, and schoolbooks being so much wanted. He has the Gospel of Luke and a work of Dr. Brown's, entitled "Scripture Extracts," almost ready for the press. The latter contains a great mass of Scripture, and will doubtless be very useful to the natives till such time as the whole Bible can be translated. He has also commenced translating historical lessons out of the Old Testament, commencing with the three first chapters of Genesis. He has also fourteen hymns in the language, which they learn very quickly, and sing very well to some of our finest English tunes."

The following is the beautiful hymn, "I think, when I read the sweet story of old," translated into the Sechuana:—

"Eare ke gopola ga Yesu Morèn,
 Ka o la tla go aga bathuñ,
 Kaha o la bitsa banyana go èn;
 Ke rata ke le ke le gon.

"Nko ke eletsa diatla, le cōn'
　Tsa gagwè ke di beilwe tlhogoñ,
Le go mo utlwa ka a bua le bōn'
　'Tlañ go nna banyana ke lon'.'
" E, rure, nka ea go èna yanuñ
　Go mmatla mo merapeloñ;
Ha ke tlhôahala go mmatla hatshiñ,
　Ke, la nna naè kwa godimoñ.
" O ile go banya kwa bontlè bo gōn'
　Helo go bōna ba' ichwarecweñ,
Kwa banyana bantsi ba phuthilweñ gōn'
　Ba bogosi yoa legodimo.
" Ba thausanta bantsi ba mo timeloñ
　Ba ba sa itseñ legodim';
Kea rata ba itse ha bonno bo gōn'
　Kwa Yesu o gōna bontleñ.
" Ke tlhologèlèlwa lobaka lo' tlañ
　Lo lontlè lo lo ratègañ,
Mogañ o banyana ba' mo merahiñ
　Ba ea go eo o ba bitsañ."

During Mr. Moffat's frequent absence Mrs. Moffat was left in charge of the station, and attended to the affairs of the mission. It is gratifying to be able to record that she was not once molested during these enforced seasons of loneliness, but looked up to and consulted by the natives as if she carried Mr. Moffat's head on her shoulders. At all times she regularly visited and ministered to the sick and aged among the people. At these visits she would read the Scriptures, and explain them, in many little addresses and exhortations, which found their way to the hearts of the people. Years afterwards these addresses were remembered, and referred to, by many a grateful hearer to whom they had been blessed. Even in the last conflict these words of the lady-teacher would rise up with instruction and comfort, so that resting upon Divine truth, the once benighted heathen hearer would confidingly cross the Jordan of death. Mamonyatsi was one of these. She was a Matabele slave, and had followed Mr. Moffat on one of his journeys from the interior. Mr. Moffat had taken her into his service, and had taught her about Christ— teaching which the poor girl received lovingly and gratefully. She made a public profession of her faith, and lived up to it most sincerely, but she was full of trouble for those of her kindred who knew not Jesus. One day Mr. Moffat found her weeping, and on inquiring the cause of her tears she sobbed out, holding up the Gospel of Luke, " My mother will never see this Word; she will never hear this good news!" Then she wept again, and wailed out, "Oh, my mother and my friends! they live in heathen darkness, and will die without seeing the light which has shone on me, and without tasting the love which I have tasted! Oh, my mother, my mother!" Mamonyatsi breathed forth many a prayer for her heathen mother, and after witnessing a good confession of faith, died triumphantly. Doubtless she welcomed her much-loved teacher to the "better land."

Instant in season and out of season, " Mrs. Moffat continued for about fifty years to labour for Christ and souls among the Bechuanas. During the latter years of this term of service her strength oftentimes failed, and again and again her husband had to remonstrate with her on the impropriety of exceeding the limits of her strength. But the aged matron could not forbear; she held, regularly, Sabbath services among the women, walking punctually amid the weaknesses of advancing life to the place of meeting. And when, in the course of years, it became desirable to return home—to relinquish active service—the separation between the teacher and the taught was most touching. For many long miles a large number of converts followed the wagons, with tears, sobs, sighs, and every expression of sorrowing affection. By-and-by the numbers began to diminish, and as the last disappeared, out of a full heart Mrs. Moffat exclaimed, " What a relief that I cannot any more look upon the faces of those I have so loved and prayed for! I now feel some relief, for the separation from so many beloved ones is most painful." She had looked her last upon the much-loved pupils, but the work remains. This little church at the Kuruman now numbers 230 members.

This loving spirit was most brave withal. Sometimes she accompanied her husband on his journeys into the interior; but at other times, to spare Dr. Moffat's services to the mission and to the work of translation, she travelled alone. On one occasion she went, with native attendants only, over three hundred miles to visit Mrs. Livingstone; and on more than one occasion she travelled to Algoa Bay, and to Cape Town, to arrange matters in relation to the education of her children. These journeys required bravery beyond description, but amidst it all the heroine exhibited an unconscious abnegation of self which added nobility to her character. Shortly after her return to England a friend said to her, " God has honoured you to be a great helper to your husband." " Yes," she replied; " I always studied my husband's comfort, never hindered him in his work, but always did what I could to keep him up to it." This reply gives the key to her character as a missionary's wife. Self-denial, self-forgetfulness, and self-sacrifice, seem to have been prominent traits. Speaking of Mrs. Moffat's letters, Dr. Moffat says, " Into whatever letter I glance there is the transcript of a soul sympathising with, and yearning to serve, the interests of the Redeemer's kingdom."

In all the relationships of life, Mrs. Moffat was the wise, tender counsellor, and the unfailing friend. We give an interesting extract from a letter written by her to her eldest grandson, Robert Livingstone. This young man was the eldest son of Dr. and Mrs. Livingstone, and after being trained at the University of Glasgow, went first to Africa to accompany his father, and thence to America, where he entered the Federal army, and engaging in the Civil War, was wounded, and ultimately died at Richmond. The letter speaks for itself, and proves what a wealth of affection welled up in that motherly heart towards the young man.

"Kuruman, October 4th, 1863.

"MY DEAR GRANDSON, ROBERT LIVINGSTONE,—How vastly were we relieved the other day by getting letters, both from Cape

Town and Natal, with the information that you were at the former place awaiting your father's direction. It is now many months since we heard from your aunt Moffat that you had arrived at Natal on your way to the Zambese. The mournful tidings of the death of your dear mother only came to our ears just when our hearts were yet bleeding over that of her brother, our own dear Robert. For some time after these mournful bereavements I did not feel able to use my pen, and when strength of mind was again restored, it was only to address those dear ones who were partakers of our sorrow. For your dear father, too, we feel much, and dread any increase of his trials. And you are my eldest grandchild—the first-born of my dearest Mary —the first of her family who lisped "papa" and "mamma" to ourselves, and I cannot but feel the deepest interest in you now, when you have no mother to look to. I now feel myself very frail, as it were tottering on the brink of the grave; but while I do live, let me know your tastes, your aspirations for this world, and for that which is to come; for I trust, my dear boy, you do not forget that after all your plans and purposes for this life, whether they may prosper or fail, there is a life to come infinitely more important, when it will be found that verily 'the chief end of man is to glorify God, and enjoy Him for ever.' Open your heart to me, as you would to the dear departed mother, were she here. I am hoping, ere long, to join her in that world of spirits, to which, in her last letter to us, she expressed a kind of anticipation of welcoming us, her aged parents. And is it not possible that she will there be allowed to inquire of the condition of those she left behind? It is now long since we heard from your dear father; we look longingly for intelligence of him, poor man, but have seen nothing for some time. Old Kuruman is much as you left it. We were long worried with fears of the Boers, but for two or three years they have been too busy contending among themselves to meddle with us; but they have sadly encroached on the lands to the east of us, and the tribes are much scattered. The beautiful valley of Mabotsa, the place of your birth, is now deserted, from its contiguity to their dwellings. Mebalwe, whom I think you will remember, is at his old business, defending the helpless from the lion, as he did your dear father many years ago. He has a lasting affection for your father, and would do and suffer much to see him once again. Your grandfather is still the hale old man, and steps about more quickly than some who are only half his age; yet he feels some of the infirmities of advanced life. He is always in danger of being overworked, and labours much at what for some time he has felt to be his chief work, the revision of the entire sacred Scriptures preparatory to a new edition, which he hopes to see before he dies. The Prices are just now at the Bamangwato, half way between Kolobeng and the Matabele; they are in a trying position, being quite alone, and the enemy likely enough to make a fresh attack. Thus, we have to exercise strong faith on account of all of them, and not less for your own dear father, who has passed through so many dangers unhurt. We know he is immortal till his work is done; but always stand prepared for a shock. O this poor Africa! how great are its miseries. But how much has he done and suffered to alleviate its sorrows!

MRS. MARY MOFFAT. 63

MR. MOFFAT PREACHING TO THE BECHUANAS.

"Now, for the present, I must conclude, and remain, my dear Robert, "Your affectionate grandmother,

"MARY MOFFAT."

Mrs. Moffat was the mother of nine children, two of whom died in infancy. Mary, the eldest, became the wife of Dr. Livingstone; Ann, the next, married Mr. Fredoux, a French missionary; Robert, a promising young man, died from over-exertion in mental and physical labours; John is still a missionary in Bechuana-land; Elizabeth married the Rev. Roger Price, a missionary of the London Missionary Society. Besides these, there are two other daughters, who are still living.

But the time was come to retire from active work. Dr. Moffat had completed the translation of the whole Bible into the Sechuana language, and was now anxious to see it carried through the press, so, in 1870, yielding to the solicitations of the directors of the London Missionary Society, Dr. and Mrs. Moffat turned their faces homeward. They arrived in England in July of that year, and were received with enthusiastic welcomes from all hearts. And the aged saint, who had borne the burden and heat of the day for fifty-one years, still looked forward to the accomplishment of her husband's life-work with yearning solicitude. Especially during the last few weeks of her life, did she dwell upon the fact, and painted bright pictures of all the joy and all the gladness which this Book would carry to the tribes for whom she had worn herself out. But she was not permitted to see this realisation of their united hopes and prospects. Barely six months passed by from the time of her landing on English soil, ere she passed away to the eternal shore. Her long African life had enfeebled her constitution, and the cold of our winter proved too much for her. On January 10th, 1871, after a few days' suffering from bronchitis, Mrs. Moffat went "up higher." She went from her work to her reward!

In contemplation of such a devoted life, the mind shrinks back in self-condemning humility, and the pen seems too feeble an instrument to do it justice. What, compared with the toils, the sufferings, the privations, the anxieties, the persecutions, and the labours of fifty years, is our poor little, whether of sacrifice or gifts? What English lady can stand side by side with Mrs.

Moffat in the matter of missionary service? We give our few poor mites, or shillings, or pounds to the missionary cause, and then complacently think that we have done our duty. Mrs. Moffat and her co-workers stand on a far more elevated plane of duty; they come nearest to the Master in serving, and doubtless they will be nearest Him in glory. O the littleness of earth's riches and grandeur! how it all shrinks into insignificance when compared with a life like this!

Some may imagine, and perhaps hint, that this foreign mission work is almost vain; that it involves a great waste of life and an almost useless waste of money; that indeed the waste far exceeds the gain. Do not such objections recall the objector Judas? And does it not, too, recall the rebuke which Jesus gave him—a rebuke which was made up of commendation to the person blamed. How the words of that commendation ring through Christendom this day! How they wither the objector's words, and exalt the noble self-sacrifice! So it is now. The noble missionary worker works not alone, or unheeded, but is constantly under the approbation of the Lord of the vineyard, and He himself will deliver His own cause from blame, and honour His servant. So also He honours those who *give* for His cause. And when we gave ourselves to Jesus did we not give our money also? If this be the case, does Christ expect us to give merely the trifle which we can give without missing, or does He not look for a measure of sacrifice? We must not offer to our God that which costs us nothing; or, while we gaze admiringly at such a life as Mrs. Moffat's, we shall be all too sadly, and too surely, heaping up condemnation for ourselves.

MRS. GOBAT.

MRS. MARIA REGINA CHRISTINA GOBAT,

Wife of the Right Rev. Samuel Gobat,

BISHOP OF JERUSALEM; OF THE CHURCH MISSIONARY SOCIETY.

"A weary path I travelled, 'mid darkness, storm, and strife,
Bearing many a burden, contending for my life.
But now the morn is breaking, my toil will soon be o'er,
I'm kneeling at the threshold, my hand is on the door.
The friends that started with me have entered long ago.
Ah! one by one they left me to struggle with the foe.
Their pilgrimage was shorter, their triumph sooner won;
How lovingly they'll hail me, when once my work is done.
O Lord, I wait Thy pleasure—Thy time and way are best;
But I'm wasted, worn, and weary: my Father, bid me rest."
W. L. ALEXANDER.

ARIA REGINA CHRISTINA ZELLER was born on the 9th of November, 1813, at Zofingen, in the canton of Aargau, Switzerland. She was one of a long family, being the second of eleven children. Her father, Christian Heinrich Zeller, was of an old Wurtemberg family; but he had gone over to Switzerland to settle, and was at that time director of the schools in Zofingen. Madame Zeller was the daughter of a Swiss clergyman, and it was gratefully recounted in her family that this lady had in her childhood experienced a very remarkable escape from peril. She was playing in the garden in front of the parsonage, when her father happened to

look out of the window, and saw a huge Lamergeier, or Alpine eagle, soaring above the child, and slowly, but surely, coming lower and lower, watching his chance to seize upon her. Snatching up his gun, which in that mountainous region was always kept loaded, the pastor fired just as the bird was on the point of catching hold of the child. The next moment the eagle lay dead at his feet, and the child was saved.

In the year 1819, Christian Heinrich Zeller received the call to begin the well-known home for destitute children, in Beuggen near Bâle; and he soon joined to it the institution for training poor schoolmasters. His great love for, and devotion to, the work, caused it to increase from year to year, and the divine blessing was granted very largely. Little Maria was six years old when the family removed to Beuggen; and in this atmosphere of simple faith, love, and self-denying work for the benefit of others, she spent her youth. Her father treated his children with love, combined with great firmness and strictness, so that it was always with a mingled feeling of love and respect that they looked up to him. Under the influence and guidance of Madame Zeller, their excellent mother, Maria and her sisters grew up, learning to put a helping hand everywhere, and to assist cheerfully in bearing the burdens of others. She spent a few years away from home, for the completion of her education, and then returned to be her mother's right hand in every department of household duty. She was beloved by all on account of her unselfish character, and her happy, contented disposition; while her younger brothers and sisters looked up to her in everything. She was very conscientious, and had often a deep feeling of her sinfulness, and her need of a Saviour. So constant and deep were these impressions, that she repeatedly and solemnly gave herself up, body and soul, to the Lord's service. Her simple faith, her trust in God, and her undivided love to her Saviour, remained unchanged throughout the whole of her long life.

Toward the end of 1833, the well-known Abyssinian

missionary, Rev. Samuel Gobat, went to Beuggen, and became acquainted with the family of the Zellers. Mr. Gobat had been engaged in missionary work and missionary studies for and with the Abyssinians, under the auspices of the Church Missionary Society, from 1826. In 1833 Mr. Gobat visited Europe in order to make known the preparedness of the land of Abyssinia for mission-work, and to induce other labourers to accompany him back to the work. On becoming acquainted with Maria Regina Zeller, he soon discovered that the young lady possessed all the necessary qualifications for becoming a good wife and a good missionary. The consent of the parents was gained; the young couple were betrothed during the last days of December, 1833, and married on the 23rd of May, 1834. Soon after, they paid a farewell visit to Mr. Gobat's home at Cremine, in the canton of Berne, and then started on their difficult journey to Abyssinia. The young missionaries had a rough time in travelling: on the Red Sea they sailed in Arab dhows, or sailing vessels; and while going through the desert they rode on camels, or mules. They could only take the most necessary things with them, and had many hardships to endure. But they bore all with willing courage; while Mrs. Gobat occupied her spare time in learning the Amharic language, and with so good a teacher as her husband, she soon made rapid progress. Very soon after reaching Massowah, Mr. Gobat fell very ill; but he resolved, if possible, to push on to Abyssinia, in order to introduce his young brother-missionary to the work. This brother was the Rev. Mr. Isenberg, who had been appointed to the mission in consequence of Mr. Gobat's representations. However, it was with great difficulty that they reached Adowa, and here they were forced to settle down for a time, for Mr. Gobat was taken so much worse that he was confined for two years to his bed. And now commenced a time when true faith, courage, and devotion, were put to the test. With the advent of the first child came a season of unparalleled trial. Mr.

Gobat seemed almost dying, and the poor young mother felt alone in a strange land. They could get no medicines but the few they had with them, and there was no possibility of getting any suitable food. But the Lord was with them, and helped them through. Writing to the Church Missionary Society in July, 1835, Mr. Isenberg thus expresses his fears concerning Mr. Gobat's life:—"Mr. Gobat's health has not at all improved; on the contrary, by the continuance of his illness, his bodily powers are daily diminishing, to the great distress of us all. May God in His mercy look upon him, and restore him to health, and enable him to resume the work of this important mission with energy and joy."

The love and kindness of the natives, who, from Mr. Gobat's former residences in Abyssinia, held him in the highest esteem, did much to make their stay at Adowa bearable. And it is strange, that, notwithstanding all the trials and difficulties they had to endure in that land, the reminiscences and recollections of Abyssinia were, with them both, to the end of their lives, the very dearest. They never spoke of the country and its people but with enthusiasm; and in after years, when some of the poor Abyssinians visited them in Jerusalem, the missionary bishop and his wife lavished willing love and kindness upon them.

Mr. Gobat's health continued so precarious that a doctor who happened to be in the country was consulted, and he said that there was no hope for the missionary's life unless he left immediately for Europe. The Church Missionary "Records" of that date refer sympathetically to this fact, but those who read such notices little imagined the trials involved in that return journey to Cairo. But there was no help for it, he must return or die, and so Mr. and Mrs. Gobat sorrowfully turned their backs on the country where they had hoped to live and labour for the Lord. Mrs. Gobat herself had several severe illnesses while in Adowa—twice she was prostrated by cholera; but it was with much regret that they bade farewell to Mr. Isenberg and his wife,

ARAB DHOWS IN THE RED SEA.

who were now commencing good work among the Abyssinians.

The journey back was most trying, but very quickly Mr. Gobat realised benefit in the shape of increased health and strength. With great difficulty they reached Massowah, and embarked in an Arab boat for the voyage up the Red Sea. This boat was so small that the only cabin measured eight feet long, by about four and a half high. They could not stand upright, and there was barely room to walk about on the deck. The sailors had laid in provisions for three weeks only, expecting to finish the voyage by that time, but instead of that they were thirty-eight days on the sea, having no food save rice boiled in half-putrid water. The goat which Mr. Gobat had taken on board in order to provide milk for the infant, died, and the poor babe having no proper sustenance, was taken seriously ill. After landing at Cossier, on November 4th, 1835, the journey through the desert commenced. To the last Mrs. Gobat could hardly speak of that journey without tears, and one particular day—the 8th of November—was found since her death, recorded in a small text-book diary as " the hardest of her life." It was no wonder that the brave heart sunk, or that endurance failed, for we find that they had to travel many days in the burning sun without a good hat, or an umbrella, with nothing save coarse food, and scarcely any water. Fortunately Mr. Gobat was better, but Mrs. Gobat was ill and worn-out; the babe got worse, and did nothing but moan and cry, while at nights no rest could be obtained. At that time she was sometimes near despair, and would frequently ask *why* God had allowed such trials to come upon her, when she had left home, and friends, and country for His sake and the Gospel's. Indeed, she records that more than once she was led almost to reason with God, and to despair of His fatherly love. But such bitter hours of murmuring were short; she humbled herself before Him, and became assured of His forgiveness. Her husband's kindness, and his meek, patient bearing of these trials were a great help to her. In order to reach Cairo, they had to travel a few days by boat on the Nile, and now hope revived that the child might yet be saved. However, this was not to be; the babe died a few hours before reaching Cairo, and the broken-hearted mother sat during those few remaining hours with her dead infant in her arms, shedding bitter, unavailing tears. Little Sofie was laid to rest in the Coptic burial-ground in Cairo, and for a season the weary, way-worn travellers found shelter in the house of the Rev. T. Leider. About five weeks after their arrival there, a second child was given to them, whom, in remembrance of their past trials, they named Benoni.

They reached home by September, 1836, and sought to recover health and strength among their native mountains. After some two years spent in Germany and Switzerland, Mr. Gobat and his wife went to Malta, being sent there to superintend the translation of the Bible into Arabic, and to take charge of the printing-press. They remained in this island for about three years, when they returned to Switzerland again, where Mr. Gobat diligently laboured for the Missionary Society in various ways. At length, in 1845, Mr. Gobat was appointed vice-principal of the Malta Protestant College, but he had not been there a year, before he was nominated by Frederick William IV. of Prussia to the see of Jerusalem. Mr. Gobat was much surprised at this intelligence, but felt bound not to refuse the call, seeing in it a summons to work in a desirable part of the Lord's vineyard. "Wherefore," he said, "I felt persuaded that the call was from God, and herein I ground my hope that God will bless me and make me a blessing."

On Sunday, July 5th, 1846, Dr. Gobat was consecrated at Lambeth, as bishop of the Church of England, by His Grace the Archbishop of Canterbury, assisted by the Bishops of London, Lichfield, and Calcutta. They then proceeded to Jerusalem, and there, both husband and wife entered into their work with their whole strength of body and mind, ever setting before them as their great aim the necessity of being really a father and mother to those committed to their charge. Mrs. Gobat, notwithstanding her many home-duties, and her large family of children, was indefatigable in her labours of love during those first years in Jerusalem. She became her husband's helpmeet in everything, taking the most constant interest in all the schools and missions. These schools were all

VIEW OF JERUSALEM.

commenced by Bishop Gobat, and prosecuted so vigorously that in the year before his death he reported that there were about 1,400 children under instruction in them. Even in the last years of Mrs. Gobat's life, when by reason of weakness and age she could not *do* so much, she was always trying to comfort the sorrowful, to help the needy, to guide the erring ones, and to "work" in peculiarly feminine departments of labour, "while it was day." The rule that guided her in all things was *love;* she could not see a case of distress without helping; she could not witness sorrow or grief without weeping with those that wept; she could not see a child without loving it, and doing something to make it happy; nor could she hear of anyone having sinned or backslidden, without going to them and praying with them. If she thought she had done wrong to anyone, or unintentionally hurt their feelings, she had no rest till she had asked pardon. Says one who knew her well, "Sometimes she would perhaps go too far in the thorough uprightness and straightforwardness of her character, and occasionally offend people by speaking too plainly; but I was told that many, though at first hurt by her words, had all the time felt that those words were spoken out *of her love* for their good, and were thankful for her friendship. Her greatest pleasure was to *give* and to make others happy. Her hospitality was well known in Jerusalem, and many travellers to the Holy Land can testify to this."

To her children she was ever a most affectionate mother, thinking of all their wants, entering into their pleasures and sorrows, and always bringing them in her prayers to the Good Shepherd. All belonging to the mission were received with invariable kindness by her; the poor, the widows, and the stricken ones, all sought her out, and were so ministered to by her for the Lord's sake, that one complaint made against her was that "she was too kind to them." She possessed the enviable art of making others happy in an eminent degree, so that everybody seemed to be at home with her after the first few minutes.

For all the schools and mission institutions she cared with a mother's interest; but she specially loved the Diocesan School and Orphanage on Mount Zion. She knew every one of the children by name, and cared most earnestly for their wants. This orphanage, as well as the other mission schools, prospered and increased abundantly under the fostering care of Bishop Gobat during his thirty-three years of labour there. Beginning at first with a small number, it now contains sixty-six pupils, of whom some are specially trained with the view of engaging in mission-work in future years. This orphanage was supported chiefly by voluntary contributions, the Bishop and Mrs. Gobat making up all deficiencies out of their own private purse, but was, three years since, made over by the Bishop to the Church Missionary Society. This society has undertaken to provide the salaries of the teachers, but, as heretofore, the expenses of the children themselves must be paid for by private contributions. The institution is carried on under the superintendence of the Rev. John Zeller, son-in-law of the late bishop, and successor in his self-denying labours. It will be seen how greatly this orphanage taxed the private means of Bishop and Mrs. Gobat, when we quote a statement made by the bishop in his last "Annual Letter." He says: "Hitherto the expenses have been at my charge, and will be for some time to come, although this year I have only received from England between £250 and £260, for boarding and clothing sixty boys, while the expenses, exclusive of teachers' salaries, will amount to about £700, on account of great dearth of bread. This institution has hitherto been richly blessed of God, and successful in raising many poor and neglected children to good positions in society; and what is more, of leading many of them to the saving knowledge of God their Saviour. Some of them have become in their turn the means of leading others to the same Saviour, as schoolmasters or catechists; while two, having been ordained presbyters of the Church of England, are now labouring—one in England and one in Jerusalem." He adds: "I began first, with nine children of both sexes, in November, 1847; and now we have in Judea, Samaria, and Galilee thirty-six or thirty-seven Protestant schools, together with twelve native Protestant communities, with perhaps as many hundred individuals professing to receive the Word of God as the only rule of faith and life."

Mrs. Gobat ever considered that she possessed the greatest cause for joy and thankfulness in being permitted to be the partner of such a man. He understood her perfectly—knew how to cheer and comfort her when sad or disheartened, and to set her right with a kind word if he thought she had made a mistake. They lived so entirely for each other, and strove so constantly to model their household life upon the Word of God, that every one coming to them felt the influence of true piety. The sudden death of her eldest son, in the year 1873, made a deep impression on Mrs. Gobat, and though she bore the blow as a Christian should, yet, as a mother, she felt it most keenly. But the separation was only for a little while.

Both Bishop and Mrs. Gobat felt that Jerusalem was their only earthly home, and the place where they would like to end their days. When, in the spring of 1878, they left for their last visit to Europe, they were not quite decided about returning; but the bishop said to her one day, "Let us go to Europe and see our children and our friends, and then come back to Jerusalem, to die here together." And so it came to pass.

They went to Europe, but in the autumn of 1878 the bishop had a shock of paralysis, which alarmed Mrs. Gobat considerably, and rendered the venerable man so feeble that it was with the greatest difficulty they could accomplish the journey back. In spite of loving care and the greatest precautions, he sank, and on the 17th of May, 1879, early on a Sabbath morning, at the age of eighty, he entered into rest. This trial was a crushing one, but Mrs. Gobat did not rebel. She tried to say, "It is the Lord!" and was most grateful for the ministrations of loving children, but it was evident to all that her love of life was broken, and that she would not survive her partner long. Their lives were too closely knit together, for they had been united for the long period of forty-five years, and had always borne sorrows, joys, and labours equally.

One day she said to her children, "Now papa has been gone two months, and I am still here." Another time she said, "I shall follow soon; I have no more work to do in Jerusalem—my task is finished." Her weakness increased, although she was not ill otherwise, and she was sometimes even in good spirits. She was as kind as ever, as anxious as ever to do good, and to help to the utmost of her feeble powers. On Sunday, July 27th, without any particular illness, she begged to be prayed for in the public services of the day, and said to different persons, "Pray for me—not that I should get well, but that I should be ready to die." Her daughter's graphic narrative proceeds:—" On Monday she was feverish, and the doctor advised her to stay in bed. She liked us to sit with her, and read or pray with her, but gradually became indifferent to earthly things. On Wednesday she asked me to read one of her favourite hymns, commencing, 'For what shall I praise thee, my God and my king?' When I came to the words, 'I thank Thee for sickness, for sorrow, for care, For the thorns I have gathered, the anguish I bear,' she said 'I have always had something to be thankful for.' On the Thursday night we found that consciousness had quite fled; she knew no one, she could answer no more questions, and probably heard neither the words that were said, nor the prayers that were offered. But we knew she was ready; we knew in whom she had trusted; her whole life had been witness enough; we needed no last assurances. She was very restless for some hours, having acute inflammation of the brain. But, thank God! she was not allowed to suffer long, and at half-past nine on the 1st of August, 1879, she quietly breathed her last. Her death occurred not quite twelve weeks after my father's. Truly they were lovely and pleasant in their lives, and in death they were not divided. We laid her beside his still new grave, under the shadow of a spreading olive tree—sweet emblem of the peace they are now enjoying. At the interment many of the poor people wept bitterly, saying, '*Now* we really have become orphans.' All felt that a 'mother in Israel' had been taken from their midst."

As soon as the tidings went forth that Mrs. Gobat had

rejoined her husband in the better land, the good of all churches mourned for the lost workers of Jerusalem. The two—husband and wife—had for so long filled such conspicuous posts in the mission in Palestine, that it seemed as if they *could not* be spared. But we may pray, and trust that the Lord of the vineyard, who endowed Elisha with prophetic power when Elijah was summoned to his reward, will also raise up labourers who will enter into their labours. An extract or two from the letters of visitors, who had spent happy weeks or months in Jerusalem, enjoying Mrs. Gobat's hospitality, will serve to show what kind of impression she made upon those who came into passing communion with her. Says one lady : " I am so thankful I saw your dear mother last year. I was then more than ever struck with her kindness of heart, and the humility which made her speak as if I had done her a favour by accepting her kind hospitality for three happy months in Jerusalem." Another says : " Never can I forget the time I spent under her hospitable roof. How good she was to me ; how edifying her conversation. I felt her to be like a mother—as if she had known me for years. What a blessing for her to be so soon called up to be re-united to her beloved partner ! How painful life would have been without him—how bitter her declining days ; but now what a gainer she is ! "

Mrs. Gobat was accustomed to pray in German as a rule, that being her mother tongue ; but among her remains were found some beautiful prayers in English. We quote one, as a sample of her devotional spirit :—
" O Lord, long-suffering, and gracious, how many years hast thou added to my life, and yet I still am an unfruitful fig-tree ; although thou, O Heavenly Gardener, hast not failed to dig, to prune, and to do all that ought to have made me fruit-bearing to thine honour and glory. Oh ! spare me yet, and continue Thy working in me till I have wholly yielded to Thy constraining love. O Lord Jesus, Lamb of God, make me feel assured that Thou hast taken my sins on Thee, so that I am now

free from condemnation. Oh, give me grace to be taught by Thy Holy Spirit, to be led by him, and not to resist his admonitions, his warnings. This is one of the causes, I am afraid, of my not enjoying more the gracious promises of Thy Holy Word, and possessing that peace which passeth all understanding. Let me wrestle and pray, and not faint till I have *fully* found *Thee*, and with Thee, and in Thee, everlasting life. Let me be a mother in Israel, a priestess in Thy house, and in my family. O Lord, let me be a true Mary, sitting at Thy feet, especially now, when I cannot be a Martha, being unable to go out and serve Thee, visiting the members of our congregation. Let me be a Mary, being Thy servant, and keeping Thy words."

Both Bishop Gobat and his wife are now gone from earth. "They rest from their labours, and their works do follow them." Heaven is richer, but earth is the poorer for their absence. They have gone from the Church militant, to unite with missionaries from every clime, and of every tongue, in the praises of God in the Church triumphant. It was but a short step from the Jerusalem of earth to the Jerusalem "not made with hands;" but from this "they shall go no more out for ever;" there is the abiding presence, and the abiding glory.

MRS. HANNAH CATHERINE MULLENS,
Wife of the Rev. Dr. Mullens,

MISSIONARY TO INDIA; OF THE LONDON MISSIONARY
SOCIETY.

" Sow: and look onward, upward,
Where the starry light appears,
Where, in spite of cowards' doubting,
Or your own heart's trembling fears,
You shall reap in joy the harvest
You have sown to-day in tears."

THE daughter of one noble-hearted missionary, and the wife of another, it was not surprising that Mrs. Mullens should possess the grace of missionary consecration from her earliest years. Some weighty words of her father's—the Rev. Alphonse Lacroix—given utterance to when Hannah was a child—furnished the key-note to her life-work, and probably determined the precise character of her labours among the women and girls of Calcutta. "Though some of the obstacles," said Mr. Lacroix, "to female education in this country have been removed, yet it is to be lamented that many still remain, and will, I fear, continue to exist until an entire change takes place in the religious and moral state of the natives. It is my opinion, that we ought to be anything but sanguine of success till Christianity has imparted to the Hindoos different

G

ideas of the female sex from those they now possess." From her girlhood's days until the hour when she laid down her life, and her work, simultaneously, Mrs. Mullens strove to advance the cause of education and religion among the native female population — both by efficient schools, and zenana mission-work in many Hindoo households. As a vigilant and unwearied labourer in this department, she realised a large measure of success.

Hannah Catherine Lacroix was born in Calcutta, on May 1st, 1826. Mr. Lacroix was a prayerful, earnest, genial-hearted missionary, doing God's work with vigilant, unwearied zeal, and making sunshine for all those about him. On this account Hannah's childish days were very happy ones. The father, by his knowledge of men and things, his vigorous mind, and his healthy tone of character, moulded the minds of the little ones; while Mrs. Lacroix directed the childish studies, in addition to caring for the comfort of the household. It seems that her youth was deficient in educational advantages, as Calcutta possessed almost no schools of the kind required at that date; so, with the exception of one year at school in that city, Hannah received all her education under the home-roof. That it was a Christian training we may be sure; that it was extensive, and in a large measure thorough, we may judge from the attainments and usefulness of her after-life.

As a girl Hannah Lacroix commenced to carry out the missionary precept—"Preach the Gospel to every creature,"—in her small measure. At twelve years of age she taught a class in a school for native girls at Bhowanipore. She could speak Bengali most fluently; most missionaries' children, in consequence of hearing their native nurses speak the language, and learning with infant lips to converse with them, gain that acquaintance with the idioms of foreign languages which favours intimate discourse. Consequently, the child of a missionary born in a foreign land, and tended by native nurses, can readily make use of all the turns, inflexions, and idioms of the language common to the natives themselves. Hannah could do this, and as the result, her labours among the Bengali girls were very greatly appreciated.

There is no doubt that the young girl was influenced greatly by her mother's example in her efforts to do good. Mrs. Lacroix for many years conducted a day-school for girls of the poorer Hindoo families with varying success. No zenana teaching was permitted in those days, and the few short years of school life could do but very little for the poor girls; still Mrs. Lacroix's work sprung up and bore fruit years after in quarters where it could be little anticipated. Although the girls were often taken away to be married at ten, eleven, and twelve years of age, they yet carried with them into their after-life some relics of the instruction gained in the school. Many years after Mrs. Lacroix's labours in this direction were ended, the following circumstance came to light, illustrating the value of her work. A little Hindoo girl, of ten years of age, already a widow, attended Mrs. Lacroix's day-school at Berhampore. After learning to read the Bible, this girl was removed by her friends; but she carried away with her several Christian books, and a few school books, promising to read them still, so as to retain some benefit of her studies. Nine years passed by, and nothing was heard of her, but one day, as the catechist of the Bhowanipore mission was passing by a pundit's house in Calcutta, he noticed and recognised this person, now a young woman, coming out of the pundit's house. Upon inquiry he found that she was acting as daily governess, *privately*, to the families of four Hindoo gentlemen, teaching them the art of reading from her own old, and well-thumbed Christian school-books. She was then earning sixteen rupees (thirty-two shillings) per month thus, and supporting herself respectably. Still, her employers were not favourable to the Christian religion, and in consequence of this the teacher kept away from the mission station, or she would have lost their patronage and her own employment. Thus the leaven of the Gospel was working silently, but efficiently, among the very classes and families shut out from purely missionary operations. What a fulfilment of the promise, "My word shall not return unto me void."

But—to return to Hannah Lacroix—although she was anxious to do good, she was not at this time a Christian. She had not as yet experienced the great change called "conversion;" but in God's providence a pious native was made the instrument of conviction. She was between thirteen and fourteen years of age when she attended a new year's prayer meeting in one of the Baptist chapels in Calcutta, taking solemn interest in all the proceedings. One of the native preachers, named Shuyaat Ali, offered up most earnest prayer for the children of missionaries dwelling in their midst, and that prayer produced a deep and lasting impression upon the young girl's mind. It led to decision of soul upon the great subject of personal salvation, earnest prayer for pardon and acceptance, sincere repentance and faith, and increased consecration to the Lord's work. In about a year from that time she was enabled to overcome her natural timidity, and offer herself to the church as a member. She was united to the church worshipping in Union Chapel, Calcutta, then presided over by Rev. Dr. Boaz, another missionary labourer.

When Hannah was about fifteen she accompanied her parents to England for the first time. During the voyage her modest manners, intelligent observations, and quiet, thoughtful mien, attracted the notice of a lady who seemed to possess that rare power of interesting and drawing out the youthful mind. This lady was a Mrs. Parsons, the widow of a missionary, and as such well fitted to engage all the youthful enthusiasm of Hannah's nature. There is no doubt but that the counsel and encouragement afforded by this lady, served to increase in the young girl that self-consecration which afterwards became so marked a trait in her character.

ON THE ESPLANADE. CALCUTTA.

On arriving in England she was placed at school for eighteen months, under wise and cultivated Christian ladies. As might have been expected, she applied herself with diligence to her studies; but even there her life-purpose displayed itself. The seminary was, fortunately, near the training-school of the Home and Colonial School Society; and, declaring it to be her fixed intention to devote her life on her return to Calcutta to the work of conducting native schools, she attended at the Home and Colonial Institution regularly, in order to gain a practical acquaintance with the best methods of teaching.

Mr. Lacroix's visit to England was extended long enough to include the period of Hannah's education at Mrs. Ramsey's school, and in 1843 he took Hannah with him to Switzerland, that she might see the beauties of his own dear Fatherland. Hannah kept a journal during her trip there, and recorded most graphically her intense delight and awe-stricken wonder in gazing on the Bernese Alps, and witnessing the sublime glories of sunrise and sunset in that region. It was a new and almost overpowering experience to the young girl, and assisted greatly in developing her powers of mind and soul. In the autumn of that year, Mr. Lacroix returned with his wife and daughter to India, reaching that land in January, 1844.

Immediately on her return, Miss Lacroix began direct mission and educational work. Forming a special class for the native female servants of the family, she taught them and their children regularly, with the most cheering results. She also took charge of the Bible-class in Union Chapel, and conducted it most successfully, having the satisfaction of hearing from some of her scholars, who passed away in early life, cheering testimony to the grace which had come to them, by means of her labours. Indeed, it is difficult to account for her striking successes in this department of Christian activity, upon any other theory than that she was a "born teacher." Teachers, no less than poets, "are born, not made;" and Mrs. Mullens was so successful in this sphere that we feel instinctively she assumed her proper post in the mission field.

At nineteen years of age she was married to the Rev. Joseph Mullens, of the London Missionary Society, in Calcutta; but her marriage did not circumscribe either her labours or her usefulness. On the contrary, the sphere of both widened and deepened. She now entered more fully upon a missionary life. Assuming the charge of the girls' boarding school in that city, she threw herself, soul and body, into the work, and succeeded in making the institution ere long a great power for good. Mrs. Mullens was accustomed to study Bengali literature; and in this pursuit Mr. Mullens, by his acquaintance with it, his researches in history, science, politics, and theology, became a most efficient helper. Husband and wife were true helpmeets to each other; labouring in one noble cause, they strengthened each other's hands, counting no labour, sacrifice or responsibility too great to further the object they had in view.

Mrs. Mullens' native boarding school became very popular, and by degrees the number of scholars increased from fourteen to sixty. In her plan of education she endeavoured, not to raise the Hindoo girls above their natural sphere of life, but to fit them for happier and holier careers in it. She inculcated upon them the refinement and purity of Christian life, while she left them free to adapt these new principles and lessons to their own native manners and customs, wherever they were of an absolutely innocent character. For instance, the girls wore the native female dress, with the addition of a tight-fitting inner jacket, which latter conduced both to comfort and propriety. They sat on mats spread on the floor during their studies, and slept on the same; eating and drinking according to the time-honoured customs of their land. In the experience of most, if not of all the zenana missionaries, this plan has been found advisable. It is not wise to attempt to make *foreigners* of natives; but they may be made Christians, without displacing many of their native manners and customs.

All innocent customs—such as those necessitated, for instance, by the requirements of the climate, in dress, food, and furniture—may remain, seeing that Eastern lands and peoples will always differ from Western, in outward conditions and modes of life. Then, too, Mrs. Mullens instructed the girls entirely in their own tongue, a fact which gained her ready attention and influence, while another, whose instructions would have mostly been in English, would not have succeeded so well. The girls gained a sound knowledge of the Bible, and of the more necessary branches of learning; after a certain standard had been reached, a little fancy work and English were added to the curriculum. In addition to all her work in the girls' boarding school, Mrs. Mullens also took charge of a Bible-class among the native women of the village. By means of these two agencies, many Christian and educated native women were added in after years to the churches of that district. It is an undoubted fact that many fruits of her labours in these quarters remain unto this day. The nurses and companions of her children were chosen out of this school, and by constant intercourse and companionship with the mission family, strengthened and confirmed the good commenced in their education.

Amid the cares of her family, and the labours connected with her school, Mrs. Mullens wrote at intervals a charming little book illustrative of native life, especially that of native women and children. It was entitled "Phulmani and Karuna: a Book for Native Christian Women." This story of Hindoo life received unmeasured praise from all quarters. Says one critic: "In reading this little work we are transported at once to the heart of a Bengali Christian village. Bengali women and children walk lifelike in flesh and blood before us. The children run about, the women gossip, and wrangle, and lie, or are honest, truthful, and industrious; but they are neither too bad nor too good for Bengali female nature as modified by Christianity. We are initiated into the mysteries of Bengali housekeeping, and begin to have becoming ideas of the value of a single farthing. We stand beside the death-bed of the righteous, and witness the awful end of the wicked, cut off unprepared in the midst of his sins. Christ, too, has a people in that little village, and the decency, industry, and good sense, the humble, active, cheerful piety which their lives show to be attainable and practicable in the poorest families, and under the most discouraging circumstances, can scarcely fail of leaving their moral in the most impervious mind. The leaven of heathenism that still lingers in the nominal Christian is delicately but clearly pointed out. Native customs and native prejudices, when injurious, are traced to their social and physical results with a happy simplicity. The story has all the simplicity and life-like minuteness of Defoe, and the reader, if he has any spiritual relish, will find himself throughout in communication with a gentler and holier spirit than is commonly to be met with in this imperfect state." We have quoted from this unknown critic at some length, because the circulation and influence of the book fully bore out this praise. It was everywhere caught up, both by missionaries and natives; it was translated into *twelve* Indian languages, becoming by this means circulated throughout India, and to this day it is read and prized by the native Christian community. And, amid all these varied labours, the one most prized and anticipated recreation of her life, was to spend each returning Saturday, together with her husband and children, at the house of her parents, where, once again, she would be the welcomed, dearly-loved child as in days of yore.

Mrs. Mullens' health partially failed in 1852, and a voyage to England was recommended; consequently she, together with her three young children, spent the year 1853 in this country, among loving friends and relatives. In 1854, after parting from her two eldest children for the sake of their health and education, she went back home again eager for work. But a sudden attack of fever threatened to snap the brittle thread of life and end her labours for ever. However, she was raised up again, and by degrees recovered strength sufficient to cope with her duties. The boarding-school—her chief sphere of action—had now increased to about sixty scholars; while, of the earlier members, some were married and settled in homes, striving to shed the light of Christianity upon those homes. They, in their turn, sent their little ones to be educated by Mrs. Mullens, so causing the training and influence to be perpetuated. She also wrote another work, which was printed in both English and Bengali, entitled "The Missionary on the Ganges; or, What is Christianity?" After this she translated Miss Tucker's popular book, "Daybreak in Britain," into Bengali.* Thus, by pen and tongue, she continued her indefatigable labours for the evangelisation of Hindoo females. Her letters to friends at this date prove that her mind was richly stored, and that out of the stores of that mind she brought forth treasures to enlighten and instruct all within the range of her influence. In some extracts from her correspondence it is easy to detect the prevailing principle of her life. Thus, writing to a friend, she says: "Nothing should be beneath us, done in our Master's service. In a worldly sense one might do better than teach the alphabet all one's life, but in Christ's service, looking at it in the light of eternity, it becomes something noble, great, and grand." Again: "Do we not feel at times how much we need a being to worship, who shall be to us a warm, loving, understanding friend, and yet God too? For a human heart is not strong enough for the burdens we impose, and there we find it. *The man Christ Jesus!* How often has this been said—how often written? but just now it comes to me with such freshness; a God-Man is so exactly what I must have to supply my present need that I could not help wishing it once again." Yet again: "I want to enjoy that sweetest of promises, to

---

* It is interesting to know that Miss Tucker (the well-known "A.L.O.E.") is now labouring as zenana missionary in Northern India.

stand 'without fault before the throne.' But perhaps it is better to wait His pleasure than to seem impatient. I only desire to be prepared for the Bridegroom's coming —to have my lamp trimmed, to be found, not slumbering, but watching. What a difference there must be in fitness for heaven. Some are saved just by grace, but they enter heaven with hardly any knowledge of it, as some travellers go to a new country about which they have never read; consequently they enjoy none of its beauties, nor understand its peculiar scenes, till they begin to feel themselves at home."

In 1858 the whole family came to England. Mr. Mullens came first, being suddenly summoned home by important matters connected with the Society, and arrangements were made for Mrs. Mullens to follow him in the next month. But just at this juncture one of the little ones fell ill, and delayed the mother's departure. She, however, arrived in England in September of the same year; and, as soon as she could, applied herself with her usual energy to advancing the cause of missions. In every possible way, she did this— by conversation, descriptions, and extempore addresses to Bible-classes, schools, and drawing-room meetings whenever the opportunity offered. The young people with whom she was thus brought in contact, learnt much of mission work in India, and drank largely of her spirit. During this visit home, however, a great trouble fell upon her, in the death of her father. She had always been specially dear to Mr. Lacroix, for the harmony of their minds had been remarkable, even from her girlish days, and the thought that she could not minister to him in his last moments, nor hear his last words, was one full of terrible grief. This event served still more to detach her affections from this world, and to cause her to anticipate with greater eagerness the reunion of spirits in that perfect home above. Mr. Lacroix's death took place in July, 1860, and soon after the bereavement the mission family returned to India. Once more, as Mrs. Mullens said she was mingling "with her Bengali

HINDOO TEMPLE, NEAR CALCUTTA.

women." Her especial work was taken up again with willing eagerness. The boarding-school was full, and openings for direct zenana work presented themselves all around. She had already, before departing for England, commenced visiting and teaching in the native homes; having, in fact, conducted two private schools in as many families for the instruction of Hindoo girls of the higher class. Now, in addition to resuming these, she adopted regular visiting among the zenanas in Bhowanipore with great success. Indeed, her work seemed to be more than ever her joy and "exceeding great reward."

But plaintively does Longfellow sing—and many in their experience have proved it true :—

> "I have marked it well, it must be true,
> Death never takes one alone, but two.
> Whenever he enters in at a door—
> Be it roof of gold, or roof of thatch—
> He leaves it always on the latch,
> And comes again ere the year is o'er."

Mrs. Mullens was to experience the bitter anguish of bereavement a second time. Her darling little Katie—the infant—was summoned away, after much suffering, to the home where neither tears, pain, nor woe, can enter. The parting was a sore trial to the mother. None but a mother who has herself buried babes can enter into the loneliness of heart which follows that bereavement. The heart aches for the little baby-smile and the baby-tongue which have made life so precious; and continually, even in the midst of friends, the thoughts wander off to the little mound of sacred earth where rests the tiny sleeper. This trial still further drew Mrs. Mullens' affections towards heaven. She had her "treasures there," in a most peculiar sense, and her heart was there also; but with a sense of the responsibilities pressing upon her, she turned for solace to the beloved work of instructing, and writing for, the women and girls of Bengal.

Her call from earth to heaven came suddenly in the midst of all these labours, but it found her ready. On the last day of her life she rose as usual, and employed the early morning hours in writing, having a book in hand for the native women which she was anxious to complete for the press by the end of the year. After breakfast, she went to the school, where she laboured with her usual bright energy, planning meanwhile to "take a holiday from one of her classes, on the morrow, for zenana work." After school was over, she again commenced writing, not allowing herself any rest between. Indeed, in response to a dear friend who urged her to take a little rest, she replied "No, no; I have just written in my book that English ladies have much to occupy their time, but they do everything without neglecting one duty for another. I shall neglect, if I leave my class; so pray don't ask me." After writing for a few minutes, she turned round to a friend who sat near, and suddenly cried out in pain. The attack was both sudden and acute; it immediately incapacitated her from any further work—indeed, almost from thought; and in the afternoon, as she lay on the couch of suffering, she said, "Is this afternoon only? It seems days to me, my pain is so acute." Still, amidst all the pain and suffering, her mind was full of her work, and she asked particulars about the zenana schools. However, as night drew on, the pain increased to agony, and she was exceedingly restless. Between the paroxysms she would fold her hands, and pray fervently to be helped. Then she would entreat the prayers of those around her, who eagerly tried every possible alleviation of her sufferings, but all in vain. The night was spent in agony by the dying one, and in tearful prayer, combined with unavailing attempts to secure ease for her, by those who stood around. When next morning dawned, she was more quiet, but evidently sinking, and anticipating the exchange of earth for heaven. Nearly all that day was passed in this way, when exceeding oppression of the breath came on, necessitating constant change of posture. But in spite of all that could be done, the agonies increased, while the dear one tried to bear them, and did bear them, with exceeding patience. As evening once more drew on, she said to a friend who was assisting her: "I do try to be patient. I try not to cry out. I know it is right. I do not wish it otherwise." Soon after, she exclaimed: "I can't breathe. Fan me." And with the words, her spirit passed away. The day which she had planned to be one of partial rest proved to be that in which she entered on "the rest remaining for the people of God."

The heart of Christian Calcutta was deeply moved at the tidings of her removal. Testimonies to her Christian worth and usefulness poured in from all sides. Said one: "I saw her grow up to become the flower of Christ's flock in Bengal." Said another: "The most respected and the most laborious among us is gone." A third added: "Hers was the most useful life in Calcutta." Medical science proved that no agency could have snatched her from the grave, because, owing to the rupture of an important artery, the hand of death was laid upon her from the first. The native converts and their families crowded around her burial, weeping that they should see her face no more. For sixteen years she had laboured among them as a pastor's wife, besides all the years of her girlhood, which, too, were filled up with self-denying efforts for their good. One of the sermons preached in her memory was delivered at the little mission chapel of Bhowanipore by a native preacher, who was, at the time she commenced her labours, sunk in heathenism and darkness. Thus passed Mrs. Mullens from her work to her reward. "They that be wise shall shine as the firmament, and they that turn many to righteousness as the stars, for ever and ever."

"Oh, Father, earth is very dark! but they
   Went on their quiet way,
Feeling Thy hand, even when they could not see
   Its mystic guidancy.
They heard earth's music, but turned not aside,
   To list its tones of pride,
But evermore their solemn vigils kept,
   Until in death they laid them down and slept."

MRS. EMILY C. JUDSON,
Wife of the Rev. Dr. Judson,

MISSIONARY TO BURMAH; OF THE AMERICAN BAPTIST MISSIONARY UNION.*

"By the bright waters now thy lot is cast,
Joy to thee, happy friend! thy bark hath passed
　　The rough sea's foam.
Now the long yearning of thy soul is stilled,
Home! home! thy peace is won! thy heart is filled—
　　Thou art gone home!"

"I dreamed of celestial rewards and renown,
I grasped at the triumph that blesses the brave,
I asked for the palm-branch, the robe, and the crown,
I asked, and Thou shewedst me the cross and the grave."

AMONG all the lives of women of worth, whether it be in the field of authorship, or of missions, we have read of none more exquisitely tender and touching than the story of "Fanny Forester" Judson, as given by her biographer, Professor Kendrick. We give her literary *sobriquet* in order to distinguish her from Dr. Judson's two other wives, and also because the name may possibly awaken in some of our readers' minds grateful recollections of the refined and cultured pen which has ministered to their delight in the pages of "Alderbrook," and other works of that class. Although

---

* Part of this sketch appeared in a religious magazine some fourteen years since. The Life has, however, been revised and enlarged for this volume.

chastened and suffering during a great part of her life, she yet contrived to accomplish a noble work in that brief span, so that her years were in reality "long, though not very many." Some characters attain ripeness long before others; they fulfil their allotted work, "and do enter into rest," while others are as yet only developing, and of this number Mrs. Emily Judson was one.

Her maiden name was Emily Chubbuck. Her birth-place was on the other side of the Atlantic. She was born in Eaton, a thriving village in Madison County, State of New York, on August 22nd, 1817. Her parents were poor, but upright, intelligent, and God-fearing; and though unable to give their daughter a dowry of worldly wealth, gave her what was far better —a religious and mental training. At eleven years of age, so poor were her parents, that she entered a woollen factory near her home, receiving something like five shillings per week. Of this place, she says: "My principal recollections are of noise, and filth, bleeding hands, aching feet, and a very sad heart." During the winters she attended the district school, and made considerable proficiency in learning.

She remained in the factory some time—indeed, until her health failed, and her medical attendant recommended country air. Just at this time we can trace the first germs—dawnings—of the missionary spirit which animated her in after years. An old copy of the *Baptist Register*, the organ of the American Baptist Missionary Society, fell into her hands one day, and her eye happened to light on a letter from Dr. Judson, describing his daughter's death. About the same time she read a Memoir of Mrs. Ann H. Judson, and this fired her heart with missionary enthusiasm. Of course, Dr. Judson was utterly unknown to her, except by missionary fame; and as she pondered, little dreaming how intimately she was to be connected with him in future years, she indulged in romantic dreams of missionary life. "And I, yes, I too, will be a missionary!" she said.

She left the factory, and very shortly became the subject of religious convictions. This was principally through the conversion of a sister, to whom she was fondly attached. About this time, too, she came under the influence of a clever, but semi-infidel teacher—a young lady, who was her instructor in English composition. While following her studies, which also included rhetoric and natural history, her mind was distracted at times by doubts on religious matters. This, doubtless, was a critical point in her lifetime. All deeply thoughtful natures have such doubt-seasons at some time or another; but, depend upon it, these seasons, if grappled with in a spirit of earnest inquiry and prayerful research, prove very "means of grace" to the soul. So it was with Emily Chubbuck.

She was devoted to her studies, and warmly engaged in everything that could improve and cultivate her mind. During this period she persisted in doing what students familiarly term "burning the candle at both ends." She says in her diary, under date January, 1832, "On Monday morning I used to rise at two o'clock, and do the washing for the family and boarders before nine. On Thursday evening I did the ironing; and Saturday, because there was but half a day at school, we made baking-day. I also took sewing of a mantua-maker close by, and so contrived to make good the time used in school. I found it, however, a difficult task to keep up with the other pupils without robbing my sleeping hours. I seldom got any rest till one or two o'clock, and then I read French, and solved mathematical problems in my sleep." In an entry dated two months' later, she says: "My health again failed, and the physician was again consulted. He said I must give up study, and leave school at once." No wonder! No human frame could possibly sustain such an accumulation of study and work. Without question she laid the foundation of future years of pain and weakness A month later, her mother insisted on her leaving school and suggested that she should commence a millinery business, but Emily rebelled against this most decidedly. Making bonnets and trimming caps might do very well for an occasional hour, but she could not seriously undertake to spend her life in it. "But what will you do?" said her mother. "Here you are, nearly fifteen, and you cannot go to school always." That was true enough, so as she says, "I went away to think." In this remark we see the character of the girl. Neither impulsive nor hasty; but calmly deliberate, and slow in resolution; and once determined on any course of action, as immovable as rock.

At last she decided on teaching a school, thus adding another to the long list of famous men and women who have ruled in village schools. Her tutor deemed her teaching abilities fully up to the required standard, but told her "she was not half big enough." Never mind; the sterling stuff of good, self-reliant womanhood was in her, and she did her best endeavour to attain her purpose. Our American cousins educate, in country districts, on a somewhat different system from ours. The teachers "board round," that is, board in turn for a week, fortnight, or month, as the case may be, with each member of the committee, during the school term, receiving besides, out of the district school fund, a certain number of dollars as a stipend. On making up her mind, she at once proceeded to act. Carrying in her pocket her credentials, she "took a short cut across lots" to a neighbouring village, as yet destitute of a "school marm." On inquiring for the principal trustee, she was shown into the presence of a raw-boned, red-headed, sharp-looking man, dressed in red flannel and cowhide boots. The young aspirant to school honours met with rather a cool reception. He questioned her as to her age, her acquirements, recommendations, and so on. He whistled when he heard her age, as well he might. Fancy a girl of fifteen becoming mistress over a school which should reckon among its scholars big, lubberly farm-labourers and rough 'prentice lads! For such would have been the case. At these Transatlantic seats of learning you may see all ages and both sexes side by side, conning the same book, and working the same sums.

Emily saw there was little chance for her there, so, betaking herself and her credentials into the woods, she solaced herself with the luxury of "a good cry." This restored her equanimity, and she trudged off again. Accompanied by a young friend, she proceeded to a district some three miles further on. Here the acting trustee seemed inclined to entertain her application. "But," said he, "the scholars will be bigger than their teacher." However, he expressed himself very well pleased with her, and promised to decide in another week. Emily went home, and tried to exercise the grace of patient waiting. In five days Mr. B. made his appearance, announcing that the trustees had engaged her as teacher at a salary of six shillings per week, and that her duties were to commence on the following Monday.

Fairly installed as teacher, she commenced working in earnest. Seven years passed in this way, her fame as an instructor spread abroad rapidly, and season after season she removed to more important schools. The winters were long vacations; only the summers—that is, the six months from April to September inclusive—were spent in tuition. But failing health and family troubles often broke her down; and her diary tells us more than once of her being compelled to close school, and return home to rest. During this period Emily became a frequent contributor to the village newspapers and periodicals.

During this period also she experienced the dawnings of "the new birth," and passed from death unto life. With the inflow of that "peace which passeth all understanding" came the renewed desire to consecrate herself to the mission cause. So fervent was the desire that she addressed a letter to the Rev. N. Kendrick, pastor of the Baptist church at Eaton, asking his counsel and assistance in the matter. One of her earliest childish dreams had been the wish to become a missionary, and the wish had remained with her through all her youth, so that now she had passed out of her teens and entered young womanhood it was stronger and more consuming than ever. Mr. Kendrick, seeing many objections in the way, advised her "to await the

VIEW OF UTICA, UNITED STATES.

openings of Providence." This she did, and by-and-by God led her by a way she knew not.

At this time a grateful change took place in Emily's affairs. A warmly-attached friend of hers mentioned to the Misses Sheldon, principals of the Utica Female Academy, her desire that Emily should be admitted to the privileges of that college. It had been customary for young ladies to go there and spend two or three years, partly in tuition and partly in study, so as to fit themselves for the position of governess; then making payment for the advantages thus secured when established in situations. Emily's fame had already reached the academy, so she was welcomed cordially, receiving also the assurance that her training should be entirely gratuitous, and that if at the end of that period circumstances favoured, she should be engaged as teacher. Emily grasped at the proposition, for the beauties of "boarding out" and the mysteries of the birch rod were not at all to her taste. Forced, as she had been, to associate with people of all intellectual grades and capacities, and possessing little or no refinement, while boarding round, she often sighed for the companionship of more congenial spirits. Still, until Providence opened the way she remained at her post and tried faithfully to discharge her duty. Aged parents and a young sister were dependent upon her, and their manifold claims could not be discharged without unremitting efforts on her part. These efforts she nobly made; and though they doubtless contributed to shorten her life, they yet cast a golden halo round her memory.

Soon after commencing her residence at the academy, she expressed a desire that her sister Kate should share also in its advantages, she, herself, of course, being responsible for the cost. Miss Sheldon, who was an ardent admirer of Emily's genius, suggested the possibility of earning money by that genius. Emily at first shrunk from the thought, as if literature would be debased by coming into contact with pounds, shillings, and pence—or rather, dollars and cents. But she had been trained in poverty's stern school. With but few friends until now, she had known what it was to need money for necessary uses, and to be compelled to use painful self-denial. So she soon got over this weakness, arriving very sensibly at the conclusion that genius, if ever so little, must eat, drink, and dress, as well as create. Thus urged she set to work, alternately teaching and writing, writing and teaching. Writing one of her short, brilliant, and characteristic notes to a friend about this time she says: "I have always shrunk from doing anything in a public capacity, and that has added a good deal to my school-teaching troubles. But, oh! necessity, necessity! Did you ever think of such a thing as selling brains for money? and then, such brains as mine? Do you think I could prepare for the press a small volume of poems that would produce—I must speak it—the desired *cash?*"

Once the idea was broached, it was not in Emily Chubbuck to rest without endeavouring to carry it out. In January, 1841, she commenced her first work, "Charles Linn; or, How to Observe the Golden Rule." This was a book for young people, intended chiefly for school libraries. It met with a very flattering reception from the circle which it was intended to reach, and Emily became favourably spoken of as a writer of juvenile books. The volume itself was written under most unpromising circumstances. It was composed and written in the hours snatched from school duties, and often those few hours were invaded by her ever-present foe, headache. Still it exhibited much creative genius, force of language, and facility of composition, indicating that she possessed the ability for her newly-found occupation. Possibly she never would have commenced authorship had not straitened circumstances compelled her; but, once before the public, she could gain no rest. Her magazine sketches, too, became popular, and engagements began to multiply. But, as may be expected, study—for she still aimed at greater proficiency in her profession—teaching, and authorship combined were too much for her slender frame. Her letters home at this time give us much insight into her toils and her weaknesses, the latter induced by the wearing nature of the former. In one of these letters she says: "The July number of the *Knickerbocker* has brought out with flattering haste my 'Where are the Dead?' for it has not been in their possession a month, and consider,

Kate, the *Knickerbocker* is perhaps the most popular periodical in the United States. My 'Charles Linn' has come—a beautiful little volume of 112 pages, worth about a dollar. My next book is also half-written, but not copied at all. I shall bring it home to finish. There is an article of mine in the *Mother's Journal* of this month. The publishers settle with me once in six months, and next January brings, if not 'golden opinions' exactly, at least silver ones."

Being now installed composition teacher, with a salary of one hundred and fifty dollars per annum, besides board, her mind reverted to her long-cherished purpose of sending for her sister. This she did; but the step entailed upon her the strictest self-denial, the severest economy, and the most untiring labour. Often, at midnight, some of her friends would find her seated at her desk, with throbbing head and marble cheeks, endeavouring to "sell her brains," as she so characteristically expressed it. On one occasion, when Miss Sheldon remonstrated with her for imprudently risking her health, her already full heart overflowed with emotion, and with streaming eyes, she said, "Oh! I *must* write! I *must* write! I must do what I can to aid my poor parents."

Soon, other children's books appeared in rapid succession: "The Great Secret," "Effie Maurice," "Allen Lucas; or, the Self-made Man;" "John Frink;" and numerous magazine articles, all of which met with most flattering approval. Encouraged by the hope of reaping pecuniary profit sufficient to cover the undertaking, she purchased, as a gift for her parents, the house and garden occupied by them. The price was four hundred dollars, and the agreement stipulated that she should discharge the debt in four annual payments. Of course, for this sum the home could not be grand or spacious; but for all that, viewed as the offering of a daughter's affection, we may fancy how precious the gift was in their estimation. In after-years, when separated from each other by rolling oceans, how sweet must have been this memento of a daughter's love. As might have been expected, however, the debt hung like a mill-stone about her neck; but while it urged her to incessant exertion, the thought that she had provided her aged parents with a *home,* supplied a sufficient stimulus to that exertion.

About this time she became acquainted with N. P. Willis, of the New York *Evening Mirror.* She became a contributor to his paper, assuming the cognomen of " Fanny Forester." Henceforth her real name became forgotten, while the assumed one became known and welcomed throughout the whole circle of American periodical literature. She became a regular contributor to *Graham's Monthly,* the *Columbian,* the *Knickerbocker,* and others, at highly remunerative prices. Every difficulty seemed to have vanished, and the country governess, hitherto, comparatively speaking, little known to fame and fortune, became celebrated through the length and breadth of the land. Like Lord Byron, she "awoke one morning, and found herself famous."

She still continued, hands and head all full—full of plans, studies, engagements, and pupils. She still resided at Utica Academy, compelled so to do by the drafts made upon her purse by her purchase for her parents. In the winter of 1844—45 her health seriously failed, and physicians and friends recommended a sojourn in Philadelphia, as the best means for restoring her health. She first sent home the money for the payment upon the house, and then departed for the "City of Brotherly Love." Her fame had already preceded her, and the warm-hearted Philadelphians gladly welcomed her whose refined and facile pen had so often ministered to their intellectual delight. "It is not in man that walketh to direct his steps," and of this truth a striking proof is given by the course of Emily's after-life. Mr. Gillette, a Baptist clergyman, and his wife, tendered the hospitality of their house so pressingly and cordially that Emily could not choose but accept. Here she remained until May, and then retraced her steps to Utica, invigorated in body, and refreshed in mind. Her brief contact with the world, and with the most polished and cultivated society Philadelphia could afford, matured and beautified her character, so that while still distinguished by that maidenly reserve which had ever characterised her, she became more genial, animated, and brilliant. During the summer she resumed her old employments, but her frail health warned her, over and over again, to spare herself all extra exertion. She was hoping to have spent the subsequent winter in Italy, "where the oranges grow, and where they have myrtles in winter time." But domestic matters prevented the fulfilment of this wish, and in October Emily again retraced her way to Philadelphia, taking up her residence with her old friends the Gillettes.

It was at length decided that she should winter in that city. She became surrounded by refined and accomplished companions. Among them she could number Dr. Rufus Griswold, the historian; Mr. Horace B. Wallace, N. P. Willis, Mr. and Mrs. Graham, Joseph C. Neal, and many others of lesser note. Life seemed *very* bright to her, and her future *very* glittering. She seemed to have finished the toilsome ascent of the hill of success, and to have arrived at its very summit. Her company was sought after, and she was courted and caressed on every side. Her genius and personal education secured her admission into the most refined circles, and her friends predicted a bright career. Possibly the things of time and sense were attracting her soul too much, and the powers of the world to come were fading into indistinctness. Be this as it may, the happy dream of earthly good was soon to be exchanged for the sweet, but self-denying reality of "bearing the cross."

In October, 1845, Dr. Judson landed in America, after an absence of thirty-four years from his native land. He had been labouring, amid discouragements and persecution, to plant the standard of the Gospel in Burmah. He had succeeded to some extent, and many seals had been added to his ministry. But he had been left twice a widower. This very voyage had been undertaken in the vain hope of saving the life of his second wife, Mrs. Boardman Judson; but she died upon the voyage, and the vessel reached St. Helena just in time for him to deposit the remains of his loved one upon that lone isle. From thence he turned his saddened face homeward, where he was received with all the rapturous applause that the churches could give. In December of the same year he was requested to attend a series of missionary meetings in Philadelphia. Mr. Gillette went on to Boston to secure his attendance, and to invite him to his house. Little did the reverend gentleman dream that the two individuals coming in contact now for the first time under his roof, were shortly to become the "all-in-all" to each other. But it was so. On the journey Mr. Gillette introduced to Dr. Judson's notice a volume of the "Trippings in Author Land," lately published by Emily, and asked his opinion of it. He cursorily examined it, and remarked that it was written with "great beauty and power"—"*great beauty and power,*" he emphatically repeated a second time; but on learning that the writer was a Christian, added: "I should be glad to know her. A lady who writes so well ought to write better. It is a pity that such fine talents should be employed upon such subjects." Next morning he was introduced to her, and after the first greetings were over, characteristically and bluntly inquired how she could reconcile it with her conscience, to employ her fine talents in writing sketches so little spiritual as those he had seen. Put on her defence, she replied by telling all. She told him how that her circumstances were necessitous, her parents indigent, her youth a constant struggle, her path up to the position she had now occupied a difficult and toiling one. She represented to him how that she considered *tuition* her life-work; authorship was only a secondary one, and assumed, in the first instance, to supplement the want of means. Besides which, she said she had striven to aid the *right,* and strengthen every good principle in her writings; and, therefore, did not imagine that her efforts could be looked upon as blameworthy. Dr. Judson was surprised and softened. His strict, fault-finding mood vanished, and he began to admire her. He detailed to her the main facts of his wife's history, with the view of getting her to prepare a memoir of the departed one, to which Emily readily consented. The discussion of this matter threw them much together during the ensuing few days; and it is by no means surprising that the usual consequences followed. Dr. Judson discovered in her the germs of true and abiding faith—fast becoming hidden, it is true, by the glitter and the glare of earthly renown, but still there it was; beside this, there was a large sympathetic heart, combined with rare intellectual power. No wonder that she won his love; while on the other hand the name of Judson had been inseparably entwined with her earliest yearnings for missionary labour—had first incited her to these noble aspirations; and now the hero himself was come just in time to act as God's messenger in winning her to another sphere of sanctified labour. But it is not to be imagined that Emily viewed such a total destruction of her plans and prospects—such a sudden change in "the spirit of her dream"—without much perplexity and alarm. She weighed herself in the balances of conscientious self-examination, and found that she was spiritually "wanting." She knew the depth of piety, the rich experience, the mellow judgment, the earnest self-denial requisite for a labourer in the mission-field, and she judged herself miserably deficient. More than all, the missionary path, which formerly she so yearned to tread, seemed now "like death for her to enter." But Dr. Judson would not resign his suit, and after much prayerful consideration she consented. It was not difficult to foresee the storm of disapprobation that would come from contending quarters. The literary world could not loudly enough express its condemnation of the wiles by which the reverend doctor had won the newly-found star of their admiration. The idea of his carrying her off into "grim Burmah," there to bury fame and talents in the night of heathenism, was to them like piracy. To the religious public, on the other hand, the matter was simply astounding. They could understand how Ann Hasseltine, and Sarah Boardman, could be fitting partners for their missionary hero; but how he could elect as a successor a young lady chiefly known as the most popular female writer of the day, was past their comprehension. Of course, the usual number of strictures were passed by both parties, but the two most interested ones quietly asserted their right of thinking and acting for themselves, leaving the outside world to enjoy its own charitable opinion. She says that one thing both surprised and cheered her: while many Christian professors stood aloof, or looked coldly on her cherished purpose, "many a worldling wished her a tearful 'God speed.'" Not one of her former pupils was surprised at her intention of becoming a missionary. There was mingled so much of quiet grace and gentle dignity in all her dealings with them that they deemed the calling just suited to her and she to it. A significant fact! young people being keen observers of character, as every teacher can testify. One of the literary magazines, referring to the rumour of her intended marriage with Dr. Judson, and consequent departure for the Orient, inquired: "Does she deem that stern duty calls her to resign the home and friends of her heart, the fame which she has so gloriously won—nay, more, perhaps even life itself—for the far-off heathen?" To this query she sang, in spontaneous and indignant eloquence, as follows:—

"There's a dearer than mother, whose heart is my pillow,
A truer than brother's foot guides o'er the billow;
There's a voice I shall hear at the grave-guarding willow,
When they leave me to sleep in my turf-covered bed.

"'Stern duty?' No! Love is my ready foot winging;
On duty's straight path, Love her roses is flinging;
In love to the Friend of my heart I am clinging;
My 'home' is His smile, my 'far-off' is His frown.

"He shaped the frail goblet which Death one day will shiver;
He casts every sun-ray on Life's gloomy river;
They're safest when guarded by Maker and Giver.
My laurels and *life* at His feet I lay down."

We think she was right. Led on, as she was, by an unseen hand, through paths intricate and doubtful, until brought gradually into the light of her assigned and chosen life mission, it was not hers to frustrate God's designs, nor to forget or ignore her early vows.

On the 20th of February, 1846, Emily returned to Utica, where she remained for a fortnight or so with her old friends. She then returned home to her native village, to remain under the parental roof until the marriage, which it was decided should take place in June, Dr. Judson wishing to return to Burmah in that month. In a few days he followed her, and remained at Hamilton for a short time, cultivating the acquaintance of his future relatives. Here arrangements were completed with publishers for the final issue of her collected works, with the proceeds of which she engaged to complete the payment for her parents' home. Doubtless, while taking her last lingering, loving farewells of the place and the people, she realised more than ever the magnitude of the undertaking that lay before her. Doubtless, too, the womanly heart sometimes sank, and the womanly faith sometimes failed in prospect of it. She says, in a sweet little poem written at this date:—

"Thou'lt never wait again, father,
Thy daughter's coming tread:
She ne'er will see thy face again;
So count her with thy dead.
But in the land of light and love,—
Not sorrowing, as now,—
She'll come to thee, and come, perchance,
With jewels on her brow."

They were married on the 2nd of June, 1846. The Rev. Dr. Kendrick—the very man to whom she had written the letter of her early days, declaring her desire for missionary work—pronounced the momentous words which inseparably linked her fate with Dr. Judson's.

As he did so he must doubtless have seen and recognised the Almighty Hand, which, by many a devious turning and winding, had led her into her soul's "desired haven."

The two bade farewell to the land of their birth on the 11th of June, having spent the intervening days in loving farewells. In a letter dated the 9th, Mrs. Judson says :—"I have been crowded to death with company. Sometimes my hand has been so swollen with constant shaking that I have not been able to get on my glove, and have been obliged to use my left hand." On the 11th, the *Faneuil Hall* weighed anchor, and the two noble hearts turned their faces towards Burmah.

After about eighteen or twenty weeks passed on the voyage, they landed at Maulmain, where, among the first objects that met Mrs. Judson's gaze were the two little sons of her husband, brought to greet her by their nurse. She at once took them to her heart; and it should not be forgotten that she had pleaded hard before leaving America that Abby Ann, the eldest daughter, should come back to Burmah with them, which proposition, however, Dr. Judson did not consider fit to accede to. In her letters home she amusingly describes "queer, ridiculous, half-beautiful, half-frightful, wholly-idolatrous Burmah" so truthfully and fascinatingly, that the reader almost fancies himself in the gorgeous East of his imagination. Her different dwellings, with their wildernesses of rooms, thick walls, and low partitions, are sometimes termed in her letters, "Green Turban's Den," and sometimes "Bat Castle." Once there, she commenced learning the language, in order to commence a mothers' instruction-class; besides which, it was her intention to translate such books as were judged necessary in the mission-work into the vernacular. After about three months they exchanged their residence in Maulmain—enlivened as it was by the presence of other missionaries and English residents— for another in Rangoon, in the very heart of heathenism. Dr. Judson longed, with true missionary zeal, to carry

VIEW OF RANGOON.

the Gospel into the very midst of the benighted Burmans. Mrs. Judson cheerfully went with him, and became his right-hand helper. She also, in the hours left free from family cares and the study of the language, commenced and completed the Memoir of Mrs. Sarah Boardman Judson. But they soon found the inconveniences of removing to Rangoon. Instead of wholesome, eatable food, such as they had been accustomed to at Maulmain, they had such dishes as were sometimes revolting to civilised stomachs. Consequently, thin, pale cheeks and weakened frames were the order of the day. In one of her letters she says they were treated to a dinner of *rats*, of which they all partook before finding out what it was. After seven months of this suffering they returned to Maulmain, the Burman Government not permitting them to do any mission-work in Rangoon. In Maulmain her first little one was born, December 24th, 1847, and baptised by the name of Emily Frances. Mrs. Judson consecrated this child's memory by a sweet little poem entitled "My Bird," which, however, our space will not permit us to give. The year 1848 was a year of mingled home-joy and happy mission-work, as Mrs. Judson was now able to converse with the women in their native tongue. Besides this, she completed a series of Scripture questions for the use of the natives, prepared a small hymn-book, and translated the first part of the "Pilgrim's Progress." 1849 was a year of much ill-health, both for her and the doctor; still, it witnessed the accomplishment of much work. In November of this year Dr. Judson was attacked by dysentery; nothing seemed to arrest the disease, and the physician prescribed a trip down the sea-coast. This the doctor tried to avoid, because of the delicate condition of Mrs. Judson's health; although, notwithstanding her own sickness, she ministered unwearyingly to him.

Some extracts from Mrs. Judson's letters home at this time will afford a good idea of the life, occupations, studies, and daily work of the mission family. Dr.

I

Judson was preparing a dictionary; and at every available moment Mrs. Judson was studying the language, perfecting herself in it for intercourse with the native women. We will give first an extract from a letter to Dr. Kendrick. She says: "Since, dear Dr. Kendrick, you were the first, and indeed, the only one, to whom I communicated my early impressions with regard to missions, it is fitting I should tell you something of my views since I have actually entered upon the field. I was very young when I opened my heart to you, full of the enthusiastic romance of girlhood, and the undisciplined zeal of a young Christian. When I remember this, I almost wonder that you should have spoken so kindly and so encouragingly; indeed, your most judicious letter, though not understood at the time, was most invaluable to me afterwards. Your advice to "await the openings of Providence," had a calming effect, and I am glad I learned so long ago how good it is to *wait*, for this is a much more difficult part of Christian duty than to labour. God has led me in a very mysterious way."

In another letter she says: "I do not know whether others find the sight of Eastern scenery and Eastern men awakens fresh interest in the narrative part of the word of God; but I really would come all the way from America for the sake of reading the Bible with new eyes. 'I have seen all this before,' was a feeling that flashed upon me more frequently at Rangoon than here, producing a momentary confusion of intellect; and then came the reflections—When? How? Where? and finally it would creep into my mind, 'Why, I learnt about it in Sabbath school, when I was a little child.' The effect was to annihilate time, and bring the days of the Saviour very near; and the strength of the ideal presence has been very profitable to me. But there I was, in the identical town of which I had read with such eager curiosity when I was a little child, away in the central part of New York, and which then seemed to me to be about as real a city as one belonging to the moon.

And, stranger still, I was associated with one of the movers in scenes, the bare recital of which had in years gone by thrilled my soul with greater power than the wildest fiction. Oh, how memory and imagination, and

BURMESE LADY.

various strangely mingled emotions, wrought together in my mind, when I looked upon a building—or rather its ruins—in which the first words of life that Burmah ever heard were spoken, more than a quarter of a century ago."

In another: "If I were sitting by you, I could give

some personal experiences. I could tell you of a time when we were hungry for want of palatable food; when we were ill, and had neither comforts nor physician; when we were surrounded by the spies of an unscrupulous government, without any earthly friend to assist us, or any way of escape. But there are circumstances in which even such trials assume a minor importance. My first real missionary trial was when, amid sufferings such as I have described, a letter came, telling of retrenchments. Schools, with the life already cramped out of them, must be cramped still more; assistants must be cut off; the workmen's hands must be tied a little tighter; and then, if they could succeed in making bricks without straw, the churches at home were ready to rejoice in their success."

To another friend: "My husband works like a galley-slave, and really it quite distresses me sometimes; but he seems to get fat on it, so I try not to worry. He walks over the hills a mile or two every morning; then down to his books—scratch, scratch—puzzle, puzzle—and when he gets tired, out on the verandah with your humble servant by his side, walking and talking (*Kaning*, we call it in Burmese) till the point is elucidated; and then down again, and so on, till ten o'clock in the evening. We are having some encouraging tokens in the church: three have been lately baptised. To-day I resume my native female prayer-meeting. The women are delighted to see me so well, and express their joy both by smiles and tears. They are very anxious to have the Bible-class commence again; and I have promised to gratify them as soon as I can use my voice a little better. Mah Zwoon came in to-day, and after looking at me for some time very sorrowfully, shook her head, and remarked, 'I am afraid we shall never have the second part of "Pilgrim's Progress" now.' Since I told the women there was another part about Christian's wife and children, they have been very anxious to obtain it, and I promised to translate it as soon as I was sufficiently well, and versed in the language."

At last it was decided that Dr. Judson *must* take an extended sea-voyage to re-establish his health, which was evidently rapidly sinking. In a letter dated April 15th, 1850, Mrs. Judson says: "I sit down to write you with a very heavy heart—indeed, heavier than I ever carried in my life before. I do not know whether my precious husband is still living, or whether he may not have already gone to heaven, and I shall have no means of knowing for three or four months to come. After I wrote you last month he continued to decline, but so very slowly that I was not much alarmed, till one evening, all on a sudden, as he attempted to go to his cot, his back gave way, and he would have fallen had I not caught and supported him. From that night he never stood on his feet. About ten days after, he was carried on board a ship bound for Bourbon, where a comfortable cot was provided for him, but poor I was not allowed to go with him. The physician said if he went to sea there would be a chance, so the question was one of duty, else all the world would never have induced him to leave me. I had watched over him night and day for five months, and it seemed as if we *could not* breathe apart. The worst of it is the uncertainty of getting intelligence. They arrive in six weeks, and in six weeks more I *may* get letters—that is, if a vessel should be coming this way." This letter gives us glimpses of the "deliciously-happy" home-life of Mrs. Judson, as she elsewhere terms it, and also of her heartbreaking sorrow in parting with the husband of her love, perhaps for ever. On the 22nd of April her second child was born—still-born, and thus he "brought no joy." We can scarcely imagine any situation more distressing than Mrs. Judson's at this time. Left alone, with three children depending upon her maternal care, her newly-given babe under the clods of the valley, herself ill, and in a situation peculiarly needing all the loving succour which kindness could bestow; and, worse than all, in total ignorance as to the fate of her husband. Under this agonising combination of circumstances she poured forth her soul's sorrow in some tender lines to her mother. These lines, entitled "Sweet Mother," are touching in their expression of mingled agony and faith. We give a few verses from the poem :—

"The wild south-west monsoon has risen
  On broad, grey wings of gloom,
While here, from out my dreary prison,
I look, as from a tomb—alas!
  My heart another tomb.

"Upon the low thatched roof the rain
  With ceaseless patter falls;
My choicest treasures bear its stain,
Mould gathers on the walls—would heaven
  'Twere only on the walls.

"Sweet mother, I am here alone,
  In sorrow and in pain;
The sunshine from my heart has flown,
It feels the driving rain—ah, me!
  The chill, the mould, the rain.

"And when for one loved far, far more,
  Come thickly-gathering tears,
My star of faith is clouded o'er,
I sink beneath my fears—sweet friend,
  I sink beneath my fears.

"O, but to feel thy fond arms twine
  Around me once again!
It almost seems those lips of thine
Might kiss away the pain—might soothe
  This dull, cold, heavy pain.

"But, gentle mother, through life's storms
  I may not lean on thee;
For helpless, cowering little forms
Cling trustingly to me.—Poor babes!
  To have no guide but me.

"With weary feet and broken wing,
  With bleeding heart, and sore,
Thy dove looks backward, sorrowing,
But seeks the ark no more; thy breast
  Seeks never, never more.

"Sweet mother, for the exile pray,
  That loftier faith be given;
Her broken reeds all swept away,
That she may rest in heaven—her soul
  Grow strong in Christ and heaven.

"All fearfully—all tearfully,
  Alone and sorrowing,
My dim eye lifted to the sky,
Fast to the Cross I cling—O Christ,
  To Thy dear Cross I cling!"

About the end of August came the dreaded tidings of her husband's death. We cannot fancy her long-drawn anguish, her anxious waiting, her painful dread, only ending in the assurance of the worst. Dr. Judson had died within a fortnight of the time that he had bidden her adieu. She says, writing home : "Now I can think of nothing, and see nothing, but the black shadows that have fallen upon my heart and life. Oh! it is terrible! my heart is aching, and I am ill with grief. I do not seem as if I should ever be well again; and then, perhaps, I do not know, I may try to bring my poor little orphans home. Oh! you do not how we have loved each other; and *now I am alone!* It was my husband's wish that I should go home with my poor little orphans; but I feel as though I can decide on nothing." At length, in consequence of her broken health, brought on by the unhealthiness of the rainy season, and doubtless also by her excessive grief, her physician ordered her home. This she decided on doing; and planned to collect the whole family together under one roof, there to act a mother's part to them. There were six children in all—Abby Ann, and the two elder boys, Elnathan and Adoniram, then studying in America, and the three younger ones with her—no small charge in her delicate and widowed condition. On January 22nd, 1851, Mrs Judson with her three little ones, left Maulmain, and sailed for America, by way of Calcutta and England. At Calcutta, among other proofs of esteem and friendship which she received was a presentation Bible from the Right Rev. Bishop Wilson, and the "Judson Testimonial Fund"—a sum of fifteen hundred dollars, subscribed by Calcutta gentlemen, without distinction of sect or creed, in token of respect to the memory of her late husband. On reaching England, she resided during her stay, chiefly with W. B. Gurney, Esq., or with Rev. Dr. Angus. But her heart longed for home, and after spending four or five weeks with her English friends, she proceeded on her voyage, reaching America in October, 1851, within a little over five years from the time she had bade her native land farewell.

Once more among her friends, she arranged all matters connected with the family. The two elder sons were at college; she placed Abby Ann under Miss Anable's care, and retained charge of the three little ones herself. She took a house at Hamilton, near her parents, and at regular seasons all the children had happy reunions there. She recommenced her literary labours, and by this means, together with the annuity allowed her from the Missionary Union, intended to bring up the little ones. She, however, very shortly declined the annuity, from high and honourable motives. In the year 1853, her health gradually but surely failed, and the much-loved employment of assisting Dr. Wayland in the preparation of her husband's Memoir became a heavy task. In 1854 she failed rapidly. About February she ceased to write even letters—an ominous token, for as long as she could, she plied the pen. Then her brother wrote from her dictation; and on May 20th we find him saying: "I fear the last of earth is speedily approaching for my sister." It was; she was sinking rapidly into the arms of death. She, however, looked forward to heaven as a place of *rest*. "It is not," she said, "the pearly gates and golden streets of heaven that attract me; it is its *perfect rest* in the presence of my Saviour. It will be *so* sweet after a life of toil and care like mine, though a very pleasant one it has been; and I am only weary of the care and toil because I have not strength to endure them."

On the first of June, 1854—the month in which she wished to die—the death-struggle commenced, and after enduring much suffering, at ten o'clock on the same evening, she sweetly dropped her head on her sister's breast, and "fell asleep."

Thus passed away from our earth one of its noblest spirits—one who nobly fought the battle of life; wore herself out in the cause of truth and righteousness; furnished a bright example of sanctified intellect; and exemplified in striking combination all the true womanly graces, united with Christian fortitude. As a missionary she entered heartily into the work; was assiduous in learning the language, and as soon as it was mastered, hastened to make herself useful in every department of effort open to her: conducting the female religious meetings, instructing in the Scriptures, guiding inquirers, and aiding the new converts to larger spiritual attainments.

We conclude this sketch with a poem, which, though short, is exquisitely beautiful, written in the latter period of her life. It is entitled "My Angel Guide."

"I gazed down Life's dim labyrinth,
 A wildering maze to see,
Crossed o'er by many a tangled clue,
 And wild as wild could be.
And, as I gazed in doubt and dread,
 An Angel came to me.

" I knew him for a heavenly guide;
 I knew him, even then,
Though meekly as a child he stood
 Among the sons of men.
By his deep spirit—loveliness,
 I knew him, even then.

" And as I leaned my weary head
 Upon his proffered breast,
And scanned the peril-haunted wild,
 From out my place of rest,
I wondered if the shining ones
 Of Eden were more blest.

" For there was light within my soul,
 Light on my peaceful way;
And all around the blue above
 The clustering starlight lay;
And easterly, I saw upreared
 The pearly gates of day.

" So, hand in hand, we trod the wild,
 My angel guide and I;
His lifted wing all quivering
 With tokens from the sky.

Strange, my dull thought could not divine
  'Twas lifted—but to fly.

"Again, down life's dim labyrinth
  I grope my way alone;
While, wildly through the midnight sky,
  Black, hurrying clouds are blown,
And thickly, in my tangled path,
  The sharp, bare thorns are strewn.

"Yet firm my foot, for well I know
  The goal can not be far;
And ever, through the rifted clouds,
  Shines out one steady star,
For, when my guide went up, he left
  The pearly gates ajar."

BURMESE IDOL.

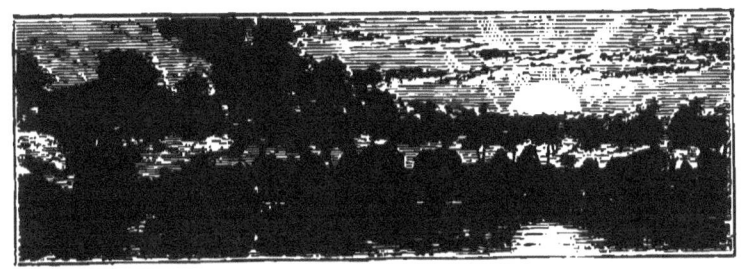

MRS. MARY WILLIAMS,
Wife of the Rev. John Williams,

MISSIONARY TO THE SOUTH SEAS; OF THE LONDON MISSIONARY SOCIETY.

"For me remains nor time, nor space,
My country is in every place.
I can be calm, and free from care,
On any shore—since God is there."

THE history of the South Sea Mission, as told in John Williams' "Missionary Enterprises," is one full of exciting interest. Its pages contain stories and reminiscences respecting the spread of the Gospel, "unequalled by any similar narrative since the days of the Acts of the Apostles." It was such a record of facts connected with the evangelisation of those far away islands of the Pacific Ocean that people read, wondered, and admired. John Williams, who afterwards filled a martyr's grave, and his devoted wife, took a very large part in the evangelisation of those islands. Indeed, there was scarcely an island of any note which he did not visit and attempt to benefit. It was in the prosecution of one of these errands of mercy that he fell at Erromanga, under the clubs and spears of the savages whom he was endeavouring to befriend. But during the years of his laborious and eventful ministry there.

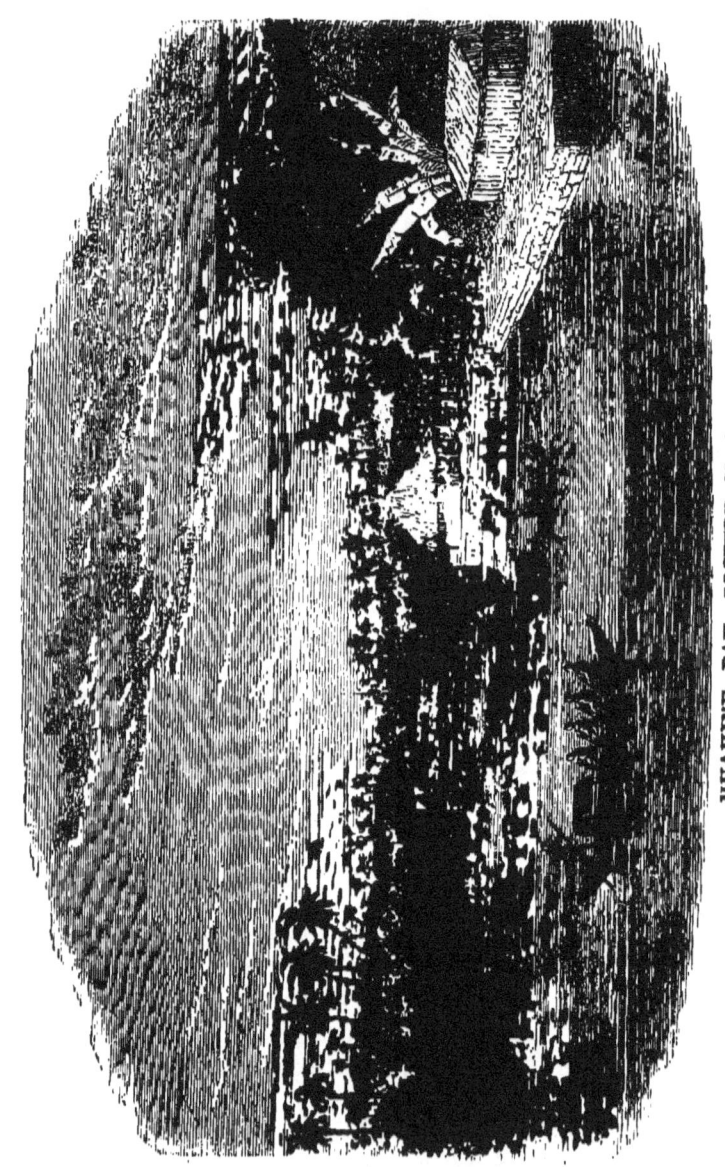

HUAHINE BAY, SOCIETY ISLANDS.

his wife, Mrs. Williams, laboured with him in the Gospel as a true "helpmeet," and succeeded in winning many of the female population for Jesus. In addition, she taught them the arts of civilised life to a large extent, and both by example and precept developed the virtues of female neatness, management, and modesty amongst them.

Her maiden name was Mary Chauner. She was connected by church-membership with the church assembling at the Tabernacle, Tottenham Court Road, London, under the pastoral care of the Rev. Matthew Wilks. Here, also, her husband attended, and consecrated himself to the service of the mission field. In Christian heroism and straightforward fulfilment of duty this lady was in every way the equal of her husband, and it was a happy day for the church when the two were united. The marriage with Mr. Williams took place October 29th, 1816, at the Tabernacle. Says Mr. Williams' biographer, in relation to this event: "This was a day which not only Mr. Williams had reason to remember with gratitude, but also many thousands of Polynesian women, whom the love and labours of his devoted partner raised from degradation to comfort, from the rudeness and vile indulgence of savage, to the manifold enjoyments of civilised life, and from pagan darkness to evangelical light."

The newly-married couple sailed from England on November 17th, 1816, in a vessel bound for Sydney, in company with other missionaries also destined for the South Seas. After some unavoidable delays, they reached Eimeo in about a year from the time of their leaving England. Nearly a twelvemonth was profitably spent at Eimeo in acquiring the language and being introduced to mission-work; but as that island seemed fairly supplied with missionary workers, Mr. Williams longed to visit and labour among those in "the regions beyond." In pursuance of this resolution, Mr. Williams, with his wife, first-born son, and other members of the mission, sailed for Huahine, one of the Society Islands.

Here the people had long desired a missionary teacher. Some beams of the Gospel light had fallen upon them, and they now sought eagerly for aid in shaking themselves free from the bondage of idolatry. Under these circumstances, their reception of the missionary party was all that could be desired. In a graphic letter Mrs. Williams records their first experiences of the people of Huahine: "The natives assigned us a good house immediately, and scarcely had we entered before the people brought to us a hot baked pig and a large bowl of yams. We then made some tea, and ate a hearty meal. Our next business was to fit up a lodging for the night, which was done by putting a piece of native cloth across one end of a very large house. Here we slept as soundly as if we had been in a palace. The next day we removed to a neat little oval house, and fitted it up with native cloth as comfortably as we could. As usual, my dear John made lime, and plastered the floors. I daresay you frequently talk of us, and wonder what we have to eat; I will tell you as nearly as I can. There are plenty of fowls here, and we dress them in a variety of ways. Sometimes we have fresh pork, and occasionally we kill a sucking pig, and get it cooked as well as you can in England, who have large kitchen fires. I only wish we had a cow, and I should then be able to make butter; but we get plenty of milk for our tea, as we have five goats." Shortly after, Mr. Williams added: "My dear Mary is a famous cook. I am sure I don't know what a poor man would do by himself in such a place as this."

From these extracts it will be seen that the work of the missionaries was no play-game. In their lot were many hardships, because they had to educate the people up to the manners and customs of civilised life, as well as to endure the greatest personal inconveniences for lack of the most ordinary appliances of English life. Mrs. Williams had to be her own cook and housemaid, in addition to fulfilling her duties to her babe, and to the native women, who crowded with curiosity around the white lady who had been brave enough to come over the ocean. In Huahine, however, it seemed that their lot was not to be cast, as a larger opening offered to Mr. Williams, and, accepting the advice of his fellow-missionaries, he, with Mr. Threlkeld, passed over to Raiatea, and made there their permanent home.

Raiatea is the chief island of the Society group, and occupies a most important position. Its chiefs exercised authority over the surrounding islands, and led the way in the adoption of any new custom. Further, Raiatea was the seat of the most abominable idolatry; and could Satan's stronghold have been shaken there, the influence would have been felt among all the other islands. Two years previously, a shipwrecked crew of Tahitians had carried the first tidings of the Gospel to Raiatea; and as a consequence, Tamatoa, the chief, had abandoned some idolatrous practices, had erected a native chapel, and now, hearing that a band of missionaries were at Huahine, went there to entreat some of them to settle at Raiatea. Messrs. Williams and Threlkeld consented to go, and without delay the two mission families accompanied Tamatoa back to his island. Here, then, at the end of 1818, Mrs. Williams and her husband took up their home.

They found much to contend with there, although the natives were just awakening from the night of heathenism and eager to receive the truth. The manners and customs of the people "were abominable," so that Mrs. Williams says, "No description could be given of them." Mr. Williams set about building a dwelling-house for his family as much in the European style as he could manage, filling up his leisure hours with all kinds of mechanical work for this purpose, while a goodly portion of each day and all the Sabbath days were set apart for religious instruction. Meanwhile, Mrs. Williams did her share of the work as a missionary's wife, among the women principally. She instructed them in making articles of clothing, and in the arts of home-management and feminine industry.

It was very curious to see with what eagerness these partly-civilised women clamoured for *bonnets*. Among all the articles of clothing worn by Mrs. Williams, none excited so much comment or stirred up such a spirit of eager rivalry as her bonnet. Not only was it so at Raiatea, but in all the other islands of the South Seas to which Christianity penetrated, the same trait prevailed. Frequently, the first outward sign of a woman's embracing the new religion, was a bonnet perched on the top of her head, while her husband would also march proudly in a *hat*, even if in other respects he retained his native style of dress.

But not only did Mrs. Williams teach the women how to make clothing, she also attended to their spiritual and moral instruction. Soon after her arrival at Raiatea, she observed with pain the sad condition of many of the old women, cast off by their friends, forsaken by their children, and perishing from lack of kindness. She sent some of the more promising of the Christian natives through the settlement, after the infant church and society had been formed, to search out the number of these despised old women. She found that they numbered from seventy to eighty, and that they were destitute of the most needful articles of clothing. Immediately she set the female communicants to prepare clothing for them, and calling them together at her own house, arranged them into classes, and placed them under teachers, reserving the superintendence of the whole matter in her own hands. Thenceforward Mrs. Williams met them every Monday afternoon, prayed with them, and examined them in reference to the teaching which Mr. Williams had given them on the Sabbath. As the natural consequence, the friends and relatives of these old women began to show them more kindness, while those who had "learned Christ," supported their aged relatives in their own households. Many of the old women became members of the Church, and after witnessing a good profession, died in peace. Twice a year a feast was prepared, at which these old members of

Mrs. Williams' classes met their teachers and the other missionaries, when the proceedings were of a most pleasing character; while every Sabbath-day they sat together on two long seats in front of the pulpit, and listened with eager delight to the blessed Word, which had made "evening-time" to be "light" with them.

According to the instructions of the Directors of the London Missionary Society, the missionaries taught the people the arts of civilised life. House-building, boat-building, cotton and arrow-root culture, among other things, were encouraged and practised. The natives were led to abolish polygamy, and the solemn rite of marriage was instituted. Incited by the example of Mr. Williams, the natives began to build themselves houses, as nearly as possible after the missionary's pattern. When Mr. and Mrs. Williams first went to Raiatea, there were only "two native habitations, and it was difficult to walk along the beach for the bushes." In a little time, however, the missionary could report that the wilderness had been turned into an open space, "with a range of houses extending along the sea-beach, in which resided about a thousand of the natives." A code of laws was also drawn up, by which every offence, according to the judgment of the natives themselves, received its fitting punishment. To crown the whole, a missionary society was formed; and the Raiateans gave out of their poverty liberally to send the Gospel to other islands. Still, as is generally the case, when good is being done, there were found a few who hated the light, and desired the destruction of the missionaries. Among these were four young men, who formed a conspiracy to kill Mr. Williams, and had it not been for a series of providential interpositions, they would have succeeded. These events caused Mrs. Williams much anxiety and suffering, so much so, that illness seized her, and for three weeks her life hung in the balance. Thus was their cup a mixed one, joy and sorrow, success and discouragement mingling therein.

But the successes atoned for the discouragements. Among the heathen customs which were gradually

J

abolished was that of infanticide. This custom reigned universally at Raiatea. Mrs. Williams had a servant in her employ, whose former trade it was to destroy infants. This woman, after her conversion to Christianity, became devoted, honest, faithful and kind, proving her fidelity to Mrs. Williams and her children by a steady service of fifteen years. Sometimes she would recount to her mistress with tears, the manner in which she performed the horrid custom. Taking a newly-born infant, she would either suffocate it by putting a wet cloth upon its mouth, or by pinching its throat. On other occasions she would bury it alive, leaving it under a layer of earth and stones in the recesses of the forest, to perish miserably. Or she would destroy it by a fourth method, which was still more brutal. Immediately after birth, she would break the first joints of its fingers and toes. If this did not kill it, she would break the second joints. If it still survived, she would break the joints of its ankles and wrists; and provided it still lingered, which it sometimes did, she would as a last resource break the joints of the elbows and knees, finishing the whole process by strangulation. This woman would recount her deeds with the greatest contrition, as, indeed, would all those mothers who had killed their infants in the former days of heathenism, and had afterwards become converted to the knowledge of the truth. One woman confessed that she had killed *sixteen* babes, her whole family; another *nine*, another *seven*, another *five*. After the introduction of Christianity into the island, however, the people deeply regretted this sin of former days. Once, at a school anniversary and examination, in which six hundred children were paraded before the king, an affecting incident took place. An aged chief arose in much excitement, and exclaimed, "I must speak. Oh! that I had known the Gospel was coming. Oh! that I had known that these blessings were in store for us, then would I have saved my children, and they would have been among this happy group, repeating these precious truths. But, alas! I destroyed them all; I

VIEW IN TAHITI.

have not *one* left. I have been the father of *nineteen* children; they are all gone—not one is left." Turning to the king, who was a relative, he said, "You, my brother, saw me kill child after child, but you never seized this murderous hand, and said, 'Stay, brother, God is about to bless us; the Gospel of salvation is coming to our shores.'"

A young woman, who became at the time of Mr. and Mrs. Williams' stay at Raiatea, a teacher in one of the missionary schools, was rescued from death some years previously in a most singular manner. Her mother and father were of different ranks in Raiatean society, and custom demanded that all the children should be destroyed as soon as born. The first babe was born and put to death, so also was the second, in spite of the father's entreaties. It seemed that his heart felt some affection for his offspring, and he renewed his entreaties that the *third* child, a fine girl, might be saved alive. But no, the mother and her friends determined to kill it; so, during the father's absence in the mountains, it was buried alive. Returning and hearing of it, the poor man hastened to the place and disinterred the babe, just in time to save its life. He then gave his child in charge to his brother and sister, who took it and brought it up at Eimeo, an island about seventy miles distant, where the custom of infanticide was not practised. Soon after, the father died, without informing the mother of his rescue of their infant. Shortly after the father's death, Christianity was introduced into Raiatea, and the mother embraced the new religion. As she grew enlightened she bewailed bitterly the destruction of her children; but one day a woman disclosed to her the fact of the saving of this one child. The mother sailed over to Eimeo immediately, and found her child—with what overwhelming feelings of joy may be imagined. The daughter was now grown up a fine girl, and became the stay of her mother. She also became a consistent Christian, and a successful teacher in the female school.

In 1822 Mr. and Mrs. Williams, compelled by ill-health, paid a visit to Sydney, New South Wales, and while there employed the time in catering for the spiritual and material welfare of their beloved islanders. Beside purchasing a small schooner for purposes of communication between the islands, we find that they laid in a stock of "clothes for the women, shoes, stockings, tea-kettles, tea-cups and saucers, and tea, of which the natives were very fond." Thus we see that the presence of Mrs. Williams acted beneficially for her poor, untutored island sisters. Having taught unto them "Jesus and his love," she endeavoured to civilise them also, and to elevate their daily life.

In the autumn of 1822, the state of Mrs. Williams' health was so full of danger that serious plans were entertained concerning their return to England. But special prayer was once and again made on her account, and her strength was so far restored that they decided to continue in Raiatea. Mr. Williams determined henceforth to watch his opportunity, and to make that island his starting-point for errands of mercy to other islands in the South Seas. Now commenced that series of visits to islands, distant and near, which have become for ever celebrated under the title of "Missionary Enterprises." There was also a prospect that Mrs. Williams' health would be established by these voyages; accordingly, on the 4th July, 1823, they set sail for Aitutaki, as the first island to which they would carry the news of the Word of Life. In addition they took with them a band of heroic teachers, in order to leave a couple on each island to teach the natives more of the kingdom of God. The Aitutaki people were very friendly, and had cherished the Word which had been left there by Mr. and Mrs. Williams on their voyage to New South Wales a little time previously. On that first occasion Mrs. Williams sat nursing her only child, a fine boy of four years old, as the natives came crowding up the sides of the vessel. As little John Williams was the first European child they had ever seen, they immediately became so excited that the chief begged to have the child for his own, offering to bring him up as his own son, and eventually to make him King of Aitutaki. This offer, however, only made Mrs. Williams clasp her boy the more tightly to her breast, while Mr. Williams courteously declined the offer. Still, however, they pressed their request, and grew so clamorous that Mrs. Williams, fairly frightened, ran away with the babe into the cabin, lest the natives should snatch him from her arms, leap into the sea, and swim with him to the shore. By this means she managed to evade the importunity of the islanders. In this voyage Mr. Williams discovered Rarotonga, and placed a teacher there, in company with some Christian natives, to teach the islanders the way of salvation. Having done this, they sailed back to Raiatea, where Mrs. Williams, with her renewed health, applied herself unremittingly to missionary work. She could dress flax, and being an excellent hand at the spinning-wheel, taught the native women to imitate her in providing garments for their households. On Sundays she also took her full share of special labours, holding, among the rest, a female Bible class, consisting of about twenty, or more, of the most pious women. This class was accustomed to read chapters, verse by verse, and to be catechised upon it, afterwards being examined as to their proficiency in relation to a subject which had been selected on the previous Sabbath. In addition, she still continued her work among the old women—full as this class was of the poor, the neglected, the blind, the lame, and the deaf. These poor old women were accustomed to say: "We thought our days were past, and that we should never come back again into the world; we were laid aside as castaways, but now we are beginning to live again. It is good we lived to see these days." To show their gratitude these old people made two fine large mats for Mrs. Williams' rooms. The younger females, especially the girls, learnt the arts of sewing, cutting-out, &c., from Mrs. Williams, while every interval was filled up with housewifely duties, which concerned the providing of sufficient and nourishing food for her husband.

In 1826, Mrs. Williams writes: "Since I wrote, we have been favoured with another sweet boy. We have called him Samuel, and pray that he may be a Samuel indeed. Our dear little John is at school at Eimeo. This is his second year. It is a great sacrifice to part with him; but as it is for his future benefit, we have committed him to the care of the Great Preserver."

After this followed a second voyage to Rarotonga, in company with Mr. and Mrs. Pitman, who were to be settled there. They remained there for about a year, during which time Mr. Williams taught the natives to build a new chapel, as their first one was not large enough to accommodate the great numbers. It was during the building of this chapel that the interesting incident occurred of "making the chip speak." Mr. Williams had forgotten his square, and taking up a chip, wrote a request upon it that Mrs. Williams would send it by bearer, who was a chief of high degree. This so astonished the bearer that he instantly exalted the chip into something very supernatural. They also suffered great privations, "being often in want of food at Rarotonga, having had neither tea, flour, sugar, rice, nor fowls for some months, and being obliged to make our own salt and soap." Here Mr. Williams constructed the "Messenger of Peace," the first missionary ship built for the purpose of carrying the Gospel alone to the islands. The story of the building of his ship is so full of interest that it would be wrong to pass it over entirely, but our space will not allow of many details. Suffice it to say that, after being detained at Rarotonga many months, hoping and looking for a ship to convey them back to Raiatea—having lost their boats by means of tempests—and suffering by reason of want, Mr. Williams determined to *build a ship*. Says Mr. Pitman, his colleague: "None but a Williams would have attempted such a thing as to commence building a vessel, not having wherewith to build her." Mr. Williams says: "I knew little of ship-building, and had scarcely any tools to work with, yet I succeeded in about three months in completing a vessel between seventy and eighty tons burden, with no other assistance than that which the natives could render." They used hatchets for adzes, bamboos for crooked planks, wooden pins for iron bolts, cocoa-nut husk for oakum, bark of trees for ropes, and mats for sails. In this Mr. Williams contemplated visiting all the islands within a distance of two thousand miles, but to this scheme Mrs. Williams had long denied her consent. At length she was visited by serious illness, and while on the brink of the grave, her missionary devotedness came out more strongly; for, calling her husband to her side one morning, she thus addressed him: "From this time your desire has my full concurrence; and when you go, I shall follow you every day with my prayers, that God may preserve you from danger, crown your attempt with success, and bring you back in safety." From that time John Williams devoted his life to the islands of those seas, only taking one short rest from labour, by means of a visit to England with his wife and family. On some of these shorter voyages Mrs. Williams accompanied her husband, while on other occasions she remained at Raiatea, to direct the work there. On one occasion, while at Rarotonga—which island always was one possessing special interest for them—Mrs. Williams nearly lost her life by a fearful tempest. It was night, and she had retired to rest, when, perceiving that the roof was bending beneath the hurricane, she hastily rose up and fled to another part of the house. She had not left her bed two minutes, before the end of the house, with the roof, fell in, covering and crushing the very place where she had lain. A thousand houses were destroyed in this hurricane.

At length, in June, 1834, after nearly eighteen years' absence, Mr. and Mrs. Williams with their three sons, paid a visit to England. They had left behind them, in various islands upon which they had resided, the graves of *seven* little infants. Bereavement, sickness, poverty, and want had all in turn been their lot; but still, nothing had daunted their missionary ardour, and they were fully prepared to return again to the scenes of their varied labours—to work, watch, and pray until life should end. After nearly four years spent in England, in the most ardent advocacy of the

SCENE IN ONE OF THE SOCIETY ISLANDS.

cause, during which time Mr. Williams published his "Missionary Enterprises," and raised the sum of £4,000 to purchase the second missionary ship, the *Camden*, the missionary party set sail once more for those islands of the South, in this new vessel. Mrs. Williams had to experience a great grief at parting, for her second son was to be left behind for the sake of his education. It is stated that "the grief of this son was so poignant and irrepressible, and created such emotions in those present, that all appeared to desire, both for the sake of the child and his parents, that the hour of departure had passed." Those who have not had to endure it cannot understand the grief of separation between missionaries and their children. It is one of the sorrows—and that not the least—of their lives. The eldest son had married, and was returning with his wife in company with the band of missionaries, for the hands of Mr. and Mrs. Williams were to be strengthened by the addition of nine missionaries and their wives.

About a twelvemonth was occupied in the return voyage, and in visiting the different islands, and introducing the newly-ordained missionaries to their work. At the end of that time, namely, about May, 1839, Mr. and Mrs. Williams settled at Fasetootai, Upolu, forming a new station there. From here, however, Mr. Williams still sailed about, visiting all the old stations, and carrying supplies by means of the *Camden*. In November of that same year he was killed, in company with Mr. Harris, by the savages of Erromanga, and Mrs. Williams was left to suffer what she had often dreaded—the bitter loneliness and sorrow of widowhood. Thus mysteriously the noble-hearted missionary fell, pierced by the spears of those to whom he was carrying the blessed Word.

It was not until the following March, that Mrs. Williams was informed of the event. So long had she been kept in suspense, though unavoidably, and now that suspense was ended only by the news of her husband's murder. The very trial, which, through all the long, weary years she had dreaded, came upon her, and she was left in lonely widowhood, to the unspeakable sorrow of her lot. Into that overwhelming loneliness neither stranger nor friend could enter; no other heart could "intermeddle." At the dead of midnight Mrs. Williams was awakened to receive the sad intelligence; and as it spread abroad, the lamentation, the mourning, the woe once beheld in ancient Egypt at the death of the first-born, were once more repeated. For many hours Mrs. Williams was unable to bear even the sympathy of friends; she was too paralysed and prostrated.

One of the first to see her in the evening of the following day was a chief named Malietoa, who exhibited the most passionate sorrow for his much-loved but cruelly-murdered teacher. At length, however, he checked himself, and kneeling down by Mrs. Williams' side, gently took her hand and said: "Oh! my mother! do not grieve so much; do not kill yourself with grieving. You, too, will die with sorrow, and be taken away from us; and then, oh! what shall we do?" Many such interviews as these fell to Mrs. Williams' share, for the natives were just like a family of children bereaved of a father. But all such lamentations were unavailing to "call back the fleeting breath;" and she who had for twenty-three years shared his labours, hardships, and trials, had now to traverse the lonely path of widowhood.

In March, 1841, after receiving on every hand the utmost kindness, and numberless tokens of good will, both from missionaries and natives, Mrs. Williams turned her face homeward. After a somewhat long voyage, and calling at various settlements of missionaries, Mrs. Williams arrived in England once more, in October, 1842. Here, after ten years' sojourning among old and dear friends, she passed away to her eternal rest, June 15th, 1852.

MISS FIDELIA FISKE,

MISSIONARY TO PERSIA; OF THE AMERICAN BOARD OF MISSIONS.

"Sow, while the seeds are lying
In the warm earth's bosom deep,
And your warm tears fall upon it,
They will stir in their quiet sleep;
And the green blades rise the quicker,
Perchance, for the tears you weep."

MISS FIDELIA FISKE was descended from the good old Puritan stock. Although a native of America, and far removed, by course of years, from those early days, the family perpetuated from generation to generation the traditions of the faith received from their fathers, and through all their descent proved the truth of the divine promise respecting a godly seed. The Rev. William Guest, the biographer of Miss Fiske, tells us that for three hundred and thirty years, the family, in all its generations, had been known to be a godly one. Her great-grandmother was such an eminently pious woman that it is recorded of her that she used to set apart whole days to pray that her children may be holy, even to the latest descent. The biographer adds that so large was the answer granted to this prayer, that in 1857 *three hundred* of the descendants of this praying woman were members of Christian churches. It is little wonder, therefore, that Miss Fiske became the devoted and successful missionary teacher that she was. May not this have been part of the answer to that pious ancestor's prayers? Beside this, the missionary spirit ran in the family. Her uncle, the Rev. Pliny Fiske, had left America to labour in the missionary field in Palestine. Fidelia was only three years of age at the time of his departure; but that event, and the periodical arrival of the "Missionary Herald" in the family, did much towards deciding her, in after-years, as to the course her Christian activity should take.

Fidelia was born, May 1st, 1816, in Shelburne, "in a plain, one-storey" American country farm-house. She was always a very thoughtful child, and distinguished, even at an early age, for thoroughness of study, as far as her limited range went. Her father, Rupert Fiske, was a pious man, a Christian of almost one book. Evening by evening, by the side of the immense log-fire, and surrounded by his family, in the large farm-house kitchen, he searched his Bible, making it the man of his counsel, and the referee in all family difficulties. From him the children learnt that invariable habit of turning to the Holy Book for counsel, guidance and instruction, which followed them through all their after-life. Fidelia attended the district school, which happened to be near her father's house; and also the sabbath school, connected with the Congregational church of which her father was deacon. There the child's teacher was the daughter of the pastor, and one day, when Fidelia was about twelve years of age, this young lady spoke very pointedly and personally to each member of her class on the subject of their individual salvation. This close appeal fastened on Fidelia's heart, and the young girl for some months carried the burden of sin. But her mother, who was a Christian woman, observing the troubled face of the child, said one day, kindly, "What is it, my daughter?" "Mother, I am a lost sinner!" was the reply; and the mother therewith counselled her child how to flee from the wrath to come. Fidelia soon found peace, and in 1831, made a public profession of her faith in Christ, by uniting with the Congregational Church in her native town. She was at this time just over fifteen years of age. After this she entered various paths of usefulness, and became the means of much spiritual good to the young people within her circle.

At the age of twenty-three, Miss Fiske entered Mount Holyoke Seminary, a noted female college, and one which had for its ruling spirit, a thoroughly educated Christian woman. After residing there for about a twelvemonth, Miss Fiske returned home, ill with typhoid fever, an illness which took her to within a very hair's-breadth of the grave. She recovered, however, but only to see her father and her youngest sister fall victims to the same disease. After her recovery she returned to Mount Holyoke Seminary, desirous of completing her education for the work of instruction, little dreaming that a career of usefulness in the great missionary field would shortly be opened up to her.

Dr. Perkins, whose labours in Persia are known to most students of missionary enterprise, visited Mount Holyoke at this juncture, and requested that a young lady might be set apart, to go back to Persia with his party, in order to instruct the Nestorian women and girls. It is a remarkable thing that the lady principal, having the missionary cause much at heart, called a meeting of the teachers and pupils, when she urged them to take this matter into their prayerful consideration, in order to see if they could not consecrate themselves to the work. Out of her band of twelve teachers, *six* of them went to the missionary field to labour, sooner or later, as the result of that meeting. On the receipt of Dr. Perkins' request, Miss Fiske was proposed; but as Mrs. Fiske objected on the score of her daughter's health, the project was for a time given up. Another young lady was chosen, but her friends *would not* give her up; and finally the request came back to Miss Fiske again. The matter was a momentous one, and as it required an almost immediate decision, no time could be lost. After a sleepless night, Fidelia said that she would go, subject to her mother's consent. Hearing of that determination, although late in the day, the lady principal, Miss Lyon, decided to drive over to Shelburne, and see Mrs. Fiske at once. They drove off through the snow and the storm, arriving at Fidelia's home at eleven o'clock on a Saturday night; and summoning the family, Miss Lyon laid the matter before them, as one requiring prayerful consideration and immediate decision. All that night and next day, the matter was thought over and prayed over. Finally, the mother's faith conquered; and turning to Fidelia, she said "Go, my child, go." Then commenced preparations for her speedy departure for Persia.

On March 1st, 1843, at the age of twenty-seven, Miss Fiske embarked for Persia, there to labour as missionary teacher. The mission party included Dr. Perkins, his wife, and daughter, who were returning to mission work in Persia; Rev. D. T. Stoddard, Mrs. Stoddard, Rev. E. E. Bliss, and Mrs. Bliss, who were going out for the purpose of labouring among the mountain Nestorians. The little party sailed amid heartfelt benedictions and prayers from sorrowing friends, and after thirty-six days at sea, reached the harbour of Smyrna. They landed here, and spent a week amid the scenery and associations of this ancient city. After this they proceeded to Trebizonde, where Miss Fiske was introduced to two devoted missionaries, who had been labouring among the Turks for years, but with such intermittent success that they often sat down alone to the communion of the Lord's Supper. After the voyage had come to an end, Miss Fiske's party had to travel, in those inhospitable regions, seven or eight hundred miles by land. But after many hardships, they at length reached Urumiah, and settled down to their missionary toils.

Urumiah is a town in Persia, near the borders of Lake Urumiah, containing about 25,000 souls. Of these 2,000 are Jews, 1,000 are Nestorians, and the rest

TREBIZONDE.

Mohammedans. According to general custom the houses present a very gloomy appearance outwardly, seeing that they are built in the true Eastern style, and, as a rule, very dirty. Zoroaster, the founder of that form of idolatry peculiar to Persia, was born here, and his followers, called Parsees, or fire-worshippers, may be found to this day even in India. The Nestorians are a wild and lawless tribe, generally at war with the Kurds, and retaining among themselves some remnants of an ancient corruption of Christianity, transmitted to them by Nestorius, a reputed saint, and bishop of Constantinople, in the fifth century. His followers have not espoused all the idolatrous tenets of Rome, and for many years kept the faith as they received it from him, in much of its pristine purity. But, during the last few centuries, the Nestorians have greatly degenerated, being Christians only in name, sunk in darkness, degradation, and lawlessness; mumbling over their idolatrous forms of prayer without any meaning whatever. This description, however, although sad, must be made a hundred times sadder, if possible, to apply to the women, for the female part of the population are so sunk in ignorance and neglect that they know absolutely nothing. In the heart of these mountains the name "woman" was equivalent to our English term "donkey," and the Moslem idea that women have no souls, appeared to be firmly believed and taught among the Nestorians. The American Board of Missions directed their efforts very much to the civilising and instructing of the females, believing that the mothers and wives possessed the largest influence upon the children, and that, therefore, to be effective, all civilising and Christian effort must commence with them. The missionaries stated that the Nestorian language contained no words corresponding to those of "home" and "wife," so degraded were the habits of the people. In her description of the manners and customs of their social life, Miss Fiske says: "The Nestorian house was formerly a large single room, and there the work of the family was mostly performed.

K

There they ate, and there they slept. Several generations occupied the same apartment, each son, as he married, bringing his wife to his father's house. Their beds are much like a good 'comfortable' filled with wool, or, more frequently, with cotton; a heavy quilt and pillow completed a set of bedding. They took up their beds in the morning, piling them upon a wooden frame, spreading them again at night. It was customary to light the house by an opening in the roof, through which the smoke made its escape. It had only a floor of earth, covered in part with mats and pieces of carpeting. There was hardly a possibility of cleanliness. Vermin abounded in most of the homes, while the *personal* habits of the people were filthy."

According to universal custom where the civilising and refining influences of the Bible are unknown, the Nestorian women were the slaves and drudges of the household. Betrothed and married when mere children, they were taken at an early age to labour for the subsistence of the lord and master. They went forth in the morning to labour in the vineyards and wheat-fields, very often carrying also their little infants, for these they must nurse between the intervals of work. Then, returning at night, tired and worn out, they had to milk the cows, prepare the supper, and then stand by until the husband had finished, before daring to partake of any. In addition to all these degradations, they often had to suffer cruel beatings at the hands of their husbands. Such were the Nestorian women without the Gospel!

It was a trial of faith and patience, to labour among such degraded specimens of womanhood; but the trial must precede the triumph. Some few years previous to this, the first American missionaries had opened three schools for Nestorian children, and had performed the preparatory work connected with the mission to Persia. This had gone on; and at the time of Miss Fiske's arrival about forty schools had been opened in the villages on the plain of Urumiah; but as these were attended chiefly by boys, the women and girls were but little benefited by the work. Mrs. Grant, one of the first missionaries, had opened a day-school for girls in 1838, but it had dragged out a lingering existence, neither being attended nor appreciated by the class for whom it was intended. Miss Fiske felt it laid upon her conscience to try to do something for the Nestorian mothers, but she adds: "I little knew the *pit* of degradation I was descending." But she was determined to *try*, and narrates the account of her first lessons. "I would seat myself among them on the earthen floor and read a verse, then ask questions to see if they understood it. For example, after reading the history of the Creation, I asked, 'Who was the first man?' Answer—'What do we know? We are women;' (meaning in English, '*We are donkeys*.') Then I told them that Adam was the first man, and made them repeat the name over till they remembered it. This was enough for one lesson. It set them thinking, and woke up faculties previously dormant." Sometimes she would visit at their houses, and, sitting down on their mats, would collect a similar party around her; but the vermin and indescribable filth, would send her home sick at heart; while the women and girls would crowd around her, examine her clothes, remark on her words, and but rarely carry away any abiding idea of good. Under all circumstances, Miss Fiske felt that it was more hopeful to endeavour to evangelise the women through their daughters. Mrs. Grant's day-school had accomplished but little towards this end, especially as she had died within the first year of its formation, leaving only native teachers to work it under the supervision of the ladies of the mission. Yet, it was not wholly dead; and it seemed as if this school presented a nucleus from which could be expanded a seminary or boarding-school. Miss Fiske decided that, having regard to the household degradation and social customs prevalent among the Nestorians, she must take some girls into a *family-school*, clothe, educate, teach, and train them, if she would raise the women of Persia. It was a bold idea, for the customs and traditions of the Nestorians were all against it; while even the members of the mission doubted if the scheme could be started, or if once started, could be carried on for a single year. Everybody feared that if they gave up their daughters to be educated they would lose the chance of marriage; neither would they be available for drudgery in the fields, to say nothing of the *reproach* which fell upon all parents who dared to differ so greatly from the majority as to think of education for their girls.

However, Miss Fiske resolved to begin, and enquired for *six* girls, who were willing to be gratuitously maintained and educated. But nowhere could she obtain promises of scholars. She says: "The first Syriac word I learnt was *daughter*; and as I can now use the verb '*to give*,' I often ask parents to *give* me their *daughters*." But at the opening day, not one single scholar had been obtained. Fifteen day scholars, however, offered themselves, and Miss Fiske feared that here her efforts would have to end. But looking from the window, she saw Mar Yohanan coming through the court, leading two little girls by the hand—one his niece, and the other a child from a neighbouring village. They were named, the one Selby, and the other Khanee, and were aged respectively seven and ten years. As Miss Fiske hastened to meet them, the old man placed their childish hands in hers, and said, "They are your daughters; no man shall take them from you." The missionary teacher wept tears of joy over these two girls, and solemnly pledged herself to educate them for the Lord.

For several months these pupils proved to be the only resident ones, although many attended the day school. If one or two girls entered as boarders, frequently their school career would end by their running away before a week had passed, or by being forcibly carried away by their friends. Yet, one by one, the desired number was gained; but only after the most stringent conditions had been made by the friends. For instance, the girls were

MISS FIDELIA FISKE.   149

PERSIAN WOMEN.

not to be allowed to go out of doors except in the teacher's company, while they were to be lodged near her night and day. All these conditions Miss Fiske promised faithfully to observe; and she carried them out so literally, that the girls were as constantly with her as if they had been her own children. The premises occupied by the missionary, furnished two large rooms for the girls. Of these, one was the schoolroom, on the mud floor of which they sat, upon mats; these, with a stove, and a few rough benches, forming the only furniture. The window was of oiled paper, and "admitted," says Miss Fiske, "far more light than I supposed a paper window could." The other room, which was larger, was the kitchen, dormitory, and parlour of the girls; and it, too, was covered with mats, upon which to spread the beds. Miss Fiske had to *cleanse* these girls, clothe them, wash them, feed, teach, train, and bear with them —duties which demanded that the Christian graces of charity and long-suffering should be in constant and active exercise. Yet there was no other way of doing good to the women of Persia. A day-school for girls, besides being scantily attended, accomplished but little good, because the girls, as soon as they returned home, went at once into the very degradation from which the teacher was trying to rescue them. But could a generation of young women be raised up to act as teachers of the next, and as reformers of the homes of the people, there would be some hope of improvement. To this end Fidelia Fiske prayed, laboured, suffered, and hoped. She says: "Our first business is to make them clothes, that they may be comfortable. These we make in the native style. They must be cared for, not less when out of school than when in. When I go out, and when I come in I take these children with me, for I dare not leave them to themselves. Oh! they are a precious charge! I find my heart going forth to them, the same as to children at home. If I can lead them in the way to heaven I shall feel that my joy is full."

Occasionally also Miss Fiske met the mothers of her girls, holding a little familiar conversation about religious things, because their prejudices prevented their hearing the Gospel from the lips of *men*. But the great obstacle to their deriving any good, was their inveterate habit of talking. Usually she was obliged to get them to keep their fingers on their lips, before she could obtain silence, and then she would tell them some interesting narrative from the Bible. So, little by little, "the good seed of the kingdom" was sown.

In June, 1844, persecution broke out, and the school was for a time dismissed, in order to prevent violence being displayed to both teachers and pupils. Their friends took them home for a time, but in November the storm had passed over, and Miss Fiske received them all back once more. Not only so, but the number grew, until at the close of the year, the seminary included twenty-five boarders; and more might have been received had there been adequate accommodation. The mothers occasionally spent an afternoon with the girls, and so favourable was the impression produced, that people who would formerly have scoffed at the bare idea, now begged that their daughters might be taken into the school. Larger premises were subsequently obtained, and Miss Fiske rejoiced over a full institution. After this date, much success was seen; many of the girls were known to use their opportunities for private prayer most assiduously, and to listen to the instruction imparted with more earnest attention. In January, 1846, a revival, or to speak more correctly, an outpouring of the Holy Spirit, was granted to the pupils, in answer to the long-continued prayer of the missionaries. Many of the girls were hopefully converted to God, and the school resounded with the voice of praise and prayer. Writing home at this juncture, Miss Fiske says: "Prayerfulness has thus far been strikingly exhibited in those hopefully converted. They love their closets; and it is one of their greatest trials that they cannot have a prayer-closet as they wish. I have many little meetings for prayer with them. It is delightful at such times to hear those who have but just begun to love the Lord, pleading for entire consecration to Him, and also, with the deepest apparent feeling, wrestling for the salvation of their impenitent friends. Can it be, I often think at such a time, that these are indeed sisters in Christ, redeemed by His blood, and made heirs of heaven? If so, what an inroad has been made on Satan's kingdom. God has brought to pass in a day what years of man's labour could never effect." Some of these dear girls grew up to be teachers of others, or wives and mothers in various domestic circles, while others were early taken home to glory. Some of the memorials of these early saved ones are very touching.

Towards the end of 1847, Miss Rice, another lady from Mount Holyoke Seminary, America, arrived to assist Miss Fiske in the female boarding school. Soon after her arrival, a new awakening broke out in the school; and while those who were converted three years before sought a fresh consecration of heart and life, bemoaning their backslidings, nearly all the new scholars experienced pardoning grace. Nor was this all. From the school the influence of the Spirit spread around through all the district, till scarcely a house could be found in some of the villages without praying members. The women, among whom Miss Fiske had laboured so long and so unavailingly, now came crowding around the premises at all opportunities, entreating to be taken in for a day or two, to learn the way of salvation. Night and day, the teachers' private rooms, as well as the schoolrooms, were crowded with women, whose one anxiety was to know how to "flee from the wrath to come." One of the servants whose name was Joseph, after experiencing conversion himself, came to Miss Fiske one day with streaming eyes, and said: "I have a petition to make; will you receive it?" On being assured that she would, he proceeded: "My village is lost, my family are going to destruction, and their blood is upon my neck. Oh! *will* you let me go to-night, and tell them their state, and ask their forgiveness for my soul-destroying example?" On receiving permission he departed, and his visit was the commencement of a blessed awakening there, also, in consequence of which many converts were added to the church.

The pupils in the school were eager to get others to partake of the same blessings. The *maleg*, or mayor, of Geog Tapa, called there one day to see his little girl, who was under Miss Fiske's care. His daughter had experienced converting grace during this awakening; and, anxious that her father should be saved, too, commenced praying with him, as soon as the first messages and salutations were over. But the old man was proud and inflexible, determined not to be influenced by the new faith. She then called in six or seven of her companions to aid in her efforts, and the girls formed a praying circle round him, as he sat in the room. There he sat and listened, till his feelings so overcame him that he sank down in their midst. This they continued, until the man himself lifted up the earnest cry for mercy, and soon he received a gracious answer of peace. This man proved his conversion by his consistent life, and his warm interest in all that pertained to the mission, up till 1863, when he died. Miss Fiske records that at the close of this awakening, all the girls in the school over twelve years of age were hopefully converted, many of them becoming, from that time, shining lights in a dark world. Some of the girls returned to their mountain homes—with great grief, it was true, but with hearts on fire with the love of God, promising their teacher, with parting sobs, to be "faithful unto death." So they proved. Many years afterward, when the evangelists of the mission journeyed among those mountains, with the message of mercy to the people, they found these girls, then grown into womanhood, in homes of their own, nurturing the love of Christ in their hearts, and ready to welcome the preachers. In this way the bread cast upon the waters showed itself, after many days.

About 1850 an attempt was made by the Persian Government to close the school, but Miss Fiske appealed to the British Consul at Teheran, and with such success that the institution was suffered to continue in its course of usefulness and blessing. It had already conferred *great* blessings upon the female part of the population. Early marriages were abolished, so that it was not now uncommon to keep girls in the school until they were eighteen or nineteen, before they left to be married, or to engage as teachers in other schools. In each case the girls were eagerly sought after, as means of great blessing to the families and districts in which they settled. The charge of fanaticism had been brought against Miss Fiske and her helpers by those who sought the destruction of the school; but she fully disposed of this charge in her sensible and lady-like letter to the British Consul. It ran as follows:—"The design of this school is to so educate Nestorian girls that they may be better daughters, and sisters, wives, and mothers, than are usually found among this people. Unless a change, and a very great change, can be wrought in the females here, all the efforts in behalf of the other sex will fail of producing permanent good. We aim to give the members of the school such a training, physical, mental, and moral, as shall best fit them for a happy and useful life among their own people. Aside from the various duties of the schoolroom, kitchen, and washroom, the pupils are taught to cut out, and make their own clothing. They also give attention to other plain needlework, and ply their knitting whenever they find a few leisure moments. Some ornamental needlework is taught the elder girls. This has not a very prominent place in our instructions, though we deem it important. It tends, not a little, to soften the asperities of these wild girls. The same hand, however, that skilfully uses the worsted-needle is found in summer among the golden wheat, holding the sickle; and in autumn, gathering the vintage."

So the cloud of persecution passed away for that time, and again, and again the school experienced large showers of divine blessing. It was extended and enlarged, too, several times, in consequence of its growing popularity and usefulness. It was Miss Fiske's increasing desire that every girl brought within the range of her influence should not only be trained to perform the duties connected with this life well, but that she should also become a Christian, in deed, and in truth. To this end, she, together with her coadjutor, Miss Rice, laboured, prayed, and believed. At this time it was nothing uncommon for the converted mothers of the girls—women, who a few years before had been sunk in darkness and degradation—to set apart seasons to pray specially for the conversion of the girls. Then they would come to the school asking: " Is there any interest in the school ? Are any of the girls praying for mercy ? Is my daughter anxious ?" This fact indicates most markedly the great change which had taken place among the Persian women. No more ignorant and stupid, like *donkeys*, the poor mothers, having found the pearl of great price themselves, yearned that their daughters might find it too.

Time passed by, and each returning year increased in blessing; but the Government again endeavoured to close the school. In 1856, Askar Khan, a Government agent, visited the school, to obtain evidence against it, and thus interrogated one of the elder girls, in Turkish :—

" Are you allowed to follow your own customs ? "

" We follow all that are good. We have some very foolish customs, which you would not wish us to follow."

" Do these ladies let you see your friends ? "

" Certainly; we always see them when they come, and we go home three times in the year ; and once we stay home three months."

" What do you do when in your villages ? "

" We go out into the fields and work, and do everything that our friends tell us to do."

" Are your teachers willing ? "

" Yes; they tell us to help our friends all we can, and are sometimes displeased because we do no more for them."

" When here, what do you do ? "

" We study and learn all wisdom."

"Are you allowed to use your own books?"

"Certainly. The book which is the foundation of our religion they have printed for us, and we use it more than any other."

"Do you fast?"

"Yes; one day at the beginning of the year, and several other days."

"Have you not forsaken your father's fasts?"

"Not any that are written in that book. We are careful to keep all those."

"Would your teachers be willing that you should fast?"

"They would be willing; but we do not wish to fast more than the book requires."

"What are your prayers?"

"Such as the book teaches us."

Although this Government agent could see nothing but good in the school, he yet spoke very decidedly against female education, and said that the only proper condition for girls and women was their former one. There is no doubt that he would have made unfavourable representations to the Government, which would have bred trouble, had he been spared. He was not permitted, however, to do this, for he was shortly after assassinated in his tent by a Khoordish chief. Thus, once more, God's providence interposed.

In 1859, however, Miss Fiske's health visibly failed. She had been labouring constantly, "in season and out of season," among the Nestorian people for sixteen years; and although the spirit was willing and eager for yet more work, the flesh was very weak. Symptoms of the disease which ended in her death set in, and it was considered advisable that she should return to America, as well for the sake of the sea-voyage as for the purpose of obtaining the best medical skill. But the affections of the people clung round her with such fervency that she felt as if she *could not* break away from them. The native converts endeavoured, by every means in their power, to cheer and aid her at this time.

She tells an affecting story of one who sat near her in a church, during Divine service, striving to bear up her weakness. Miss Fiske was sitting on her mat, pensively thinking of the coming separation, and striving against her pain, when a Nestorian woman sat behind her, so as to support the invalid's frail strength, whispering: "If you love me, lean hard." She did lean, and rest too; winning so much rest and refreshment, indeed, that she was able to give the native women another lesson of an hour's length, before retiring home that evening.

Although greatly against her will, Miss Fiske had no alternative but to return to America. Her disease seemed to be of a cancerous nature, and quickly sapped the foundations of her strength; so, weary, worn, and broken in health, she decided to go. Others of the mission were going home too, to rest and recruit, and it became her settled intention, after doing this, to return to Persia—there, if it became her Lord's will, to end her days. The last few weeks of her sojourn at Urumiah were full of tender ministries on the part of those who had learnt the way of life from her lips. She mentions that in one meeting *ninety-three* converted females met to wish her "God speed," with all of whom, save one, she had prayed alone. Finally, with the promise of coming back again as soon as strength permitted, the devoted missionary tore herself from her much-loved pupils.

Returning home, she was welcomed by Christians of all ranks and denominations. During 1860 she used all her failing strength for the advancement of missions —speaking at drawing-room meetings, consulting with missionary labourers destined for the Nestorian mission-field, and stirring up the female colleges, especially her own loved Mount Holyoke, by her touching recitals of what the Lord had done. Many positions of usefulness were offered to her, but to all the requests for Christian service in this form her reply was "*Persia.*" In truth, she hoped and expected to sail for that land in the summer of 1863; but her evidently failing strength forbade it. With much sorrow of heart she relinquished this dearly-cherished design, and assumed the direction of Mount Holyoke Seminary. Here her Christian graces were called into play, and as far as her strength allowed she threw herself, heart and soul, into the beloved work. Such a blessing descended upon the institution that in one year it is recorded, "out of three hundred and forty-four scholars only nineteen left it unconverted." She succeeded, too, in sowing the seeds of missionary consecration among the young ladies, and some of them, upon whom her mantle descended, carried on the great work after she had passed into the skies.

She was not, however, spared very long to labour in her native land. Her disease progressed rapidly at the last, and she was compelled to lie by altogether. Precluded from writing, from the pain and inflammation of arms and chest, she dictated a last faithful yet affectionate message to the young people at Mount Holyoke. It closed with these words, words which come home to every Christian heart: "Live for Christ; in so doing you will be blessed for time and eternity." She experienced no doubts; her assurance was complete; her peace flowed as a river, for she knew in whom she had believed. One of the neighbouring ministers called to see her on the morning of her death; and while he was praying, her spirit, upborne on wings of faith and love, soared to realms of endless day, on the morning of July 26th, 1864.

Those who knew her bore the highest testimony to her Christian character. Dr. Kirk, the eminent Congregational minister of Boston, said: "I wish to speak carefully, but I am sure I never saw one who came nearer to Jesus in self-sacrifice. If ever there should be an extension of the eleventh chapter of Hebrews, I think that the name of Fidelia Fiske would stand there. That is a list of those who either had remarkable faith, or who suffered for the truth. She was a martyr. She had made the greatest self-sacrifice. She had given up her will; and when you have done that, the rest is easy. To burn at the stake for awhile, to be torn in the rack, to be devoured by wild beasts is as nothing when you have torn out your own will, and laid it on God's altar." Said the venerable Secretary of the American Board of Missions: " In the structure and working of her whole nature, she seemed to me the nearest approach I ever saw, in man or woman, to my ideal of our beloved Saviour as He appeared on the earth." This is high praise; but the labours and the life of Fidelia Fiske combine to bear it out.

"What then? Eye hath not seen, nor ear hath heard!
Wait till thou, too, hast fought the noble strife,
And won, through Jesus Christ, the crown of life!
Then shalt thou know the glory of the word,
Then as the stars, for ever, ever shine,
Beneath the King's own smile, perpetual zenith thine."

MRS. MARY M. ELLIS,
Wife of the Rev. William Ellis,

MISSIONARY TO THE SOUTH SEAS; OF THE LONDON
MISSIONARY SOCIETY.

"Open, O Heaven! No morrow
　Will see this joy o'ercast;
No pain, no tears, no sorrow,
　Her gentle heart will borrow;
　Sad life is past;
Shielded, and safe from sorrow,
　At home at last."

AMONG our English hymn-writers the Rev. Joseph Hart occupies an honourable place. In almost every selection of hymns, some of Hart's are to be found, while his sound "Guide to a Young Christian" has directed many into the path of life and counselled them when there. The subject of this sketch was the granddaughter of the Rev. Joseph Hart; in fact, for many generations the family had been noted for godliness, so that Miss Moor was the descendant of an ancestry renowned for piety and good works.

Mary Mercy Moor was early left an orphan. When she was only an infant of three months, her father, Mr. Alexander Moor, died, and before the child had completed her eighth year, Mrs. Moor also passed away, leaving her daughter to the guardianship of a pious friend, living in the metropolis, who engaged to supply, as far as possible, the lack of a mother's care. The little girl remained with this lady for some years, receiving in the school which the latter carried on, a sound education, adapted to train her for future usefulness as a governess. On her attaining the age of eleven, she felt the stirrings of the Spirit to such an extent that her Bible became her companion by night and day. She would even sleep with it under her pillow, so as to have it at hand on awaking in the morning. Beside this, she engaged in Sunday-school teaching in connection with the Silver Street Chapel, and in various ways tried to work for her Saviour. Still, it seems that she did not, at that time, make any public profession. However, in 1812, when Mary was nineteen, she went to reside with her only brother, who, being two years older than herself, had commenced business in London; and during the next year she was admitted into church-fellowship with the Silver Street Church, then under the pastoral care of the Rev. Mr. Jones. At the date of this profession of Christianity she was about twenty years of age, and known to all with whom she mingled as an earnest, sincere follower of Christ, and a devoted Sunday-school worker. But Providence so ordered it that her sympathies were not to be confined to this path of Christian labour, although the means by which Miss Moor's mind was directed to the contemplation of mission-work, were somewhat staggering to faith.

In the year 1815, she was laid on a sick bed by an illness which at first threatened to cut her off. But in answer to many earnest prayers—as she always believed —she was again raised up; and with renewed health came renewed and deepened consecration to the Master's service. The mission-cause engaged very much of her attention; she read, talked and prayed about it, longing to be permitted to go to the untaught heathen. It was only after the most earnest counsel on the part of her friends that she consented to forego her purpose of *going alone* to the heathen. In deference to their wishes she relinquished that idea, but laid the matter before her God, and awaited the openings of Providence; and very shortly Miss Moor was led "by a way that she knew not" into the mission-field.

Among the youthful members of the church at Silver Street, was William Ellis, then filling a situation as gardener in a gentleman's family. About the time when Miss Moor's missionary aspirations commenced, the Rev. John Campbell gave several addresses concerning the work of missions in South Africa. He had just returned from a two years' visit to the missionary stations there, and his accounts of the wretchedness of the Africans, and their willingness to receive teachers, made a very strong impression on the minds of all who heard him. Among the rest, William Ellis decided to devote the remainder of his life, provided the directors of the London Missionary Society accepted him, to the work of preaching the Gospel to the heathen. Mr. Ellis's friends were not greatly in favour of his going out; indeed, the mission-cause was then in its infancy, comparatively speaking, and "the madness of the missionary enterprise" occupied people's thoughts more than its utility or glory. However, nothing daunted, William Ellis persevered and was accepted, being afterwards appointed for service in the South Seas. About the same time Mr. Ellis became acquainted with Miss Moor, who willingly consented to join him as his partner both in life and service. Accordingly, after about a year's preparation, the young missionary, having been previously ordained, was married to Miss Moor on the 9th November, 1815. On the 8th December, the young married couple bade farewell to their friends in London, and proceeded to Gosport, but in consequence of various delays, did not finally sail until January 23rd, 1816. It also added to their trial that no passage could be obtained for them save in a transport vessel, crowded with mutinous convicts, and commanded by an insolent and disobliging captain. Along with their fellow-missionaries, Mr. and Mrs. Threlkeld, Mr. Ellis and his wife experienced the utmost discomfort from this man's incivility and cruelty. The food was insufficient and coarse, and sometimes consisted of the flesh of sheep which had died of disease or starvation. Yet, in view of all this, as a brief extract from one of Mrs. Ellis's letters written at this date will show, her missionary ardour was in no degree abated.

"Did we not believe that an over-ruling Providence

IN THE SOUTH SEA ISLANDS.

orders all things for the best, we might be inclined to murmur at being sent out in a convict ship, but we know we are in the hands of God, and that He has the hearts of all at His disposal, and renders all things subservient to His own glory; therefore we cheerfully go forth, assured that if the Lord has anything for us to do among the heathen, we are safe until our work is done. We rejoice that our minds are kept stayed on God, and we can say, with our dear missionary sister, 'Onward in the strength of the Lord, is our motto.' Indeed, the hope of being useful among the convicts animates and reconciles us to the prospect of danger. But why do I talk of being exposed to danger? If our Saviour be at the helm, we need fear no evil."

After a delay at Rio Janeiro, the vessel proceeded on her outward course, reaching Sydney on the 22nd July. It was not until the following December that a passage could be secured to the South Sea Islands; and during this interval the missionaries remained the welcome guests of a missionary who had returned from Tahiti because of the hostility of the natives. Here Mrs. Ellis's first child was born.

In December they sailed for the scene of their future labours and came in sight of the island of Kapa, about the 26th of January, 1817. At this place they first made acquaintance with the predatory habits of the islanders. Although shy at first, the natives gained courage, crowding up the sides of the ship, and swarming over the decks like bees, laying hands on whatever they could find. One powerful fellow tried to seize a youth, but the lad was too nimble for him. He then clutched at the cabin boy, and attempted to drag him off, but the sailors made the native relinquish his prize. A second attempted to carry off a large mastiff, and a third succeeded in stealing a little kitten. Only a few minutes previously, the nurse was playing with Mrs. Ellis's little infant on deck, having just retired to the cabin as the islanders commenced to swarm around the ship; thus the infant was providentially preserved from probable kidnapping, and that before its parents' eyes.

In February, just thirteen months after their departure from Portsmouth, Mr. and Mrs. Ellis arrived at Eimeo, the scene of the first part of their labours. The first night on shore was spent in "a slender, birdcage sort of a structure," thatched with leaves, and with a floor only of earth, stones, and pebbles. This first night's lodging shadowed forth their subsequent career in the missionary-field—self-sacrifice, suffering, and lack of much personal comfort. Still, Mrs. Ellis never once murmured, such was her singleness of heart and her desire to be useful. And when, in obedience to the counsel of the other missionaries, her husband removed to a station called Afareaitu, on the opposite side of the island of Eimeo, she journeyed thither without a delay, and resided in the rudest shelter until the mission-house could be built.

Here she at once commenced the special work of a missionary. She studied the language, so as to hold communication with the natives, and instructed the native women in sewing as well as in other feminine arts. This was no light labour, for the ignorance of the native females was only equalled by their stupidity and obstinacy. And among the minor trials which they had to endure, not the least was the entire change of food—a change which, to some extent, affected their health. As soon as the dwelling was erected Mr. Ellis set up the printing-press, and with the assistance of his brother missionary, struck off a native spelling-book, a Tahitian catechism, and an edition of St. Luke's Gospel. It should be mentioned that Mr. Ellis spent four months out of his twelvemonth of preparation in England, in learning printing and book-binding. After the printing was done, Mrs. Ellis, along with the other missionary's wife, laboured at book-binding, teaching the natives also this necessary art. Mrs. Ellis further undertook, for several hours daily, the education of the six children of Mr. Crooks, their fellow-missionary labourer, so that with the care of her own babe, domestic duties, the book-binding, and the instruction of the native women, she never knew an idle moment. In 1818 a second son was born to them, a child of so delicate a constitution, that the parents had to make frequent and wearisome journeys to Papetoai, on the opposite side of the island, for medical assistance. Afterwards, through the carelessness of the native nurse, this child fractured his arm; and on more than one occasion both the lives of infant and mother were in danger. One day, Mrs. Ellis, with her infant, narrowly escaped drowning, through the upsetting of her canoe. All were plunged into the raging sea, but by the exertions of the natives were rescued.

VIEW IN HUAHINE.

In the same year Mr. and Mrs. Ellis, with Mr. and Mrs. Barff, removed to Huahine, with the intention of settling in that island permanently. Here Mrs. Ellis resumed her works of love among the native females, with varying success. Nothing was more common than for the women, after receiving instructions in needlework, to turn round and demand pay for the trouble of learning. Among the rest, a young woman who had gained great proficiency in the art applied for payment. "For what?" asked Mrs. Ellis. "For learning," was the answer. "You asked me to learn, and I have learnt; what am I to get?" Of course it was explained to her that she had *received*, not conferred, a benefit, and was also shown how she might turn her newly-acquired knowledge to account by working for wages. In 1820, a little church, consisting of fifteen members, was formed in Huahine. Several of these were females, and had been won over by Mrs. Ellis's labours. She also commenced a class for giving Biblical instruction to those women who were anxious to unite in church-fellowship; and along with Mrs. Barff she visited the sick and aged females, according to a regular system.

Soon afterwards, Mr. Ellis sailed for the Sandwich Islands, in order to accompany two native teachers, who were prepared to settle in the Marquesas, leaving Mrs. Ellis and her four little ones alone among the infant church. At this date Mrs. Ellis writes: "Sister Barff and I continue our meetings with the females. We often find it a season of refreshing to our own souls, and do hope it is beneficial to the dear natives. We had a very affecting meeting at the parting of our two dear sisters, the wives of the native teachers. Many of the women could not speak for tears; indeed, there was not a dry eye in the room. 'We grieve to part with our dear sisters,' said the native women. 'We shall never again see their faces at our meetings for conversation, at our meetings for prayer, at our meetings for public worship. We have been used to listen to them with delight when they have exhorted us with affection, and prayed with, and for us; but we shall not hear their voices more. But we will not keep them back; the work is God's, and if teachers had not been sent to us we should now have been dwelling in darkness, and the shadow of death. We should now have been killing one another, and murdering our dear babes, and sinking into hell; but God had compassion on us. He has sent His good word to us, and caused our hearts to believe that Jesus Christ alone is the Saviour of sinners, and to desire Him for our Saviour; and shall we not be willing that others may know this good Word and Saviour also?' This, and much more to the same purport, was the language of their lips, and we believe also the language of their hearts. It reminded us much of those delightful meetings we had in our native land on the eve of our own departure."

Mr. Ellis did not anticipate that his absence would extend to more than three months, and during that time Mrs. Ellis visited Borabora, at the request of Mrs. Orsmond, who was the only European female there, to assist her in the work of the station. After remaining about nine weeks, Mrs. Ellis, with her family, set out on her return voyage. But contrary winds forced the boat back, and the boatmen were compelled to put in at Raiatea. Here she remained for a fortnight, waiting for another favourable opportunity. On the first calm day they accordingly left again, but the wind rose, and after battling with the storm all night, they found themselves still near to Raiatea, and landed, although this time it proved to be another part of the coast. The natives carried Mrs. Ellis to the nearest hut, for she was too weak and faint to stand. At first sight this hut appeared empty, but on looking round Mrs. Ellis descried a poor native woman kneeling by the side of a corpse, and praying to God. As soon as the first outbursts of her lamentation subsided, the newly-made widow came forward, and explained that the corpse was that of her dead husband; that all the other inmates of the hut were gone to attend a missionary meeting, but that she had stayed at home to attend on her dying husband, who had passed away as the boat approached the shore. Mrs. Ellis was still lying on the mat, where the natives had placed her, and, indeed, during the whole of the day and the next night she was too worn and feeble to rise, but she tried to comfort the poor, lonely widow. Telling her of Him who is a "Husband to the widow, and a Father to the fatherless," Mrs. Ellis endeavoured to lighten the load of sorrow pressing on her hostess. And this poor woman, but recently snatched from heathenism, rose from out her great sorrow and tried to minister to her heaven-sent guest. This was self-renunciation, as taught by the Bible; and Mrs. Ellis never looked back to that time but with feelings of grateful interest. On the next day the boatmen made another attempt, and fortunately succeeded in reaching the island of Huahine. Here, however, her troubles were not ended, for owing to some unknown cause Mr. Ellis had not returned, and his absence was prolonged to *eight* months. During this time the natives vied with each other in attending to the comfort and safety of "the little lonely widow," as they designated her. At length, after eight anxious months, the vessel in which Mr. Ellis had sailed returned, and husband and wife were safely re-united. But this voyage was the commencement of another change of home. An important opening offered to Mr. Ellis in the island of Oahu, and late in the same year he, with his family, set sail. This event was the breaking-up of many ties. The women, especially, crowded around Mrs. Ellis, with many tears, while those who had acted as nurses to the children, or had been more constantly associated with Mrs. Ellis in domestic matters, were overwhelmed. One poor woman went on the beach and watched the vessel far out at sea, waving the last farewell to her teacher and friend, now gone for ever.

At length they reached Oahu, and here Mrs. Ellis commenced work among the females, pursuing the same course as at Huahine. She says in a letter of this date: "We were welcomed with the greatest cordiality by the missionaries, the king and the chiefs, and were happy to find that though there is plenty of room for improvement, the people give the hearing ear, and seem willing to receive instruction. I do not like these people so well as I do those of the Society Isles; but perhaps I may like them better when I know more of them. There is a great work to be done here, and plenty of room for many labourers." Mr. and Mrs. Ellis spent all the time possible in the acquisition of the Hawaiian dialect, so as to be able to proceed with the instruction of the natives. As soon as she had gained proficiency enough, the females of the royal family attached themselves to her for instruction; and every day some one or more of them visited her for this purpose. It was curious, too, to observe how these half-taught females aped the manners and customs of the missionaries' wives. At that time it was the fashion for ladies to carry their handkerchiefs in small reticules; and one of the native women, high in rank, having observed this fact, resolved to emulate the practice. So, during the week she procured a *new covered pail,* and on the following Sabbath marched to chapel with a long train of attendants, one of whom, strutting nearest her mistress, carried this pail. The missionary wondered what could be the purpose of this article, but, of course, proceeded with the service as usual. The party calmly took their seats, and presently, at a sign from the lady, the attendant, lifting the lid of the pail, took out a white pocket handkerchief, which she handed to her mistress. This lofty specimen of heathenism used the handkerchief very ostentatiously, and then returned it to the pail, surveying the congregation meanwhile with great complacency. Still, in spite of many humorous incidents of this kind, much good was accomplished, and many of these sable daughters of the South Seas were won for Christ. Among the number was Keopuolani, the queen-mother of the king of the island of Maui, who had been a most consistent Christian for some time, and who was the first to receive the rite of baptism in the Sandwich Islands. This woman died a most triumphant death, after a long illness; and in accordance with her own request, Mr. Ellis buried her with the simple rites of Christian burial. And this enlightened queen was only the first-fruits of a long accession to the crown jewels of the Redeemer, from those southern seas.

ISLAND OF MAUI.

But a severe form of spinal disease developed itself in Mrs. Ellis, consequent, as it was supposed, upon one or two disastrous voyages between Huahine and Raiatea, taken soon after the birth of her youngest child. This disease forbade active service any longer, and compelled Mrs. Ellis to remain in her own house, confined to her couch for many hours every day. Here, whenever her strength permitted, groups of female natives would gather around her to listen to her words, while she would discourse to them of the love and faithfulness of Jesus Christ. Indeed, she was eagerly sought out by those whom she had been accustomed to teach; and although now laid aside in great measure, she continued as far as possible her oral instructions to the women. But there was no prospect of recovery, and the medical opinion was that nothing but a voyage to England, and life in her native air once more, would restore her. Accordingly, all the cherished missionary-work and the long-planned mission-schemes had to be renounced, and on the 24th of September, 1824, Mr. and Mrs. Ellis left Oahu, amid the weeping and lamentations of the chief women, who had stood and knelt around Mrs. Ellis' bed all day. After a month's sail they touched at Huahine, the scene of their former labours, and as soon as the natives knew who was on board they crowded round with many tokens of affection. They stocked the ship with provisions until the captain declared he could accept no more, while the little ones in the Sunday-school brought arrowroot, sugar-cane, fruit, and fowls for the children—all from love to Mrs. Ellis. Not content with this, the natives got up a social gathering; Mrs. Ellis was present, having been carried to the place of meeting on a couch, and made the special guest of the queen and the young princess. After this short stay they passed on their way, and reached America, whither the ship was bound, in March, 1825—little more than nine years from the date of sailing from England. After another rest among sympathising friends in America, and the prosecution of mission-service by Mr. Ellis, in giving lectures and holding meetings, they once more sailed, and reached London on the 18th of August in the same year.

Mrs. Ellis's expectations of relief and cure by a return to England, were not realised. Bodily weakness and mental depression united to do their worst, and the trial of her faith was severe. She says in her diary: "Still, dear Lord, thou seest best to visit this feeble body with pain and languishing; wearisome nights are appointed unto me; and distressing have been the seasons of pain Thou hast called me to bear these last two months—seasons which sometimes induce the thought, 'Why are His chariot-wheels so long delayed?'

"Cast down, but not destroyed, I bless the hand,
My Father's hand, which strengthens while it strikes;
And should the furnace rage with sevenfold heat,
My Father's even there: mighty the waves,
But mightier He above, who calms the storm."

In 1827, however, her disease assumed a favourable appearance, and she was able to attend public worship, as well as to ride about. Indeed, it was hoped at one time that her physical improvement would be such as to permit herself and her husband to return to the South Seas. But no improvement continued long enough to carry out these plans: the continual fluctuations prevented even the thought of a return to foreign mission-work. Consequently, for five years Mr. Ellis travelled and lectured for the London Missionary Society. At the end of that period he assumed the post of Foreign Secretary to the Society, and was discharging the duties of that office at the time of Mrs. Ellis's death. The last four years of her life she was confined to her room with continued suffering. Yet even there she continued the same patient, loving, ministering friend as ever. One touching instance proves this: a little boy—a missionary's son—was sent to England for his education, and taken home for a short time by Mr. Ellis. Mrs. Ellis admitted him to a share in her motherly love and sympathies. Writing about it many years after, this gentleman says: "You perhaps forget the kindness of your mother to the stranger boy that had drifted to the haven. Do you think I can? With all her pain and weakness, and the cares of her own children, she at once found room for me in her thoughts and anticipations. I shall never forget that white, thin, patient, loving face. The tears gather and drop as I write these lines. Nor was this all. Her thoughts followed me to school, nearing, though she was, the hour when heart and flesh should fail; she remembered the lonely boy in the distant school, and sent him at Christmas a box of schoolboy's cheer." This was at Christmas, 1834; in the following month she passed away. A sudden change took place, and on the evening of Sunday, January 11th, 1835, the beloved sufferer exchanged earth for heaven. Her patient endurance, saintly self-sacrifice, and loving ministry, form still a sweet savour among those who knew and loved her. From Huahine, and from Oahu, ransomed souls have long ere this, been "presented before the throne of God," as the result of Mrs. Ellis's labours there. Now she rests from these labours, but through all eternity her "works do follow her."

MRS. DOROTHY JONES,
Wife of the Rev. Thomas Jones,

MISSIONARY TO THE WEST INDIES; OF THE WESLEYAN
MISSIONARY SOCIETY.

"Mysterious to our reason seems your doom,
Yet not less merciful that doom might be;
And when the silent chambers of the sea
Shall hear the echoing trumpet rend the skies,
With them to meet the Lord in glory, ye shall rise.

"Then shall the wisdom of Omnipotence,
To our illumined vision be made clear;
Marvels and mysteries unto mortal sense
Shall great, and good, and merciful appear."
BERNARD BARTON.

THE lives of few female missionaries have been more eventful than that of Mrs. Jones. During the short period that she was permitted to labour in the foreign field, she suffered more in the cause of missions than many who have been spared to toil much longer in the work, her whole career being marked by striking interpositions of the providence and grace of God, and filled up with thrilling dangers and sufferings.

Dorothy Hobson was born at Cobridge, a Staffordshire village, on August 17th, 1802, being the youngest of four daughters. Her father was in business as a master potter, and by the exercise of industry and economy, managed to bring up his children respectably, and to give them a fair education. Dorothy was trained under her mother's eye, in the fear of God, and in the strict observance of the Sabbath. She had several remarkable escapes from peril in her early childhood, and these escapes she was accustomed to call to mind in afterdays, with deep emotion. Once she was stolen by gipsies; but her father assembled a company of his workmen, and started in pursuit. After some time, little Dorothy was found in the gipsy camp, sitting in a hamper of straw, and contentedly eating gingerbread. At another time, she and her little brother were lost, while walking in the fields, having strayed too far, and in their childish way they repeated their evening prayers for preservation and direction, until they by-and-bye reached home.

When Dorothy was about fifteen, her mother died. Mrs. Hobson was a sincere Christian, a wise parent, and a far-seeing woman. As if apprehending conflicts between Dorothy and her father on the score of religion, she made it her dying request that if she or any other of the children after her death should prefer another church to the one in which they were brought up, he would permit them to attend. This bereavement was greatly blessed to the young girl; indeed, it finally led to her coming to "the great decision." She was for some time in great distress of mind on account of her sins; her health suffered, so that she was compelled to go for a season from home, and while away was induced to accompany a friend to the Wesleyan Chapel at Burslem. She continued her attendance on the Wesleyan ministry, and after long and earnest struggling with sundry difficulties, she was enabled to believe with her heart unto righteousness, and obtained a blessed sense of forgiveness, and acceptance with God, through the merits of Christ. Miss Hobson soon after became a member of the Wesleyan Church, and in the warmth of her first love, engaged in Sunday-school teaching, and missionary collecting, as well as in other works of faith and usefulness. During the week she was employed in hand-painting on china at a neighbouring pottery, thus earning her own living. This circumstance was a fortunate one for her, seeing that very shortly a heavy trial came upon her. Her father, feeling annoyed at his daughter's devotion to religious work, and her attendance at the Wesleyan chapel, determined to turn her out of doors, unless she acceded to his wishes, and renounced her connection with these things. It was in vain that she pleaded her mother's request. One night, upon returning home, after she had been collecting for the missionary society, he said to her: "Dorothy, I wish to give you a choice as to which way you will take, and you must let me know your decision within a half-hour. You must give up praying, visiting the sick, collecting for those blacks and attending the missionary meetings, or in half-an-hour you must leave this house, and find another home." Dorothy looked frightened, and full of sorrow; but her faith was firm. She said: "Father, I cannot promise these things; I must serve Jesus first." "Then you must go," said her father. She says: "It was a great trial to me, but my heart was kept, trusting in the Lord. I left home at the end of the half-hour, the servant girl going with me, to carry my things. I had no relatives within many miles distance, but I went to the house of a poor widow, who was detained at home that evening by the accident of spraining her wrist, and her consequent inability to lock her door." Dorothy settled down here for a little time, and continued her engagements as usual, trusting that God would soften her father's heart towards her. As she prayed, it was done unto her. Mr. Hobson sent her very soon a cordial and pressing invitation to return home, promising that he would never more interfere with her conscientious convictions of duty. She returned home at once, glad and thankful at the reconciliation, and only the more eager to work for Christ.

Shortly after, Miss Hobson became engaged to the Rev. Thomas Jones, who was preparing for mission-work, and this circumstance gave rise to further trials at home. In spite of all his past harshness, Mr. Hobson regarded Dorothy as his favourite child, but so incensed was he at the prospect of losing her that he intercepted Mr. Jones' letters, and even threatened personal violence towards him should he appear on the premises. One evening the matter came to a crisis, and Mr. Hobson entered the room where Dorothy was sitting, in order, as it appeared, to talk matters over. Having silently lifted up her heart in prayer, she quietly told her father that Mr. Jones had passed his examination, was appointed to the West Indies, and was anxious to know whether she could accompany him. "I suppose," rejoined Mr. Hobson, "if I say *no*, you will go?" "No, father, I should not think it right in that case to engage; nor would the committee allow it. The rules forbid it." "You don't know what you are doing," said he. "You would never be happy with those blacks always about you. And then the climate is so sickly, you could not live long in it." She replied: "Yes, father, I have thought of all these things, and read all I could on the subject." "Then, what do you want? Cannot you be happy at home?" She said with deep feeling: "If I could but be useful to the heathen I should be happy." He paused, and then replied: "Well, I neither say yes nor no; please yourself." "Father, I shall think it my duty to go," she replied, "as you do not forbid;" and so the matter was decided.

The young missionaries were married at Burslem, October 22nd, 1824, and sailed on December 21st. After various delays they reached Antigua safely, on February 7th, 1825, and landed at English Harbour. A friend, who saw Mrs. Jones land, writing of her, said: "She and her husband had all the vigour of English health, and presented every indication of lives of usefulness and honour. She had all the bloom of her fatherland, and her amiable and gentle manners, as well as her consistency in dress and deportment, attracted the attention of all with whom she came in contact." They were stationed at Parham, six miles from St. John's, and both became speedily favourites with the negroes. Anxious to be at work, Mrs. Jones gathered together a class of negro women, in order to teach them to read; and so great a favourite was she that women of all ages came from long distances seeking admission. Among the number was an old woman of seventy-two years of age, bent, and decrepid. Mrs. Jones hesitated about receiving her, seeing that she had already as many young and hopeful scholars as she could well manage. But the aged negress pleaded pitifully for admission, saying, among other things: "Yes, missy, I know my head is thick, but I asked the Great Massa to help me read, and to put it into your heart to teach me." Mrs. Jones asked her, "What do you wish to read for?" "Oh!" said the poor old woman, "I wish to learn that I might read the Great Word. Perhaps, missy, I may be sick and have the fever; and you know massa have plenty to do, and I live eight miles off. Den I think if I can read the Great Word it will tell of Jesus, and comfort me." As the result, Mrs. Jones gave the old woman permission to come twice a week, in order to learn her letters, giving her at the same time an easy reading book. Twice, weekly, the poor old woman trudged to Parham, walking the sixteen miles, and each time she succeeded in gaining a little additional facility in the art of reading. After some months of this effort, as she was with Mrs. Jones in the study one morning, she succeeded in spelling out the name LORD. A sudden awe seemed to strike her. "Missy," she said, "that is the Great Massa's name." "Yes," was the reply. Overcome with emotion, she let go the book, and stood up; clasping her hands together, she lifted up her eyes, full of tears, saying: "Lord! Massa! Great Massa! I can read your great name." Then she dropped on her knees, and prayed so fervently for blessings to rest upon the work of God, and upon her teachers, that Mrs. Jones could not restrain her tears.

In addition to this class of women she also taught a class of girls, in the hall of her house nearly every

NEGRO HUT IN THE WEST INDIES.

evening in the week. These poor girls had, in many instances, to labour at field-work all day—for this was during the time of West Indian slavery—and then to walk distances of several miles to the mission-house. But the love of learning so stimulated them that they attended with surprising punctuality and regularity, although the accommodation was so restricted in proportion to the numbers that the little ones had to sit or lie in the corners of the room, and "even under the table." Mrs. Jones was permitted to see many pleasing instances of good done by means of these two classes.

About a year was spent in faithful service for Christ among these "little ones" of the flock, when a painful and crushing dispensation of Providence put an end to her missionary joys. The district meeting was to be held at St. Christophers—another island in the West Indian Archipelago—and as many missionaries were to meet on that occasion, Mr. Jones wished much his wife to accompany him. She decided to do so, but appears to have suffered much beforehand in consequence of a remarkable dream, which seemed to forebode evil. She could not shake off the impression, but felt willing to suffer whatever might be in store, and especially to accompany her husband into whatever danger or sorrow might be appointed for him. The mission party proceeded to their destination in safety, however, and after going through the services, and calling at Montserrat, prepared to return home. At Montserrat these terrible forebodings of shipwreck were repeated, so much so that Mrs. Jones almost felt her courage fail in the prospect of the return voyage. The missionary party now numbered five missionaries, three missionaries' wives, four children, and two nurses, making a total of fourteen individuals. They left Montserrat on Monday, February 27th, 1826, in the *Maria* mail-boat, instead of their own vessel, hoping thereby to secure a quicker passage back to Antigua. All seemed fair when they embarked, but during Monday night a storm arose, which increased in rapidity until it became a hurricane. The passengers were roused, for the vessel was blown over on its side, the waves dashed frightfully over it, and the only boat the ship possessed was carried off with two sailors in it. The passengers were dragged up on the deck, parents clinging to their children, and husbands to wives until morning broke, hoping that then the storm would lull. But before day had dawned the vessel broke in two. Mrs. Jones says, in her deeply affecting story: "The captain, with four sailors, the brethren Hillier, Oke, and Jones clung to the bows of the vessel; myself, brother White and family, brother Truscott, wife and child, two nurses, one gentleman passenger, and several of the sailors, who were holding on by the bulwarks to the quarter-deck, at once went down with that part of the vessel to which we had trusted ourselves. When the waves had passed over him, Mr. Jones called out for me. I heard him, and cried out, 'I am going!' but my feet were entangled in the rigging, which was the cause I was not washed away with the rest. Mr. Jones, finding by my voice that I was not far off, said, 'Put out your hand.' I reached it out above the water, and he brought me up from a watery grave. I now heard the heart-rending shrieks of the dear children. Their cry was: 'Oh! mamma, I am drowning!' 'Oh! papa, save me!' The little baby's cries were distressingly distinct."

As Tuesday broke, its light found Mr. and Mrs. Jones, together with the persons before-named, clinging still to the bows of the wreck, all the others having gone into eternity! "But I thought I should soon be exhausted," says Mrs. Jones, "being extremely cold, through sitting so long in the water, with my head only just above the surface. I had no bonnet on, and the pieces of wreck which came dashing up against me soon tore up my dress, so that I had nothing to keep me warm. Mr. Jones pressed me to take his jacket, but to this I could not consent; the captain, however, gave me an old jacket, which I thankfully received. Twice I lost my hold, in consequence of a large dog that had been on board attempting to get on the wreck. The poor animal, seeing my head out of water, came and set his feet upon it, and I was very near being drowned before the brethren perceived my danger." On Wednesday the storm abated, and the survivors hoisted their cravats as signals of distress; but the long day wore to a close, and still no succour came. The dead bodies of their friends and companions floated around them, being entangled in the rigging, making Mrs. Jones "shrink from the prospect of a watery grave, and long to die on shore." This shore was only about three miles away, but the look-out man was at the other side of the island, and neglecting his duty, consequently they were not discovered. The poor sailors, one by one, were washed off the wreck exhausted; but ere they were so lost the missionaries pointed them to Jesus, and earnest prayers for pardon and acceptance ascended up to heaven. The night passed in cold and misery, for the wind was very boisterous; but when Thursday morning dawned the hopes of rescue had well nigh died out of every breast. On that morning, Mr. Hillier, one of the missionaries, endeavoured to swim to land, but the current was too strong for him, and he was soon carried away. Mr. Jones said: "Brother Hillier's sufferings are at an end; and this will be the case with us, for we cannot live much longer." But Mrs. Jones could not answer; her "heart was too full." Towards sunset the captain planned to make an attempt to get to Sandy Island on the mast, but on making the trial found he could not succeed. Mrs. Jones urged her husband to go with him, saying she would remain in the rigging till he brought back help; but Mr. Jones said: "No, my dear, I cannot leave you. We will remain together as long as we can." But the time was drawing on when he, too, was about to sink into the arms of death.

Continuing her story, Mrs. Jones says: "The wreck now began to unjoint, and before morning we expected it would quite separate. We suffered much from pieces of wood, with nails in them, which, by the force of the water, were driven against us, and tore our flesh. On that day also the sun greatly scorched me, for as I had no bonnet to screen my face, that, as well as my hands, was blistered, so that my skin and finger-nails afterwards came off. On Friday morning my pain and faintness increased, so that I thought I was dying. Our sufferings now were so great that death seemed desirable, though our minds were, by the great mercy of God, kept in perfect peace. There were now but three of us left. Mr. Jones could scarcely speak distinctly; sometimes he would say, 'Let me go, for I am dying!' Sometimes he asked me what could be the matter with him. Every time a wave came it washed him almost from me; he had no power to assist himself. I called to the captain: 'Mr. Jones is drowning. Oh! if you can assist me, do. Do not let him drown, for he is dying. Raise him, and let him die in my arms.' The captain turned round and attempted to assist, but could not; he said, 'It is all over. I am almost dead myself. I cannot assist you.' I then, by a last effort, got his head on my shoulder; but how I collected strength for the exertion I cannot tell. I continued to hold him in my arms, but frequently thought I must yield him up. Then again I thought: 'Oh! if I can but hold him till death has ended his sufferings I shall be satisfied.' He spoke after this, but I could not answer him for weeping, and I now felt as though my heart would break. Mr. Jones then gave a struggle, and cried aloud, 'Come, Lord Jesus!' I held him several minutes, but he neither spoke nor moved again. I spoke to him, and begged him, if still alive, to move his hand, but life had fled. I well remember feeling thankful, amid all my sorrow, that I had been enabled so to help him as to keep him from drowning, and that he had not to struggle with death in the water."

The captain next passed away, and Mrs. Jones fell into a state of insensibility, which would quickly have ended in death, had not two gentlemen just then come to her assistance in a boat. After they had recalled her to partial consciousness, she told them her name, and asked for water. They carried her on shore very tenderly, and delivered her into the care of kind friends, who nursed her back into life and strength again; but her dearest friends could not at first recognise her, on account of the frightful distortion of her features. But while in that semi-insensible state, on a friend's asking her for the address of her father in England, she gave it correctly, and then added : "*If you write to my father, tell him that I have never regretted engaging in the mission-work.*" This was the ruling passion of the brave Christian heart, even in the midst of hardship, shipwreck, and death.

As soon as her health was sufficiently established, Mrs. Jones returned to England, a widow at twenty-four years of age, and the sole survivor of as terrible a shipwreck as the annals of seafaring life can furnish. She was received in England with much enthusiasm, as one come back from the dead. After some years of widowhood she married Thomas Hincksman, Esq., of Preston, and after a career of twenty-seven years spent in useful and Christian service for the good of those with whom she was brought in contact, she passed away to her everlasting rest, on April 17th, 1859.

MRS. JANE CHALMERS,

Wife of the Rev. James Chalmers,

MISSIONARY TO RAROTONGA AND NEW GUINEA; OF THE
LONDON MISSIONARY SOCIETY.

"Thou, Jesus Christ, our Head and Lord,
  Through suffering went to God,
And leadest, who believe Thy word,
  With Thee the self-same road.
Let, then, O Lord, all that are here
  Thy sufferings and Thy kingdom share.
Thro' Thy death's door, from death and night,
  Exalt us to Thy heavenly light.
    Thro' night to light;
    Thro' night to heavenly light."

SWISS MISSION HYMN.

IT was said of the subject of this sketch that "New Guinea and the missionary society had lost one of the brightest heroines the mission-field had known." This praise was not too high, for a reference to the annals of her twelve years' missionary service will show that her best was given to the Lord of the vineyard. She proved herself to be a heroine in the midst of danger, as well as self-denying and laborious in the midst of duty.

The Rev. James and Mrs. Chalmers sailed in the *John Williams* for Rarotonga, on the 29th January, 1866. The young couple were eager to commence direct missionary work, and looked forward with intense interest to the time when they should "enter into" the labours of Williams, Ellis, and other pioneers of the South Sea Mission. But from the outset they were destined to encounter trials and difficulties. These trials assumed the form of "perils by the sea," for that voyage of the *John Williams* was characterised by disasters almost as soon as the vessel reached the South Sea Archipelago, which disasters finally culminated in the total shipwreck of the vessel, before Mr. and Mrs. Chalmers sighted Rarotonga. The *John Williams* arrived safely at Adelaide, Australia, in May, 1866, touching also at Melbourne, Geelong, Hobart Town, and Sydney in turn. On August 21st, the vessel sailed for Aneiteum, where it struck upon a reef, and was forced to return to Sydney for repairs. The other members of the mission-party remained at Aneiteum during the return of the *John Williams* to Sydney, but Mrs. Chalmers and her husband fearlessly accompanied the ship back. The needed repairs having been accomplished, they returned with the vessel to Aneiteum, and after receiving on board those missionaries and their wives who had tarried at that island, proceeded first to the Loyalty Islands, and thence to Niué.

They reached Niué on January 3rd, 1867, having been nearly a year on the journey, and not yet having seen Rarotonga. To the dismay of all the mission-party, however, the *John Williams* was wrecked off the coast of Niué on the 8th of that month. Those of the missionaries who had not yet reached their appointed stations were still on board, and among this number were Mr. and Mrs. Chalmers. Not only was the vessel wrecked, but the missionaries lost nearly everything in their possession, besides the stores intended for Samoa and Eastern Polynesia. In an interesting letter written by Mrs. Chalmers, she says, in reference to this misfortune: "We left Sydney on the 15th of November, with our vessel fully repaired and as strong as ever. In four weeks from the day we left Sydney we had finished all our work at Aneiteum and the Loyalty Islands, and with high hopes we went on our way to Niué. We had to beat all the way, and for nine days before getting to Niué we had to sail amongst most dangerous reefs.

. . . . During the night of the 8th the wind changed. . . . All means were at once resorted to to keep the vessel out at sea. All the native teachers on board wrought well with the sailors, but all was of no avail: nearer and nearer we approached the dreaded reef. About nine, Mrs. Williams, Mr. and Mrs. Davies,

VIEW IN NEW GUINEA.

Mr. Chalmers and myself, went to the saloon for prayer. The two gentlemen offered up prayer in turn, while at the same time the native teachers offered up prayer on the main deck. Fervent were the prayers offered that the Lord would save our justly-prized ship—His own ship—from the doom we saw threatening her, and that she would be spared for many years to carry the good news of Salvation to these lovely isles. After prayer, we went on deck and fired off some rockets and blue-lights, to warn our friends on shore of our danger, though well we knew they could not help us. Oh! the agony of that hour! None but those who have experienced it can realise how we felt. It was sad to see our floating home being drifted on to destruction, and we unable to save her. The night was densely dark, the lightnings began to flash, and now we think surely the wind will come up to save her; but not a breath of air could be felt. About ten the gig was ordered alongside, and the ladies dropped from the side of the vessel into it. No time for ceremony: seventy-two souls, among whom were several native women and children, were on board; and already could the back swell of the reef be felt. By twenty minutes past eleven all were in the boats, and in a few minutes after, the vessel struck with a crash, which quickly dispelled all our hopes as to her safety, and sent a pang through our very hearts. We loved the vessel, and it seemed like losing a friend to lose her. To the last we clung to the hope that ere she struck, a breeze would spring up and save her."

After a short delay Mr. and Mrs. Chalmers proceeded to Rarotonga by another vessel, reaching their destination on May 20th, 1867. Two months later the resident missionary returned to Europe, and the sole conduct of the mission consequently devolved upon Mr. and Mrs. Chalmers. They immediately set about acquiring the language, and while Mr. Chalmers assumed the care of the Training Institution for the native ministry, Mrs. Chambers assembled the wives of the students at her house daily in classes, teaching them reading, sewing, and Scripture, in addition to labouring among the children. With the children of Rarotonga she seems to have been a prime favourite; and her occasional communications to the *Juvenile Missionary Magazine* afford many pleasant glimpses of her life and labours among them. She took special interest in the schools and classes, adopting that as her chosen work. As might have been expected, she attained large success in this congenial employment, and succeeded in leaving her mark upon the schools of Rarotonga. A vivid description from her pen of an annual examination in one of these schools will be perused with interest. She writes: "All is now quiet. A hymn is read out and sung, prayer offered up to our Father in heaven, and a very short address follows from the missionary. And now begins the true business of the day—*class examination*. Each teacher is sitting beside his or her class, looking almost as excited as the children themselves. The youngest class is called on first to stand up and read out of Primer I. in the Rarotonga dialect. Soon their courage rises, and we are not long in seeing who have been attentive to their lessons, or who have been careless. After each class has been examined, a hymn is sung by all, but led by one of the class. Some of the younger children sing little rhymes on the alphabet instead of a hymn. In this way we go on till all the classes are over, which takes three or four hours. The elder scholars are examined in geography, arithmetic, and the multiplication-table, beside reading, dictation, and spelling."

Mrs. Chalmers acknowledges the help which a female chief gave to the mission by means of her power and influence. It seems that this woman Tepaern was connected with the family of the head chief of Rarotonga, but was by some means carried off in her youth to Aitutaki. During the Rev. John Williams' stay on that island he met with her, and on his visit to Rarotonga brought her with him, and restored her to her friends. Tepaern had heard of the Gospel in Aitutaki, and partially believed it; but after coming back to Rarotonga she gave in her full adhesion to it. She aided the missionaries and teachers of Rarotonga in many ways, proving herself a valuable auxiliary, as well as a consistent member. Mrs. Chalmers writes concerning this old lady: "She is now an old woman; her hair is grey, her hearing is very defective, her memory is not so good as it was, her limbs are very stiff, and she finds it difficult to rise from her seat, or sit down again, but still her teeth are beautifully white and strong, not one is broken; her back is as straight as can be, and she walks with a very majestic step. She has a great influence over all the people, and always exerts it in the right direction. It is amusing to see how all the evil-doers, old and young, of both sexes, fear her. It is a poor look-out for any wrong-doer when she hears of their shortcomings. They would much rather that the missionary should hear of their sins, than old Tepaern. Sometimes her severity to offenders carries her too far, and then the missionary has to mediate between the parties. Still, she is a great favourite of all, and unless when she considers it her duty to apply the lash, she is a kind, happy old body."

The work which fell to Mr. and Mrs. Chalmers as superintending missionaries at the Rarotongan station was somewhat onerous, and one which required great tact. On account of the disastrous loss of the mission-vessels, the native teachers on the out-stations had not been visited for eight years, and had consequently gone without their accustomed supplies. It seems that their wages are not paid in money—which would be of no use on these isolated isles—but in *goods*, such as drapery, hardware, food, and other necessaries, while the missionary at Rarotonga has to superintend the division and appointing of these supplies. It is amusing to read of the labours of Mrs. Chalmers in this direction. When the new *John Williams* arrived at Rarotonga with the greatly-needed stores for the scattered labourers, the two set to work, and very quickly divided the cargo into the destined portions, giving, in addition, from their own supplies, "to each student a shirt and pair of trousers, and to each of their wives as much print as would make a dress." After the careful division and assignment of the stores, it became necessary for Mr. Chalmers to go by the departing *John Williams* to visit the out-stations, as well as to carry the goods, while Mrs. Chalmers remained at home to welcome the *Dayspring*, the Presbyterian Mission ship, which was on her way to Rarotonga, and then to despatch by her, six of the students, with their wives, as teachers to new out-stations. In all these duties Mrs. Chalmers acted with a self-denying heroism worthy of admiration. The lonely white woman in Rarotonga was preparing for the time when she should be once more left alone, among a horde of New Guinea savages.

Although visitors were few and far between, Mrs. Chalmers gratefully records that on one memorable communion Sabbath, when an American ship was lying in harbour, "there were assembled representatives of Christ's church from fourteen different lands." That was doubtless "a time of refreshing."

But, after ten years' work on the island of Rarotonga, Providence seemed to point out a new channel for labour. New Guinea, or Papua, one of the largest islands in the world, offered a most inviting field for missionary operations to those brave spirits who looked out for "other worlds to conquer" for the Prince of Peace. This island, which extends about 1,300 miles in length, and 200 in breadth, is a tropical land, inhabited by tribes of savages who are totally ignorant of civilisation and religion. The island lies to the north of Australia, being divided from that land by Torres Straits. It was visited by Captain Cook in 1770, but has since been somewhat shunned by sailors. Indeed, the barbarous treatment shown by the natives toward all strangers, effectually prevented intercourse; for if it happened that a ship's crew found themselves cast, by the accident of shipwreck, upon the shores of New Guinea, the natives immediately murdered and ate them. But native teachers from the various groups of the South Sea Archipelago, anxious to spread the news of that Gospel which had blessed them, had ventured forth to New Guinea, carrying their lives in their hands, and had stationed themselves among the people at different points, in order to tell of Jesus. They had attained partial success, inasmuch as the natives learnt that the intentions of the white missionaries towards them were good, and that by

VIEW OF THE MISSION STATION, PORT MORESBY.

opening their land to strangers, they would receive spiritual and temporal benefit. Messrs. Murray, Macfarlane, and Lawes went forth on a pioneering expedition into New Guinea, in order to report upon the land and the people for the Missionary Society, and found that to some extent the natives were willing to accept teachers. Still, the experiment promised peril to those who should attempt it.

In May, 1877, Mr. and Mrs. Chalmers were transferred to New Guinea. Dangers awaited them in the shape of murderous conspiracies by the natives, who had been ill-used by the crews of trading vessels shortly before Mr. Chalmers' landing, and who vowed to be revenged on the first white man who should fall into their hands. Only the care of an overruling and watchful Providence can explain the fact of Mr. Chalmers' preservation during those perilous days of exploration among the New Guinea natives. In the spring of 1878, Mrs. Chalmers accompanied her husband on a cruise along the south coast of the mainland, from east to west, visiting about two hundred villages. In ninety of these villages the white man was unknown; accordingly, it needed the greatest circumspection and discretion to establish friendly communications with the people. New Guinea was a hotbed of malignant fever, and peopled by cannibals whose only craving was for human flesh. Under these circumstances, Mrs. Chalmers appears in her true character, as a heroic Christian woman, in consenting to live in such a land, and in the midst of such a people. They settled down at South Cape, established the mission station, and won their way among the natives until the name "Chalmers" acted as a talisman among the different tribes. The work was progressing successfully, when the *Mayri* schooner called at the island, and the crew became embroiled in a quarrel with the natives. Blood was shed on both sides; and the savages, intent upon revenge, were bent upon murdering their teachers. They especially threatened the lives of Mr. and Mrs.

Chalmers, and surrounded the station in large bands, night after night, yelling and clamouring for the blood of the inmates. But prayer, heroism, and fearlessness conquered. The savages were quelled at last, and quiet and peace once more reigned at the mission-station. God had restrained the wrath of man, and wrought out a deliverance for his servants.

Soon after these disturbances, Mr. Chalmers made a voyage to Thursday Island to bring back necessary stores, and to obtain the assistance of the new mission-steamer *Ellangowan*. He wished much to take Mrs. Chalmers with him; but the heroic woman chose to remain behind as a kind of hostage for the return of her husband to South Cape. Beside this, the recently-settled native teachers were in peril; for at some of the villages in which Mr. Chalmers had placed them, a desire on the part of the natives to obtain their property had led them to call in the aid of a sorcerer or medicine-man, who had succeeded in poisoning several of the teachers. On looking at all the circumstances, Mrs. Chalmers preferred to remain, believing that her presence would act as a defence to the native teachers, as well as evidence the good faith of herself and husband toward the people. It was well that she did so. After being absent a month, Mr. Chalmers returned to South Cape to find his wife safe and sound, and pleased to report that the savages had treated her with unexpected kindness during his absence. Mr. Chalmers wrote of this critical time to the directors of the Society in the following terms:—

"We left South Cape, on the 5th February, for Port Moresby, Mrs. Chalmers remaining with the teachers. There was really no accommodation on board for her, and she thought it was not well for us both to leave the teachers so soon after the disturbances, and in the unhealthy season. The natives of the place were highly pleased with her remaining, and promised to treat her kindly: they saw we had confidence in their friendship. On my return home, I found that Mrs. Chalmers was well, and had been treated right kindly by the savages; they bringing her food, and saying that she must eat plenty, so that when Tamate (Mr. Chalmers) returned, she might be looking well and strong. Mrs. Chalmers says it is well she remained, as the natives saw we had confidence in them; and the day following our departure, they were saying among themselves: 'They trust us; we must treat them kindly; they cannot mean us harm, or Tamate would not have left his wife behind.' Had Mrs. Chalmers not remained, it is very probable one of the teachers would have died. She nursed him, and under God's blessing he was restored. She attended to them all, and saw that they had proper medicine and tonics when required, and also saw that they had good, warm food twice a day. One little child—the only child in our company—died after some weeks' illness, and was buried the day after we got home. The natives were highly delighted at my return, and came in crowds to meet me; but their delight was greatest when they got presents of arrowroot, hoop-iron, and a few beads."

Soon after Mr. Chalmers returned to his courageous wife, the shadow of the final separation fell upon them. She was struck down by the fearful malarious fever which is so prevalent in New Guinea, and remained so ill that her husband decided to take her to Cook Town. A few months' rest and change of air partially restored her, and she longed to return to South Cape, there to take up her chosen work again. But her frame was so evidently shattered that Mr. Chalmers persisted in refusing to allow her to return to the station, sending her instead to Sydney, to visit among dear friends, who were glad to minister to her wants and weakness. But in spite of unintermitting attentions, it soon became evident to all that Mrs. Chalmers was daily becoming weaker and weaker. Daily the poor feeble frame grew more exhausted, but the mind was ever bright and vigorous, and the affections dwelling constantly on the beloved work in New Guinea. She never saw her husband again in this life, although her wifely love longed sorely for one last interview; she was unwilling that he or any of her relatives should be informed of the truth until the day came that the last sad news must be told. So she sank, gradually, but surely, until she fell asleep in Jesus, on February 20th, 1879. Mr. Gill, writing in April of the same year, from Mr. Chalmers' old station at Rarotonga, says: "We have just heard with profound sorrow of the death of Mrs. Chalmers, at Sydney. She was a noble woman. Her talent was very versatile. She possessed great courage and tenacity of purpose. Her power of organisation was admirable; she was heart and soul a missionary. The sensation produced throughout the island is very great; the whole population is in mourning. Everybody who knew Mrs. Chalmers when she was going to New Guinea, felt that she was going to certain death. But although it was the wish of the directors of the Society that they should first visit England, they went on to New Guinea for the sake of the teachers."

This was heroism of the first order! To go to possible, and in the end to certain, death, for the sake of the Gospel and the defenceless native teachers labouring there, was bravery such as few could have displayed. Verily "the world knows not its greatest heroes;" "the day alone" shall declare them before the assembled nations. This humble woman, far away from home, friends, and civilisation, patiently winning the hearts of savage cannibals toward the good news of salvation by Jesus Christ, has, all unknown to worldly fame, finished her course, entered into rest, and won the guerdon of immortal renown.

MRS. ANNA HINDERER,

Wife of the Rev. David Hinderer,

MISSIONARY TO IBADAN, WEST AFRICA; OF THE CHURCH MISSIONARY SOCIETY.

> " It is thine own, O Lord,
>   Who toil while others sleep;
> Who sow, with loving care,
>   What other hands shall reap.
> They lean on thee, entranced,
>   In calm and perfect rest;
> Give us that peace, O Lord,
>   Divine and blest,
> Thou keepest for those hearts who love thee best."
>
> A. A. PROCTOR.

ISS ANNA MARTIN was early deprived of a mother's tender care. Born in March, 1827, at a peaceful village-home in Hempnall, Norfolk, her childhood presented almost nothing to indicate the future importance of her life-work. About a year before her death, the prematurely broken-down missionary penned a few touching recollections about the far-off days when her mother was yet alive. She says: "I lost my dear mother when I was just five years old. I have just the remembrance of a form in bed, as white as a lily, with rather large, bright, blue eyes; and I know she taught me to sew; and when I was not by her bed-side, I used to sit on a

low, broad window-seat, and when I had done ten stitches I was rewarded with a strawberry; and I used to say tiny little texts to her in the mornings. I was only allowed to be in her room twice a day. But though I knew so little of her on earth, if God, who is rich in mercy, will have mercy on me, and admit me to his blest abode, I shall see her again, for she rejoiced in God her Saviour. I have been told that her last breath was spent in singing a few lines of a favourite hymn:—

'I want, oh! I want to be there,
Where sorrow and sin bid adieu!'"

She appears to have been a very thoughtful child, "pining," as she says, "after something beyond this world, but could not yet grasp it." Changes succeeded her mother's death; and after residing for some time with a grandfather at Lowestoft, she eventually became an inmate of the vicarage. The Rev. Francis and Mrs. Cunningham seem to have been the most active agents in forming her character, and to them she was ever accustomed to look with the deepest love and reverence. They were her parents in the faith, and dealt with her through the restless, changeful period of her teens with that wise, tender, judicious, stimulating love, which alone could form a character and life of such rich, rare promise. Her own account of this period is so intensely interesting that we transcribe the portion which relates more particularly to her religious convictions and yearnings. She says: "I loved Sunday above every day. I loved church, and was soon permitted to enter into the beauty and solemnity of the service. I felt that I was in a holy place, and that holy words were being used. The *Te Deum* carried me to heaven; I longed to be a martyr, to be one of that noble army. I cannot tell of times and seasons; but I became more and more happy. I longed to do something. I had a strong desire to become a missionary, to give myself to some holy work, and I had a firm belief that such a calling would be mine. I often thought if I might have a few little children in the Sunday-school to teach, it would be an immense pleasure. I was afraid to ask it; but having obtained my aunt's consent when I was between twelve and thirteen, I ventured, one Saturday, after passing dear Mrs. Cunningham three times, to make my request, fearing all the time that she would say I was too young and small; but what was my joy when she smiled kindly upon me, and told me to go to the school at eight o'clock the next morning, and she would give me a class. I was up early enough; a heavy fall of snow was upon the ground; but that was nothing. I went, and six little ones were committed to my care, and thus commenced that interesting work, to which, I may say, I more and more intensely devoted myself. As I said before, I was seeking for something solid; I felt the want of something to make me happy, something that this world could not give, and I think, while talking to these little ones of Jesus, it entered my mind, "Had I gone to Him myself?" I went on, seeking and desiring, and often said and felt, "Here's my heart, Lord; take and seal it—seal it for thy courts above," and I was comforted in the sense that God would do it. This was, doubtless, the movement of the blessed Spirit in my soul; and amid all my failings, my sins of thought, and word, and deed, the craving of my mind was that I might be made the child of God. I saw my need of a Saviour, and in the Saviour I felt there was all I needed, and I was by degrees permitted to lay hold on eternal life. Notwithstanding all my sinfulness, infirmities, and shortcomings, the blessed hope of salvation in Christ Jesus was mercifully given, with the secret assurance that I was adopted into the family of God, made nigh by the blood of the Cross, and sanctified by the Spirit."

Soon after this, Miss Martin became a member of the family at the vicarage, for Mrs. Cunningham cherished a deep and tender affection for the young lady whose willing fingers and eager spirit strove to lighten other people's burdens, so fulfilling Christ's law.

This vicarage home was a very bright and happy one; Mrs. Cunningham possessed in a great measure the spirit of her sister—the distinguished Mrs. Elizabeth Fry—and strove to make her home a centre of Christian usefulness and happiness in Lowestoft. Miss Martin became a district visitor in one of the largest and most needy districts in the town, while a Sunday-school class of neglected children, which she formed when about fourteen years of age, grew in process of time into a large school of more than 200 children under her superintendence. In addition to these duties she devoted an hour each Sunday to teaching the boys in the workhouse, and engaged in every scheme which had for its objects God's glory and man's good. So, surely and gradually, was she being trained for her future mission-life.

It might have been thought, perhaps, that while so constantly busy with holy and useful work, Miss Martin would forget her old aspirations after foreign mission-work. But, no; she herself records her feelings at this time: "Notwithstanding all, my old desire for a missionary life would never leave me, and though so much of my work at home was of a missionary character, yet I felt that to heathen lands I was to go, and that such would be my calling some day, though I never saw the least shadow as to how it was to be accomplished. Yet although all this time no way in the smallest degree seemed to open for such a thing, He who only knoweth the future steps of his children was preparing me in a way I understood not."

In October, 1852, Miss Martin was united in marriage to the Rev. David Hinderer, of the Church Missionary Society. Mr. Hinderer was a native of Schorndorf, in the kingdom of Wurtemberg, and had been labouring in the Yoruba country, in West Africa, for about four years previously. The affairs of the mission requiring him to visit England, he came, and there met with Miss Martin. Then, feeling that they were led by God's guiding hand, the two young Christians decided to bear the Gospel together to the Yorubas; and so commenced Mrs. Hinderer's life-work among the heathen. The Yoruba country is situated in Western Africa, near the kingdom of Dahomey, and has a population of about 3,000,000. Mr. Hinderer was about to

VIEW IN WESTERN AFRICA.

be stationed at Ibadan, a warlike city, of about 100,000 inhabitants, and situated about fifty miles to the northeast of Abeokuta—having penetrated thither and found both chiefs and people anxious for white teachers. The work was, however, heavy, although inviting, and with the object of seeking help he came to England. The society granted him assistance, in the person of Mr. Kefer, and on December 6th, 1852, Mr. and Mrs.

Hinderer sailed for Africa. So God answered her early prayers.

They reached Lagos on January 5th, 1853; and scarcely had they landed, before Mrs. Hinderer was assailed by the malarial fever of the country. The West Coast of Africa has proved so fatal to Europeans that it is known as "the white man's grave;" and the Church Missionary Society, which has nobly devoted much of its energy to the evangelisation of that coast, has lost a large number of missionaries in the attempt. It is a question whether new-comers are able to survive the early attacks of this fever, which manifests itself in all degrees, from ague up to yellow fever; but supposing that they do withstand its first onslaughts, they continue to be liable to it as long as they remain in the country. Referring to her first illness, Mrs. Hinderer writes: "I had a very sharp attack of fever indeed; but through the mercy of our tender Father, on the eighth day I was able to get up a little. I suppose few people ever had the first fever last so short a time; but when I got up, I felt my weakness. My poor limbs tottered and trembled fearfully. I am still weak, and expect to be so for some time yet. Indeed, I dare say I shall never regain the same strength that I had before —I believe no one does; but one will soon forget it, and go on by slow degrees."

At first, the newly-married missionaries took up their sojourn in Abeokuta, pending the preparation of a suitable home at Ibadan; and here Mrs. Hinderer commenced work, during her husband's absence at the latter town. As there was a flourishing mission at Abeokuta, Mrs. Hinderer was among friends, but the loneliness was something trying to a young wife; beside which she had a second attack of fever, sharper than the first. But she was near the Rev. Henry Townsend and his wife, who both showed the young, lonely Englishwoman "no little kindness." Meanwhile, although feeling the enforced separation, Mrs. Hinderer strove to get acquainted with the best methods of missionary work, as well as to become familiar with the habits of the people. In March, all was ready for removal to Ibadan. A temporary home had been gained in a native house, while their own should be built; and the young couple prepared to "endure hardness" for the sake of the Gospel. But the mission-party which had sailed to West Africa only three or four short months previously was to experience severe trials, and even death. Most of them had been destined for Abeokuta; but by the end of April two or three were dead, and of the rest, nearly all were seriously ill. Mrs. Hinderer had "her hands full" with nursing Mr. Kefer and Mr. Maser, and until they recovered, she could not travel to Ibadan.

At last, during the closing days of April, 1853, Mr. Hinderer and his wife departed for Ibadan. Their road lay through the African bush, so that Mrs. Hinderer was now first introduced to the experience of African travel. The journey was safely accomplished, either in hammocks or on horseback, and in due time the missionary party reached their destination, much to the astonishment and delight of the people. "The white mother," as the people of Ibadan named Mrs. Hinderer, was welcome from the first, and the demonstrations of astonishment and kindness continued during every available hour of daylight, for some days. Especially were the *women* surprised at the wonderful courage of the white woman, who had come so far to teach them. The house was a long, narrow, low structure, of one storey, without either door or window—"a curtain serving for a screen at the entrance"—but it was as comfortable for the emergency as any native dwelling could be; and after making allowance for hurricanes, insects, and reptiles, was pretty fairly situated. It stood on the side of a hill, overlooking gardens, in which flourished palms, orange, plantain, and banana trees, while at a little distance away spread the town, with its numerous picturesque compounds. A Yoruba compound—or house and court combined—is composed of a low, dark, square building, enclosing a courtyard open to the sky, and having one gate or outlet leading to the street. Horses, sheep, goats, and poultry share the compound equally with the family, while most of the business of the daily life is transacted in the open air. Mrs. Hinderer strove to accommodate herself to the conditions of Yoruba life, adding, of course, such improvements and ameliorations as her English tastes rendered possible, and commenced benevolent Christian work at once. She took four little boys, in order to feed, clothe, train, and teach them; and this number proved to be the nucleus of a school, which ultimately did much good in developing agents for missionary work among the natives. Not content with this, she opened up communications with the women, who quickly began to perceive that Sunday was a different day with "the white mother" from what it was with them. The Sunday classes were well attended, and almost from the first Mrs. Hinderer taught them through an interpreter. She says, writing about a month after her arrival: "I have had many visitors this week, especially women. Their tenderness over me is touching; if they see me hot, they will fan me; if I look tired, they want me to lie down. I have had much talk with them through my little maid Susanna; they do, indeed, receive us with joy and gladness, and we have r any regular attendants on Sunday. They are quite b ;inning to understand that it is a holy day with us, and I feel sure some are trying to give up Sunday occupation. One woman, who is very fond of me, was missing last Sunday; she came on Monday, and with tears in her eyes, told me, 'Too much work live in her house on Sunday; her hands were too full, and she could not get them out.' On her way home, she met four of her friends, and came back again with them; so after talking a little with them, I wished them to go, as I was very tired. My old friend said she wished me not to speak another word, but rest; yet if they might sit down quietly and look at me they should like it. I mention this to show their kind, and respectful, and really polite way of speaking, and to describe their tender and affectionate feeling towards me, which must be seen to be fully known. I am still somewhat of a curiosity; the novelty has not yet worn off, and our house is pretty well surrounded all day long."

Beside the four little boys who were given to Mrs. Hinderer by their native friends, she started a day-school for others. As may be supposed, all the children were wild, uncivilised, and possessed of a good share of heathen unruliness and intractability. But they were wonderfully docile at times also, and learnt eagerly the new Christian ways. They were also amenable to the power of music and singing. Mrs. Hinderer had carried out a nice harmonium, and played it constantly in the classes and services. The ministry of song was never more powerful than in the midst of these heathen people. A large shed, covered with palm-leaves, was erected as a temporary church, and here Mrs. Hinderer conducted Divine service regularly. The people came, as a rule, in good numbers, and sat on the ground, asking questions frequently, and showing by their attention great interest in the Word of Life. So the work progressed, broken frequently by illness on the part of some of the missionary party, but still pursued faintly, even then. Not unfrequently Mrs. Hinderer had to nurse both her husband and Mr. Kefer, while she herself was almost prostrate by the terrible fever. At such times the love and attention of the people were very cheering. They would weep bitterly when danger was present, and do all in their power to lighten the sad and heavy burden. Still the prejudice of heathenism manifested itself at times; Mr. Kefer was frequently interrupted while preaching among the natives in the town, and the parents of the children drew back from sanctioning the attendance of their boys at school, for fear "book" should make them "cowards." Mrs. Hinderer's few female scholars were exposed to much persecution at times for their attachment to their teachers and the books. Writing of this, Mrs. Hinderer says: "The story of one young woman is most touching and interesting. She stands with the courage of a dependent child on the love, mercy, and help of a gracious God. Her marriage was hastened by her parents, who thought it would prevent her coming to church. Her husband treated her even more cruelly than her parents, who had been hard enough. When told by him, 'You shall never enter white man's house again,' she said, 'Very well: as you wish, it shall be.' 'Neither shall you go to his church.' To this she replied: 'I cannot, and will not submit; it is God's house; I will go.' She was then cruelly beaten with sticks and cutlasses, and stoned, till her body swelled all over; a rope was tied round her neck, and she was dragged as an ox to the slaughter, to her father's house. Mr. Hinderer went to beg them to cease their cruelties. He found her lying prostrate before the idols, which had been brought out for her to worship; she was held there by furious people, who were shouting: 'Now she bows down; now she bows down!' She exclaimed: 'No, I do not! it is you who put me here. I can never bow down to gods of wood and stone, which cannot hear me. Only in Jesus Christ, the only Saviour of poor sinners, can I trust.' She was then dragged up; they took a rope to put round her throat, saying, 'Well, we will take you away, and kill you.' She replied: 'Kill me if you will, the sooner I shall be with my Saviour in Heaven; but I will not, I cannot, serve those foolish things.' They did not kill her; but for months she endured every kind of ill-treatment, and at last ran away to Abeokuta. The history of her journey is little short of a miracle, and reminded me of the angel opening the door to Peter."

Still the work proceeded; men, women, and children, chiefs, and slaves, united in hearing and believing the wonderful Gospel, which the white man had brought. Mrs. Hinderer had more serious attacks of illness, and at last went away for a short season to Abeokuta to recruit. On her return the mission-house was complete, and fit to enter upon; so also was the new and substantial church. From this time they had more comfort, more freedom, and more success. Mrs. Hinderer relates some amusing experiences of the natives, as they came to look at the new house, and examine into the appurtenances of English civilisation. To the women, especially, the toilet-table and washstand presented wonderful mysteries, far above their highest flights of thought. These poor creatures, grateful for the instruction which they received, were most teachable, and brought all sorts of offerings, to show their gratitude, declaring, at the same time, that they meant to serve only the white man's God. A good day-school was also established, taught by one of the early converts, named Olubi. Mrs. Hinderer also increased the number of her school, by adding some little slave children, who were absolutely "thrown away"—left to perish by the roadside. The mother of one of these poor waifs discovered her child, quite by accident, some time afterwards, in the mission-compound, and manifested such thankfulness of heart, that Mrs. Hinderer redeemed her from slavery, and made her cook to the establishment, so that mother and child might not again be parted. This mother—"Lucy"—became a sincere Christian, and died, years after, in the faith, gathered safely home, we may believe, through Mrs. Hinderer's instrumentality.

In November, 1854, the first confirmation in Ibadan was held; and in the June following, five of the converts were formed into a visible church, and received the Lord's Supper. This was an event not to be forgotten; but, prior to this, heavy afflictions and bereavements had fallen upon that West African mission. Mr. Kefer, their colleague, was dead; the bishop who had but so lately confirmed the converts was dead; and, indeed, so many had died, that Mrs. Hinderer sorrowfully writes: "Of the fourteen who sailed together in one ship two years ago, only *four* were left to labour here." Beside all these trials and bereavements from without, Mr. Hinderer had been laid so low by the dreadful fever, that for weeks during that spring his life had been despaired of. Surely it was amid tears and sorrows that they learnt to count

A YORUBA SCENE.

their successes. Towards the close of 1856, Mr. Hinderer suffered so severely and constantly from yellow fever, that it was judged best for them to return to England for a time. This they did; but before leaving they had the intense happiness of seeing that the work of the Lord had prospered in their hands. The day-school was progressing encouragingly, the Sunday-school numbered between forty and fifty adults; the services were well attended, and the ordinances of religion were observed. Christian baptism and marriage were instituted among them; and Daniel Olubi, the first mission-schoolmaster, was married to Susanna, a Christian convert who had faithfully served Mrs. Hinderer, only a few days before the missionaries returned to England in search of renewed health and strength.

After about a year, spent in England and Germany, during which time they made known the story of their work, and gained many friends, Mr. and Mrs. Hinderer returned to their beloved post in Ibadan, reaching there in January, 1858. The work had proceeded well in their absence; and on their return, the people manifested their delight by overwhelming them with presents. Mrs. Hinderer says: "For three weeks or more we had visitors constantly, and such kind presents. We have still quite a farm-yard from them. The chiefs and people seem as if they could not give us welcome enough. They are bringing their idols, too; we have a large basketful of idols; and last evening, a man who had been a large dealer in slaves, brought the irons with which he used to chain the poor creatures, saying that, 'having been made free by the blood of Jesus, he never should want such cruel things again.'" This, surely, was showing their faith by their works. Mrs. Hinderer's school increased by thirty children; and by her teaching and ministrations she succeeded in checking the tendency to infanticide, which manifested itself among some portions of the people.

But darker days were coming. Mrs. Hinderer was taken seriously ill of fever again, and lay for many weeks between life and death. Then Mr. Hinderer had to take long journeys eastward, upon mission affairs; and trials from continued, harassing warfare between the neighbouring tribes, were added to their lot. The King of Dahomey inaugurated this war, and very quickly the chiefs of the Ijebu and Ibadan people followed his example. A general war was proclaimed; and human sacrifices were offered on all sides in the Yoruba country. This war commenced in 1860; and although the missionaries were well aware of the difficulties and dangers which would of necessity encompass them, they resolved to continue at their post. As, one by one, the roads were closed for general traffic, their supplies would be stopped, and the distance from Lagos being about eighty miles, it will be easily seen that famine would in course of time stare them in the face. Still they were too greatly beloved by the natives to be in actual danger of life; and keeping close around them those who were faithful, they still prosecuted their work. Mrs. Hinderer wrote at the time: "Troubles increase; but sufficient unto the day is the evil thereof. We have plenty of yams and corn, but our people are troubled for want of cowries (little shells which are used by the natives for money), and we have to open our store in faith, hoping they will last till peace comes. European comforts and what in a general way appear, and are, necessaries, we must do without, and be thankful for what yet remains in our hands. With tea, coffee, and sugar, we think ourselves rich. What we most regret is our flour, when that is gone. You can soon be weary of yams, if you have to take them as the staff of life. But by Christmas we hope the war will be over. It looks dark indeed, just now."

But the war was not over by Christmas, nor anything like it. On the contrary, it continued for five or six years, dragging its slow length along, and bringing misery and destruction to all the land. In 1861, their flour was finished; their food consisted principally of a handful of horse-beans daily, flavoured with palm-oil and pepper. Everything that could be spared was used or exchanged for food; and with all their efforts they sometimes were so hungry that "they cried themselves to sleep like children." Missionary life was no pleasant pastime to Mr. and Mrs. Hinderer, but rather the testing, through hardship and suffering, of their faith. In addition to deprivation, both of them fell ill, at different times, partly, no doubt, through want of proper food; and Mr. Hinderer had to take one or two long journeys to the coast, through the enemy's country, to endeavour to purchase necessaries. Then sometimes, when these things were despatched, they were either stolen or wasted, so that the missionaries had still to bear with the pangs of partial famine. Kidnapping, war, semi-starvation, and occasionally persecution, made up the tale of their lives for a long time. Mrs. Hinderer says: "European necessaries and comforts we have long been without, and can never have again. My last pair of shoes are on my feet, and my clothes are so worn that if the war does not soon end I shall have to come to a country cloth, like a native. These would be small troubles if we were in health, but my dear husband is a sad sufferer, and every bit of remedy or alleviation, in the way of medicine, has been for months entirely finished. I had two severe attacks of fever—one in August, and one in November." Yet still the mission-work went on, and Mr. Hinderer translated portions of the "Pilgrim's Progress," hoping for happier times. But these did not come for a long time; during 1863 and 1864, the roads were shut up, and their isolation was complete. Little news of them reached their friends in England, for letters were constantly lost or intercepted; and few supplies or letters reached them. Their writing-paper was done, and they were forced to use printed sheets; while the contents of the work-box were reduced to "two rusty needles, and half a ball of cotton."

At length, help unexpectedly came. The Governor of Lagos was determined to rescue the isolated missionaries, and set them forward on the road to England. Captain Maxwell, a brave volunteer, and a band of determined young men made forced marches, and reached Ibadan one night in April, 1865, with supplies of food, and a hammock in which Mrs. Hinderer could be borne back to Lagos. They would gladly have conveyed away both husband and wife before morning, so that the enemy should not be able to intercept them; but it was seen to be imperative that Mr. Hinderer should remain at his post for a little time longer, in order to provide for the safety of the mission. Accordingly he remained behind, while Mrs. Hinderer prepared, all through the night, for her journey to Lagos, and from thence home to England. At five in the morning the little party started; and we may fancy the fears and anguish of both husband and wife at the parting. It was agreed that Mr. Hinderer should manage the affairs of the mission, and then seize the first opportunity of making his escape to the coast, from whence he was to follow his wife to England. By the gracious help of Providence this was accomplished: Mrs. Hinderer reached England in May of that year, and her husband some two months later. Here, however, they could not settle down while the Lord's work was to be done, and having gained strength of mind and body, were on their way back to Ibadan by the end of 1866.

Work had been done in the interval, of which the mission reaped the benefit. The "Pilgrim's Progress" had been finished and printed, and the books were now used by the converts. The war was not over; still, in 1867, we read of cheering progress among the heathen. There were three churches and mission-stations in as many different parts of the town, and native helpers were rising up to do the work. Converts and schools multiplied; and Mr. Hinderer was deeply engaged in training native catechists, who should act as schoolmasters and pastors, when another emergency drove him off.

This emergency arose in 1869. Mrs. Hinderer's health failed again, and she planned to go to Lagos for a change. But the enemies of the people in Ibadan plotted to take away her life on the journey. This caused her to hesitate; still, life was sweet, and unless she could get to the coast she could not recover. Providentially, the journey was accomplished before the plotters were aware, and Mrs. Hinderer succeeded in gaining the haven which she desired. From Lagos she sailed for England once more, arriving in January; and in September Mr. Hinderer again re-joined her. He had left the mission in charge of three tried and faithful native teachers, and now turned to England to prolong his own enfeebled life, as well as to shelter his suffering helpmeet.

She was truly suffering as the result of her devotion to missionary work. She lost the sight of her right eye, but with a small measure of renewed health, was still eager for Christian work. In 1870, Mr. Hinderer was offered the curacy of Martham, in Norfolk, and the two settled down, hoping once more to be of use in their generation. This was in March; but barely three months passed by, before the Great Reaper gathered her home. Mrs. Hinderer had planned and commenced womanly Christian work for the women of her husband's parish; but the toils and hardships of the long years in West Africa had exhausted the springs of life, and almost suddenly she passed away. Only a few days of illness and weakness, and then, on June 6th, she entered into rest. She was lovely, composed, and Christian in her death, as she had been in her life.

She passed away in her forty-fourth year, having done good service for Africa. Her seventeen years of labour there have undoubtedly left their mark. Many of the women and children of West Africa have found Christ through her instrumentality; many were gathered home during her lifetime, and many more will be gathered home as the years go on, to swell the song of redeeming love and dying grace.

MRS. SARAH SMITH,

Wife of the Rev. John Smith,

MISSIONARY TO MADRAS, SOUTH INDIA; OF THE LONDON MISSIONARY SOCIETY.

" From Britain's green and flowery isle,
To India's bright and burning soil,
Gently transplanted, bathed in dew,
A lily of the valley grew.
Death, wafted on the eastern blast,
Swept by, and kissed it as it passed.
A few days gone, and those who sought
The blighted floweret, found it not.
For there came One who loved the flower,
And took it home to deck His bower:
Bore it away beyond the skies,
To blossom in His Paradise."

MRS. SIGOURNEY.

THIS lady was, by marriage, sister-in-law to Mrs. Moffat, and, as far as we can judge of her by the few memorials left behind, possessed the same spirit of self-denying earnestness in the mission-cause. Her maiden name was Sarah Marsden. She was born in London, on October 2nd, 1798, of respectable parentage, her father being a hop-merchant, residing in Southwark. It seems that Miss Marsden possessed a great quickness of apprehension, and diligence in study, even as a child; and as she grew up into girlhood, became distinguished for her attainments in history, geography, astronomy, and music. Indeed, the correctness of her historical knowledge was such, that, in a mixed company, she was frequently appealed to in order to settle a disputed point, or render information. But astronomy was her favourite science, and to it she devoted all the leisure of her youthful days. Her own opinions on this science are well expressed in a letter to a young friend at this time. She says: "The study of this sublime science has a great tendency to raise our conceptions of the immensity of the Deity, and to give us proper ideas of our own comparative insignificance in the scale of creation. While it exalts the greatness of that condescension which deigns to watch over our concerns, we should exclaim with the psalmist: 'Lord, what is man, that Thou art mindful of him, or the son of man, that Thou visitest him?' It is in this way only that any description of knowledge can be truly useful. Without this, were we to employ our whole existence here in the pursuits of literature, we should be compelled to adopt the language of Grotius: 'Alas! I have spent my life in learned nothings.'"

From about twelve years of age, Miss Marsden was the subject of serious impressions. Brought up in a pious family, and favoured with attendance on the ministry of the Rev. Alexander Fletcher, it was scarcely possible that it should be otherwise. Her correspondence and private papers, penned during her teens, prove this most abundantly. Like many other thoughtful young persons, she was the subject of doubt at times, arising from sceptical notions. But she strove to free herself from these, instead of nursing them, as too many do, to their souls' detriment. An extract from her diary, written in her seventeenth year, will prove this: "I find more and more reason to lament that sin of unbelief which dwells within me. When I would have faith in the dear Redeemer, I am tempted to doubt my interest in His salvation, or else the world takes off my attention, and I feel too indifferent about it. Gracious God, leave me not in this state, but manifest Thyself unto me, that I may be enabled to say, 'Return unto thy rest, O my soul, for the Lord hath dealt bountifully with thee.' May I never desire to pry into those mysteries connected with redemption, which I can never understand here, and which are not essential to me to know; but may the Spirit of truth guide me to a right understanding of those things which are of so much importance." Yet, with all this anxiety and research, there was a large measure of timidity in her character. And after she had most truly experienced the greatest of all changes, she still hung back, fearing to avow her faith and love, by an open profession at the table of the Lord. At length, grace conquered her natural timidity, and when in her twenty-fifth year, Mr. Fletcher received her into church fellowship. From that time she grew more humble, watchful, and prayerful, her conduct was strictly governed by Bible rules, and all around her took notice that she had not only been with Jesus, and learnt of Him, but that she was endeavouring to live to His glory.

In 1827, the prospect was offered her of accompanying the Rev. John Smith to India, as a partner of his life and work in the mission-field. Mr. Smith was then preparing for his departure, which was expected to take place in the spring of the following year. At first Miss Marsden's friends were violently opposed to the step; indeed, there were not wanting those who accused her of destroying her mother's peace and happiness, by taking the step. It is true that Mrs. Marsden was at first prejudiced very strongly against the prospect, but afterwards she gave her cordial assent and blessing. The Rev. Alexander Fletcher, and other friends, placed the claims of the missionary field so strongly before Mrs. Marsden, that at last she was not only able to say, *Go,* but to cheer her daughter when trembling at the idea of separation. The two young people were married on the 11th March, 1828, by the Rev. Rowland Hill, and received his hearty blessing. They sailed for India on April 15th, and arrived there on August 20th. The voyage was profitably occupied, in uniting with other mis-

218   HEROINES OF THE MISSION FIELD.

sionary passengers and friends, in studying the languages of the people among whom they were appointed to labour, and in reading such works as were most calculated to strengthen and refresh the soul, in prospect of arduous duties. The novelty of Indian scenes and cus-

MADRAS, FROM THE SEA.

toms presented itself very strikingly to Mrs. Smith's mind, but, ever intent upon the great end for which she had gone out, she commenced studying at once. Her first letter, written the week after landing, says : " I felt as if indeed entering the territories of the prince of darkness, and desirous to be made, in some humble measure, useful to the inhabitants. Being desirous of commencing as soon as possible our Tamil studies, we took our first lessons with the Moonshee last Wednesday, and intend occupying ourselves with him every day."

After getting settled in their own home, Mr. Smith was appointed to the pastorate of the English Church in Madras, in addition to his strictly missionary work, while Mrs. Smith was made superintendent of the Black Town Female Free School. These schools—for they also included one for boys—were founded by a previous missionary, and were blessed by God to many of the scholars taught there. The girls received a plain education, as well as instruction in Divine things. In addition, they were taught needlework, and other domestic arts; but better still, many were rescued from a life of suffering, vice, and heathenism. After the training ended in this school, Mrs. Smith was in the habit of obtaining situations for the best behaved girls in such families as had received Christianity; and it was remarked by the residents in Madras that very few of the girls educated at the Free School afterwards proved guilty of misdemeanour or crime. In addition to all the other duties which devolved upon Mr. and Mrs. Smith, two young students came to reside with them in 1829, in order to be more fully prepared for missionary work. It was in this year that Mrs. Smith's first child was born; and this event was followed by an illness so severe, and so prolonged, that it was doubtful whether she would ever be raised up again. But she was so raised up, and with renewed strength came increased devotion to the work of missions. In a letter written about this time, in reference to the condition of the native women, among whom she was labouring, Mrs. Smith says: "Such of the native women as I have seen have generally an oppressed and degraded appearance, indicative of the servitude of their condition. They are fond of adorning themselves with nose and ear jewels, also with bracelets, anklets, and rings on the fingers and toes. It is very rarely you see a man and woman walking together; the latter seem to be considered beneath such companionship. Their employments are, cooking rice, drawing and carrying water, cutting grass for use of the horses, with other laborious work, and few of them can either read or sew. The women have a singular mode of conveying their children about, by carrying them on the hips. May not this custom illustrate the Scripture which speaks of the children being 'nursed at the side?' Were there not *an adequate end in view* I do not consider that, on the whole, a residence in India would be desirable. Among other peculiarities of Indian life—leaving out insects and reptiles, which are trying enough—is the plague of native servants. The continual disobedience of your domestics, and their propensity to cheat you, are certainly very vexatious, as they are circumstances of perpetual occurrence. I find my time completely occupied, between domestic duties, reading and writing Tamil, and giving instruction."

In the midst of manifold labours, Mrs. Smith was suddenly taken ill. At first, a favourable ending was anticipated, but fever and delirium supervened. Only four or five days passed by, and it became known that *death* would end the sufferings of the stricken one, who, although so frequently delirious, ever and anon prayed for herself and others. Not long before her death she said, "I feel as if I were just entering into the gulf of death. My eternal rest is in Jesus Christ. I shall die, and be with Christ." Then, falling, as it were, into a deep sleep, she passed away to be for ever with the Lord, whose servant she was. She had spent about three years in India; and although the time for missionary work was short—especially after deducting the necessary attention to household and maternal duties, she had made her mark upon the great work of female education there. There were not a few among the girls educated in the Black Town Free School who looked back upon Mrs. Smith's labours with and for them, as being the means by which they were raised from degraded heathenism into a nobler, better, more womanly and Christian life.

MRS. REBECCA WAKEFIELD,
Wife of the Rev. Thomas Wakefield,

MISSIONARY TO RIBÉ, EAST AFRICA; OF THE UNITED
METHODIST FREE CHURCH MISSIONS.

"I would the precious time redeem,
   And longer live for this alone,
To spend and to be spent for them,
   Who have not yet my Saviour known.
Fully on these my mission prove,
And only live, to breathe Thy love."
                        C. WESLEY.

THE story of Mrs. Wakefield's life fills an intensely interesting page in the annals of modern missions; and for single-heartedness, devotedness, and important, although brief service, her memoir stands pre-eminent. It is a touching story of womanly and Christian devotion.

Rebecca Brewin was the daughter of Mr. Simeon Brewin and his wife Rebecca, a worthy, godly couple, who were connected with the Wesleyan Methodists, in Mountsorrel, Leicestershire. In this quiet and romantic little town, Rebecca, the subject of our sketch, was born, on August 19th, 1844, the youngest of the family. She passed the first twenty years of her life in that rural retreat, surrounded by the comforts of an old-fashioned country home, and being trained by loving hands and patient hearts for a useful and blessed after-life. She was physically robust and healthy, although very nervous, and shy as a child; but was very lovable, earnest, and attracted to things which pertained to the religious life.

When only about thirteen years of age, she experienced the change which is known as "conversion to God," and her testimony upon this point is very clear and decisive. In that year, bereavement had spread its black shadow over the home, for the father and elder brother were both summoned away by death. The brother died in the glorious spring-time; he was a hard student, and promised to obtain honourable distinction; but at seventeen he was cut off; and in the December following, Mr. Brewin followed his son to the grave. It was in the autumn of this sad year that Rebecca decided to serve the Lord, and to cast in her lot with God's people. She gives her account of the matter in these words: "The time of my decision for Christ was on October 27th, 1857, the year in which dear Iliffe and my father died. I had, for a long time previously, felt the powerful strivings of the Spirit of God, and I was not ignorant of the way of salvation; but I did not yield until this night. After hearing a sermon from the Rev. J. W. Ackrill, from the text, 'My son, give me thine heart,' I went forward in the prayer-meeting as a seeker of salvation, kneeled as a penitent at the foot of the Cross, and was at once made happy by believing in Jesus. Blessed for ever be his glorious name! Oh! may I ever live to His glory."

After completing her education, at Loughborough, she took charge of a young ladies' school at Mountsorrel, and discharged the duties of her post as mistress for about three years. She taught, meanwhile, in the Free Methodist Sunday School, distributed tracts, and was a diligent missionary collector. The mission-work and cause lay very near her heart, and all the more, because a much-loved aunt was at that time occupying a post in the West Indian mission-field, as the wife of a devoted missionary. Without doubt, the letters which this aunt sent home did much to stir up the "gift Divine" in her niece Rebecca, and infuse into her young soul renewed devotedness to the glorious cause.

When about eighteen years of age, Miss Brewin lost her only remaining parent by death. Mrs. Brewin was a consistent, earnest, Christian woman, and had proved the sincerity of her profession by a long life spent in the service of God; therefore the daughter felt her loss to be no common one. The only remaining members of the family were Rebecca, and her brother Robert, but he was out in the world preparing to enter the Free Methodist ministry; consequently, the poor girl's loneliness was very bitter. She, however, continued school-teaching for about a year and a half after her mother's death, residing meanwhile with an aunt, whose loving care made up for the lost mother in some measure. When about twenty years of age, Miss Brewin renounced her school, and removed to Birmingham to live with an elderly lady who was related to her mother, and who offered her a comfortable home in exchange for helpful companionship. About this time, however, she became engaged to the Rev. John Mitchil, an early friend and playfellow, and then a missionary of the Wesleyan Missionary Society in Ceylon, so that her thoughts contemplated the mission-field with keen interest, as being in all probability the one destined for her own occupation at no remote time. During her residence in Birmingham, she also strove to employ her leisure and opportunity in doing good to cabmen and others. He that is faithful in the least, is also faithful in that which is greatest; and Miss Brewin proved her fitness for increased service by discharging, earnestly and prayerfully, the duties which were nearest to her.

But she had yet to pass through the crucible of trial. On December 14th, 1866, and while she was contemplating the nearer approach of her farewell to English life, tidings came that the Rev. Mr. Mitchil had died of Asiatic cholera, after a few hours' illness. This trial was indeed crushing; it needed all her faith and endurance to bear it, or to recognise it as coming from the hand of the Lord of that vineyard which she was so anxious to enter. In the following February she writes: "For the last week I have been suffering most acute sorrow on account of my severe loss. My grief was most painfully renewed by the receipt of one of my own letters, which was returned to me by the last mail, with the word '*Dead*,' written upon the envelope. For several days I have scarcely been able to look up. Oh! how hard these things would be to bear, if in the midst of our sorrows we had no sympathising Friend above, who was once Himself the man of sorrows and acquainted with grief."

In the autumn of the year 1867, Miss Brewin removed to London in order to reside with her brother, who was minister of the Beresford Street Church, Woolwich. She carried on zealous Christian work there, being engaged in the Sunday school, and also in leading a class. Writing to a friend, she says: "I have been much blessed of late in working for Christ. I find there is nothing so blessed as living for others. God does, indeed, abundantly reward me. My brother is thinking of removing to Louth next year, and if so, I shall go with him." Accordingly, in 1868, they removed thither; but in the spring of 1869 they were again in London, and attended the annual meetings of the United Methodist Free Church Missions, held in Exeter Hall. Here, for the first time, they heard and saw the Rev. Thomas Wakefield, as he recounted the story of his labours in the East African mission.

During the sittings of the Annual Assembly, held during July and August of the same year, Mr. Wakefield was introduced to Miss Brewin, and, discerning in her the sterling Christian faith which longed for active service in Christ's cause, requested her to become the companion of his life. He was eight years Miss Brewin's senior, and had been engaged in the East African mission, in conjunction with other helpers, among whom was the Rev. Charles New. Miss Brewin decided to accompany Mr. Wakefield back, and to accept the trials and labours of a missionary life. Accordingly, on December 2nd of the same year, they were married at Louth, and sailed for Zanzibar, on February 24th, 1870. It was a very painful parting with her brother, when the time for embarkation came; and had it not been that it was for "Christ's sake, and the Gospel's," her endurance would have given way. In describing that parting, Mr. Wakefield says : " Long ago had my wife and her brother been left orphans, the last members of a loving family. They had faced the world, and fought its battles together; their sorrows, sympathies, and sentiments had been one. For some time past they had tabernacled in the same fugitive habitations, travelled from circuit to circuit together, gathering daily round the same hearth, and bending together at the same altar. The warp and woof of their lives were closely interwoven. It seemed cruel to tear them thus asunder, and put seven or eight thousand miles of land and sea between them. But the time of parting came. One long lingering embrace, as they stood on the steps near the water's edge, a rush of tears, a reluctant unclasping, and the loving brother and gentle sister were separated. I do not wish to witness such a farewell again."

The *Emily*, the ship in which they sailed, was a vessel of small size, poor accommodation, and possessing wretched arrangements for passengers. In fact, she was not intended to carry passengers at all, being only a cargo vessel. Add to these things, the facts that she was going by way of the Cape, that her crew numbered only eight seamen, and that she carried forty tons of gunpowder, and it will easily be seen to what a miserable experience of voyaging they were destined. In justice it should be stated that they would have sailed by the *Malta*, a large steamer, had not circumstances compelled the countermanding of this arrangement ; but by the time they arrived at Zanzibar, they had reason to look upon this disappointment as a kind providence, for the *Malta* reached Zanzibar in the height of a visitation of cholera, and nearly all on board died. Meantime,

P

the *Emily* was slowly and painfully ploughing her way through the stormy ocean, for our travellers had a tedious voyage of ninety-seven days, many of which were full of storm, tempest, and danger. However, they reached Zanzibar on the 2nd of June, and heard with grateful emotion the sad story of the cholera visitation on board the *Malta*. The voyage had been most trying to Mrs. Wakefield; she suffered so severely from sea-sickness, that fears were entertained by all on board the *Emily*, that she would not survive the voyage. However, she rallied slowly towards the end of the voyage, and landed at Zanzibar in partial health and strength.

A pleasing incident occurred in connection with their arrival at Zanzibar, which illustrated the Christian charity of the episcopal Bishop of that town, toward the missionaries of another society. As soon as they had cast anchor in the harbour, a boat went out to meet them, containing the Rev. Mr. Pennel, of the English Universities Mission, and he conveyed to them a letter from Bishop Tozer, couched in the following kindly terms: "Shangain House, English Mission, Zanzibar, May 17th, 1870. My dear Mr. Wakefield,—I am leaving this letter to welcome you back to Africa, on the eve of my departure for the coast. We have made arrangements for taking you and Mrs. Wakefield, Mr. Yates, and your Galla boy, in at the mission-house, where you will find rooms prepared for your reception. I only regret that I am not able myself to assist at your landing. Pray make up your minds to take sufficient rest before starting for Mombas. I do not propose being absent more than a month, even if so long, and I shall be cruelly disappointed to miss you. I do not think there is any house in the town where you can be taken in with less inconvenience than here, and I am sure there is none where your sojourn will give the inmates so much pleasure. Believe me, with kind regards to your party, my dear Mr. Wakefield, always yours sincerely, WILLIAM GEORGE TOZER, Missionary Bishop."

COAST SCENE, ZANZIBAR—LIVINGSTONE'S HOUSE.

They remained in the Bishop's house until about July 16th, when Mr. Wakefield and his colleague departed for Mombas, while Mrs. Wakefield took up her abode with Dr. and Mrs. Kirk, at the British Consulate, until his return. It was necessary that the gentlemen of the missionary party should go on to Mombas, and thence to Ribé, to see after the interests of the mission, but Mrs. Wakefield's health forbade her taking the trying journey. She was going through her first experiences of African fever, of which she had three severe attacks, each one following closely on the heels of the other; and it was impossible to leave European society and life wholly until she had become in some degree acclimatised. After Mr. Wakefield's return from Ribé, where he was pleased to find the affairs of the mission prospering, they took up their sojourn for some time in a little two-roomed cottage, while he occupied himself in translating the little work, "More about Jesus," into Kisuahili, for the boys and girls of the mission-school at Ribé; and Mrs. Wakefield learnt to adapt herself and her strength to the conditions of African life. They had a "raw, big, fierce-looking black boy" for a servant, according to the custom of the country, for the females did all the manual labour. The little household was increased in October by the arrival of their first-born child, "little Nellie," and she became immediately, although unconsciously, the great attraction to the natives. She was visited, inspected, and praised, by native ladies and gentlemen, as the greatest novelty. Mrs. Wakefield writes: "One night a messenger came to say that some ladies wished to come and see me and the baby. No less than six came, accompanied by a young Arab gentleman, a regular swell. I could scarcely find seats for so many persons; but they were very polite, and would not allow me to rise to wait upon them. Nellie was handed round to them, and seemed to enjoy the fun. I was amused at the way in which the young gentleman made use of the arm-chair. After sitting in it in the English style for a minute or two, he lifted his feet on to the chair, and sat with his knees touching his chin for the remainder of the time. After chattering and smiling for about twenty minutes, all took their leave."

Early in January, 1871, Mr. and Mrs. Wakefield, with their infant daughter, removed to their permanent home at Ribé. The journey was tedious and exhausting to one so fearfully weak, for they had to travel in an Arab dhow for about one hundred and twenty miles, then for twelve miles in a small boat, and lastly, six miles overland to the mission-house; while their goods and chattels were scrambled for, quarrelled over, and finally taken in charge by natives, who asked exorbitant fees, and only appeared with them at the mission-house, days after, at their own convenience. Mrs. Wakefield says of this journey: "The voyage to Mombassa was, of all miserables, most miserable. I never met anything to equal it in my life, for lack of all comfort. It was wretched to the last degree. For several days I lay cramped up in a wretched place, the roof of which was far too low to allow of one's sitting upright, the boat itself pitching and tossing on the raging sea with every wave, and the most abominable stench from bilge water arising the whole time. When, on reaching Mombassa, Nellie and I emerged from our dark cell, I was almost too weak to stand, not having tasted food for about four days. On landing, I was regarded as a great curiosity by the natives, and as, accompanied by my husband, I took my first walk through the town, the whole place seemed moved at our coming. It was as though a menagerie had been passing through an English village for the first time. Hundreds of children were shouting, racing, screaming, like wild things, and making the poor innocent fowls that were strutting about the street run and fly for their lives. Indeed, men, women, and children alike, came scampering after us in one general stream, and, after staring after us for a while, some would, anticipating our route, cut the corners, and stand waiting to get another good view when we came up again. Nellie, however, seemed to be the great attraction. Now and then, cries of 'Let me see the baby;' 'Bring the baby here;' 'I want to see the baby,' reached us from some of the wealthy Arab or Hindoo ladies, who stood in their dark doorways. Once or twice we stopped, that they might come and look at Nellie; but we were at once shut in by a crowd of wondering gazers, all eyes being turned on the novelty in long, white dress, and little pink bonnet. The women leaned over, and, in Kisuahili, addressed baby in this fashion: 'Oh, very beautiful, yes.' 'Are you like milk?' 'Are you like sugar?' 'Are you like gold?' 'Are you like honey?' 'Are you like pearls?' And then, if Nellie happened to crow in her childish way, they burst into roars of laughter."

At Ribé, after many delays, they succeeded in getting their home into some sort of order, in spite of the fact that many of their things had been stolen by thievish natives at Zanzibar. Mrs. Wakefield was for a long time visited by natives who came long distances in order to see the wonderful phenomena of a white woman and baby, and they all asked for, and expected, presents, contrary to the custom of many other heathen tribes. About two months later Mr. and Mrs. Wakefield went down to Mombassa to look after some of their lost luggage, and while there Mrs. Wakefield was seized badly with fever. As she lay in bed there, she records that the rats were so numerous that they ran over the bed, dressing-table, and walls—that they ate up her pocket-handkerchiefs and hearthrug, and that they got inside the piano and ate the cloth on the hammers. Yet she did not seem alarmed; these were among the every-day incidents of residence in that country, and in spite of these and many other drawbacks she commenced learning the language, with a view of instructing the women. She, however, made a beginning, holding sewing classes for the Galla women, and teaching them easy lessons through an interpreter. She also led the singing in the public service, a task for which her musical abilities and excellent voice well fitted her. She endeavoured faithfully to adapt herself to the requirements of the mission, and strove to fill her own particular niche, although "in trials oft" from the visits of the large rats, depredations of white ants, constant attacks of fever, and the numberless other disagreeables which go to make up the lot of a missionary's life. It was a matter of frequent occurrence to find that everything wearable had been destroyed by white ants, while the nightly visits of jackals, hyenas, and leopards to their dwelling, rendered the most careful vigilance necessary to preserve life.

Yet, amid all these discouragements the principal object of their residence in East Africa was ever kept before them, and the spiritual welfare of the natives sought after by every means. It was curious to notice that they commenced to adopt European customs and dress, as far as possible, as soon as they began to understand a little about Christianity. Even the men would adopt hats, and wear them to chapel, in their eagerness to imitate white people; but, unlike them, would forget their hats in coming out, and leave them behind in their pews. This forgetfulness involved a hasty run back for the missing hats, to the amusement of the Europeans. Some of them, however, looked beyond the bare civilisation, and longed for "the pearl of price." As one very interesting instance of this, Mrs. Wakefield says: "A young woman was sitting with me one day at her work, making herself a plain dress, which I had just cut out for her, when some one came in and said to her: 'Why, you'll be like a Musungu, exactly, and you'll like that.' She replied, modestly: 'Never mind being like the white man; if I am like Jesus, that is better.'"

The institution of slavery was a great hindrance to their people, and many harrowing instances came under their own knowledge, in which youths were stolen by man-stealers of other tribes and sold far away. Yet the Word of God prospered. On one Sunday Mrs. Wakefield records that four of the young men—native Christians—made their second attempt at exhorting, with the view of becoming local preachers. Yet the progress was slow, and the population small, and easily scattered. Sometimes Mr. Wakefield, together with his wife, felt discouraged at the little progress made, and contemplated the possibility of removing to the Victoria Nyanza territory, in order to influence the vast masses of the heathen in the interior. Mrs. Wakefield expressed herself willing to "go anywhere for Christ," and had any opening occurred, would cheerfully have accompanied her husband into the interior. An interesting note just here gives one an idea of the utter childishness of the people. She says: "The children constantly come begging for toys, or something to play with. Toys cannot be bought here. Nellie's dolls are very much coveted. Many grown-up men at Ribé have asked me for one that they might take it away to their far-off home *to play with*."

Beside ministering to the souls of the natives, the missionary and his wife strove to imitate the Great Healer in doing good to their bodily sicknesses and infirmities. We find that the people came to them from long distances, complaining of being bewitched, "possessed of devils," beside suffering from other and more tangible ailments. Mrs. Wakefield says: "Not merely is medicine given to the sick on the station, but strangers come from all parts to be treated, making journeys of twenty, thirty, and forty miles, and even farther, trudging all the way on foot. A poor old woman, whose home is forty miles away, came some time since, and is still taking medicine three times a day, for what I think is deep-seated consumption. She has a fearful cough, and her body is much wasted. Another patient who is staying here, and for whom I have made linseed-meal poultices every day for months, comes from a place thirty miles distant, with large wounds of six years' standing on his hands and legs. He has tried many remedies, among others, conversion to Mohammedanism; but all have hitherto failed. Kamnazo, the boy whom I have been teaching to read, has had a wound on his leg for a long time, which keeps getting better, and then worse again, because I can't keep him from running about till it is quite healed. I have another boy with a bad cold on the chest, a little boy to have two teeth pulled out, a Galla man with bad toes, and many other cases. One day a man and his wife brought their little three-year-old child to be cured. His case was beyond our power to assist, for he was an idiot boy."

All these ministrations of mercy *told* in the end; and many listened the more eagerly to the Gospel, because of the kindness shown to them by the missionaries. Converts multiplied, until every Sabbath six or seven of the young men were sent out into the neighbouring villages, to re-deliver, in their own quaint fashion, the story of the Saviour's love. These young evangelists also visited among the huts, inviting the natives to come to the mission-chapel. "But," said one old man, "I am willing to come when I hear the news that you people who read the book *don't die;* but at present I see no difference between you and ourselves." The young evangelist then explained to the poor old Wanika man, but without much result, the difference between bodily death and spiritual death.

In March, 1873, Sir Bartle Frere and a large party of English gentlemen and officers, with a suite of about fifty soldiers and servants, paid the lonely mission-station a visit. On the Sabbath Sir Bartle attended the Sunday-school, and preaching service in the little schoolroom, and not content with listening, gave a "nice little address to the people," which Mr. Wakefield translated to them. The native Christians greatly appreciated this address, remarking afterwards: "We thank you very much, sir, for your words; they are very good, and they have filled our hearts with joy."

One more extract will tell a little of her daily duties and cares. All through Mrs. Wakefield's experience in East Africa, it seems that the outward circumstances of the mission were such as added to her trials. The prowling hyena or leopard at night, reptiles by day, the constant inroads of vermin, such as rats, and ants, the lack of congenial society, the deprivation of nourishing food for long seasons, the malarious and pestilential air, all contributed to make her lot, together with that of her husband, hard and difficult. Nothing but strong, abiding love to Christ could have sustained their sad and weary hearts; they longed, too, to do the Master's work there, and would fain have rejoiced over large numbers brought into the fold. True, a little church was gathered out of the wilderness; but compared with the teeming multitudes in the interior of Africa, these few were as nothing; and when the heroic husband and wife contemplated the vast work yet to be accomplished, was it very wonderful that they should grow discouraged? Yet that sense of sad discouragement never once caused them to slacken at their tasks. They were working under the Master's eye, and for His glory; what need then to doubt the final result? Mrs. Wakefield says: "I had to leave my letter yesterday, and go to bed with fever, and now the messenger is waiting to carry this down to Mombas. I am sorry for this, for my heart was full, and I was about to tell you some of our trials. However, I hope they will pass away, and that we shall be spared to be a blessing to the people. My time is very much occupied; in fact, I have a great deal more to do than I can find strength for, and I think this is why I get fever so often. These black boys do not know enough of European life to render me much assistance. By doing so much sewing for the boys of the school, and overlooking the making of all the women's garments, my own personal sewing gets far behind, and I often get troubled about it, especially when I see my little Nellie outgrowing her frocks, and I am unable to make more. We have had some dreadful losses in the matter of clothing lately. The white ants, cockroaches, and moths, in spite of all precautions, have been among my dresses, and destroyed many pounds' worth of our things. Mr. Wakefield has had two suits of clothes eaten up, besides hats, and socks, vests, and woollen things of all sorts. A good strong box in my bedroom, containing my whole stock of calico, has just been attacked by white ants. They have got inside, and pierced the calico through and through, so that out of about a hundred yards there are only a few yards left whole. I could have cried when I opened the box, for I had been to it only a week or two before, and all was right; and even on the outside there was no appearance of anything wrong."

In the last letter ever written by Mrs. Wakefield, she says: "When I last wrote we were suffering the intense heat of the hot season; now the weather has entirely changed, and we are having the unhealthy wet season, with all the mists, vapours, and malaria, rising out of the valleys and jungles which surround us. I am glad to make daily use of that grey, thick, woollen shawl of mother's—the most useful article we brought out here. The natives themselves get very bad colds and coughs at this season of the year. Even we sometimes envy them their bright fires in their little huts of an evening, for they look so snug and comfortable, while our little cottage is feeling all damp and cold, and consequently unhealthy." The dark bereavement which was slowly but surely coming on, was casting its fearful shadow before. Mrs. Wakefield's strength was fast failing, and her worn frame and depressed energies told the sad tale to her anxious husband. According to her later letters, the music of her life was pitched in the minor key; although the missionary spirit still animated her, yet hardship, fever, privation, and loneliness were working their legitimate results upon the tender frame.

On Sunday, June 8th, 1873, the little mission-family was gladdened by the addition of a son, whom Mr. Wakefield baptised by the name of Bertie. But immediately after, fever came on again—that insidious foe, which ever lurks in wait in tropical climes—and this was followed by delirium, abscesses, rheumatism, with pain and swelling of the face. Her constitution was naturally vigorous, and her spirit brave and hopeful, else she would not have battled so long. Six weeks of this terrible time passed by, and Mr. Wakefield was for a time sole nurse and medical attendant, for, with the exception of the Rev. Mr. Rebmann—an infirm missionary at Mombassa, connected with the Church of England missions—there were no Europeans in the country within 140 miles. The heathen native women had no idea of rendering gentle and kind attention to the sick, and all the women at the station were heathen. A few days after, the most alarming symptoms appeared; however, a Christian native woman, named Polly, who had been educated at a mission training institution at Bombay, came from another mission station at a great distance off, to proffer help. News of Mrs. Wakefield's dangerous illness had travelled abroad, and as soon as this good woman had heard of it she resolved to go and do what she could for the help of the sufferer. Her help was eagerly accepted; but no amount of skill availed to stay the ravages of illness upon a weakened and exhausted frame. It seemed that Mrs. Wakefield herself felt that she should not recover, for she said to her husband one day, "There is one thing which I ought to tell you. It is this: though I have prayed a great deal for recovery, all seems dark." The words sank like lead into her husband's heart, but he strove to combat the hopeless feeling, and suggested that God was only trying their faith. He adds: "I think I soothed her, but it was a dark hour for us both. During the whole of Mrs. Wakefield's illness, my prayers for her recovery were frequent and earnest; and when I had impressions of her possible removal, they were prayers of agony and tears. I retired to the iron house, where no one could possibly see me, and poured out my soul to God as I never prayed before. I pleaded the Divine promise, 'The prayer of faith shall save the sick, and the Lord shall raise him up.' Sometimes through the darkness there were faint gleams of an answer, but I was never fully satisfied, although I continued to hope on till the day of her death."

So June passed by, with alternations of hope and fear. Mrs. Wakefield, however, rallied a little, and was able to sit up for a few hours; but Bertie was now dangerously ill, and not expected to live. Polly, the nurse, was fetched home on July 1st by her husband; and now Mr. Wakefield resumed his sad office, without rest for any length of time, either by night or day. The means for her recovery were diligently continued, but with very little beneficial result. On July 12th, little Bertie died, and on the afflicted father devolved the sorrowful task of breaking the sad intelligence to his wife. She craved that the babe might be given to her for a few minutes once more; this was done, and then, after a last longing embrace, accompanied by a flood of tears, she handed it back again, as if resigned to God's will concerning it. In the evening of the same day, when the coffin was ready, the stricken parents laid their little one in his narrow bed; for although almost paralysed by rheumatism, the mother longed and tried to render yet some little ministration to the lifeless form. Then, sitting down upon her bedside again, with Mr. Wakefield supporting her, she breathed forth her sorrow and her resignation in this touching prayer: "*O Lord, look mercifully upon us in our deep affliction. Thou hast sorely tried us. One sorrow has come upon another. But, O Lord, if Thou canst, stay now Thy hand, and let us learn all that Thou wouldst teach us by this dispensation. Heal and comfort us. Spare and raise me up again, if it be in accordance with Thy purpose; but if not, not my will, O Lord, but Thine, be done. Amen.*"

Mr. Wakefield says: "The daylight was now fading, and having gently laid my wife down, I left her, to perform the funeral ceremonies of my child. While one of the boys tolled the bell, I took little Nellie by the hand, and led her into the chapel. This was hard work. With great difficulty I read the service in the chapel, and then we slowly proceeded to the grave, Nellie and I following the coffin as chief mourners, the boys and the mission people completing the procession. Here I buried our darling boy, beside the grave of Mr. Butterworth. Nellie, and I, and the rest cast our flowers into the grave, and we came away, the people to get their suppers, and to go to bed, and I to light up our gloomy cottage, and to sit beside my dying wife. We wept together, as we conversed about our great loss; and I afterwards read to her the ninetieth Psalm, and prayed with her. Then, about one A.M., thoroughly exhausted, I lay down to rest." On the following day, Polly, the nurse, returned again, and Mr. Wakefield welcomed her assistance; for, what with watching and sorrow, his strength was well-nigh exhausted. Mrs. Wakefield now grew at times more delirious, and in her incoherent sentences, talked of things and friends in far-off England, occasionally also singing snatches of hymns in the Galla and Wanika languages. On the fourth day after little Bertie's death, it was too evident that the parting was near. Mr. Wakefield brought their little Nellie to take a farewell of her mamma, and the dying mother kissed the little girl most tenderly. Then the missionary sang part of the hymn, "Jesus, lover of my soul!" very softly to his dying wife; and finally, several of the natives residing on the station were admitted to look at their departing friend. Mrs. Wakefield could not speak, but her countenance expressed pleasure at the words she heard; and she was too securely calm, under the shelter of the Rock of Ages, to be fearful or mistrustful now. So she remained until a few minutes before seven o'clock that evening, when, with her right hand clasped in her husband's, she gently exchanged earth for heaven. Her death occurred on July 16th, 1873.

Mr. Wakefield superintended the preparations for her burial, assisted by a catechist, and on the following day she was committed to the tomb. The bereaved husband and child looked upon "the last of earth" with feelings which cannot be described, and as he read the service for the dead his voice was choked with emotion. The little chapel was crowded with people, and among other things they sang a translation of the hymn, "Canaan, bright Canaan," which had been prepared, and adapted, and taught to the school-children by Mrs. Wakefield before her last illness came on. They had about forty hymns translated into the Galla and Wanika languages, and Mrs. Wakefield had importuned her husband until he assisted her in adapting this one also. After the singing, which was mingled with tears, the missionary and his little child returned slowly and sadly to their desolate home.

Said a critic: "Mrs. Wakefield was only the wife of a Methodist missionary, but she had a loftier courage than Joan of Arc." This was true. Tears dim the eye, and emotion chokes the utterance, as one reads of the trials, the conflicts, the chastening, and the victory which fell to the lot of this sainted woman. She was sorely missed, and mourned, not only by the stricken husband, but by the converted natives. So lovingly and so tenderly had she ministered to the wants of the heathen that they bore abundant testimony to her worth. A few extracts must suffice. The catechist wrote thus: "All the Christians and the inquirers at Ribé are deeply afflicted with the loss which has befallen them. She was their 'piano' in singing, and she will never be out of their minds. I have heard some of the boys of the station saying: 'We have lost our voice,' that is to say, they have lost their best teacher in singing, whose voice elevated above all the rest." A boy from the school wrote: "Oh! I am very sad. It was she who taught me the way of eternal life. If she had remained till now she would have taught me more, but now God has called her, and she has answered. And I wish to hold fast the words which she taught me. When I could not read it was she herself who taught me, and to write also. And to *sew* she also taught me. And when I had an ulcer she herself applied the poultices to it. And if I had a torn jacket it was she who mended it for me. But now she dwells on high in heaven. She came with a torch here, to the land of Ribé, that all the people might take it, and each one be enlightened in his mind, and when the last day shall come be prepared for the Son of Man, when He cometh." Said another: "We are sad, for she was our good one." Said another: "We feel very much bitterness in our hearts, for she left home and all things else to come and teach us the way of everlasting life."

So passed away one who counted not her life dear unto her, that she might win souls for Christ, from dreary, fever-stricken East Africa.

> "Strong ties withheld thee here. A full array
> Of hope and bliss. But what were these to thee,
> Who on God's altar laid the thought of self,
> With prayerful incense, duly, night and morn!
> What were such joys to thee, when duty bade
> Their crucifixion!
>   Therefore the grief
> Born at thy grave is not like other grief—
> Tears mix with joy. We praise our God for thee."
>
> L. H. SIGOURNEY.

MISS SUSAN B. HIGGINS,

MISSIONARY TO YOKOHAMA, JAPAN; OF THE AMERICAN WOMAN'S FOREIGN MISSIONARY SOCIETY.

"Not we alone have tears to shed,
The dark-eyed children of the land,
Whose hope was in thy helping hand,
  Have wept above thy coffined head.
Oh! hearts that bleed, and well nigh break,
'Good cheer,' I whisper you once more;
She sings it, on the heavenly shore.
  This land is fairer for her sake;
  And could ye note the perfect peace,
  That rounds her toil, the sweet release,
Then would your own, like angel-eyes,
  See but a crown, not sacrifice."

JAPAN, and the Japanese, have of late acquired great interest in the eyes of Europeans. As we read of that strange land, where the language of the women differs from that of the men so largely, that it is impossible to reach the women, except by a special study of their peculiar forms of expression—where they commence reading at the end of a book, and read backwards from the bottom of the page to the top, and from right to left; where the heat and dampness make the glue of the furniture so soft that things fall to pieces before you are aware; where pedestrians strut about under big umbrellas; and where the people are so excessively clean that they sit for an hour at a time in huge baths, with earthen furnaces at the bottom, to keep the water up to nearly boiling-point, we seem to be transported to the region of fairy-tales. But then, again, as we read of the new institutions of Japan—of her press, her schools, her laws, her government, of the grafting of Western civilisation upon Eastern customs, and the national desire for knowledge, we begin to realise the fact that the land is waking up from its long night of superstition and error, that the isles are waiting for God's law, according to ancient prophecy. In this strange land, and among this interesting people, the Americans have a flourishing mission. The female members of this mission are among its most successful and self-denying workers, winning many trophies for the Redeemer, among the ranks of their ignorant and benighted Japanese sisters. In this work the Woman's Foreign Missionary Society, operating in connection with the different churches, has done noble service.

Miss Susan B. Higgins was one of their most devoted workers, for the little space permitted to her. She was only in the field of labour some eight months, but such was her success, her loving consecration, and her Christ-like spirit, that all who knew her, mourned her loss as that of a sister not easily replaced. It seems that Miss Higgins was of godly parentage, her father being a preacher in the Methodist Episcopal Church, and her mother an earnest, discreet Christian woman, whose best powers were devoted to the training of her family for God. It was remarked of Susan, that she possessed fine intellectual powers, an acute perception, a breadth of comprehension, and a strength of memory, not often seen in a girl. In her education she was distinguished for earnestness and thoroughness, being the favourite of her teachers, and the honoured pupil of the academy. After graduation, she became a teacher in one of the large public schools of America, in which sphere she was known as a remarkably successful teacher. She was known, too, as a Christian woman, for she had been converted at the age of fourteen, and from that time had lived a thoroughly Christian life. Disdaining mediocrity in religion, as in all else, she strove after "perfection;" was "mighty in the scripture," and constant in prayer. Indeed, from the commencement of her spiritual life until her sudden departure for the "glory-land," she habitually sought for, and received, answers to prayer. *Duty* was to her a pole-star; and nothing could tempt her to deviate from the straight course. It will easily be understood that with these qualities Miss Higgins was a successful teacher. Always feeling it her duty to teach her scholars morality, as well as purely scholastic matters, and to exercise over them a pure influence, she gained their loving respect and accord, in a degree not often seen. As a consequence, her fame spread abroad among the surrounding country, and she received an invitation from an adjoining State to take charge of another school, at a salary which amounted to nearly double the sum which she was then receiving. But she preferred to remain with dear friends; and, in accordance with this preference, wrote, declining the offer. Then, those who were around her—who knew and loved her—deemed that they should rejoice in her presence for many years. But the love of Christ was to prove a far more powerful constraining influence than love of home, or friends, or country. At its summons she arose, and swiftly hastened to obey. She could, and did, leave America for Japan, at the call of the Master.

About this time a little nephew and niece—both dearly beloved by her—were suddenly snatched away by death. Miss Higgins felt their loss severely, and so sanctifying was the effect, that a newer consecration seemed to come upon her from that date. The Executive Board of the Missionary Society made an appeal to educated women to go unto other lands, bearing "the lamp of life" to their benighted heathen sisters. In response to this appeal, Miss Higgins wrote offering her services, stating also that her interest in missionary work had grown with her growth, but that it had been strengthened and quickened by various recent events, chief of which she noted her little nephew's death, Dr. Alden's sermon on the need of workers in the missionary field, and the appeal of the Board. She further said: "June 12th, 1878, brought our quarterly meeting, to which I had been looking with much interest, but a sudden and heavy shower came about the time for me to start, so I carried the matter to the Lord (who drew very near), asking Him to show me what to do, and to find my answer in my Bible. Turning to the wonderful Book, I opened immediately to Acts xxii. 10 : 'And I said, What shall I do, Lord? And the Lord said unto me, Arise, and go into Damascus, and it shall be told thee there of all things which are appointed for thee to do.' Nothing doubting, I took the next car to town. At the close of the meeting Mrs. Daggett crossed the platform, came down the aisle where I was standing, and as she passed said, 'I expect we shall send you as a missionary, some time.' I replied, 'I am ready.' She took my hand, and looking at me, said, 'Apply, then, apply.' The following week, on Friday, I met with the Executive Committee, where the Lord let me roll the responsibility of this over to other hands, and I leave it as I do myself in His hand, praying, above all things, that He will guide your deliberations, for I had rather be kept in my native land by the direst calamity, than undertake the care of souls unless sent and used by God."

In response to this honest, heartfelt, Christ-like letter, Miss Higgins was chosen by the Board of the Woman's Foreign Missionary Society to go to Japan. Three months intervened between her appointment and her departure, months full of deep, self-sacrificing joy on her part, and of loving, devout benedictions on the part of all those Christian hearts who knew her. In September, 1878, Miss Higgins, together with a band of missionaries, numbering five, departed for Yokohama, Japan. She went out to Japan "for life," as she said, intending and hoping to consecrate a long and laborious life to God's service there. And no sooner had she landed in Yokohama

YOKOHAMA.

than she commenced work among the foreigners drifted there, in the prisons and hospitals of the city. While working away thus, in the English tongue, she devoted her mornings to the study of the Japanese language, and her afternoons to the superintendence of a day-school among the natives. This school commenced at first with about three or four pupils; but during the short time that Miss Higgins superintended it, its numbers swelled to fifty-two. Further, she directed and overlooked the work of a Bible-woman among the Japanese females, and with the help of her instructor in the language, carried on a weekly Bible-class for women. It was her intention, in accordance with the wish of the Society, to devote herself specially to the work of training teachers and Bible-women, seeing that these agencies would have had special fitness for Japan, and that Miss Higgins was in a very high degree fitted for such a work. While engaged in her necessary recreation, such as walking or talking with dear friends, her mind was busy, planning for the welfare of those around her. It is recorded of her, that she never passed an old shrine or temple dedicated to Buddha without entering, and praying to her Father in heaven. And, with all her practical sound sense, her business-like capacity for work, she possessed a loving, sympathising heart, which endeared her to all who came within the sphere of her influence. One sentence spoken by her at this happy, busy time affords the key to her character. Said she, "I gauge my spiritual growth by the time I spend with my Bible." And she won strength from that Book every day. Referring to this period of her work in Japan, a fellow-missionary, writing home, says, "'Lord, what wilt Thou have me to do?' was her constant prayer. And a path was made plain, opening up to her a new and unexpected field of usefulness—a field upon which, though dead, she lives. That she was diligent, and successful in the study of the language, others will bear testimony. Often she regretted that her progress was so slow; still, when a little success came to her, she was so pleased and happy. I well remember when she first used successfully a few words in Japanese, such as 'God,' 'good,' 'loves;' she called it her first sermon in the language. And as her vocabulary increased, and she practised on the children she met in her daily walks, when their faces lit up with intelligence, she was as happy as a child. Her manner with the natives was pleasing and winning. That she would have made a grand successful worker, none could doubt. Once I called on her at her school. How well I remember the scene; sitting on a low seat, surrounded by Japanese children, who watched her every motion, how patiently she taught them, how lovingly she drew them to her heart. There were no more sincere tears shed than that of her Japanese teacher. Sobbing aloud, when he heard she was going home, he said to me, 'All night I cried before God to make her well, and let her stay in Japan to work for my people.'"

Miss Higgins spent much of her short time in *visiting* among the people, attended, of course, by an interpreter. Writing home, she says: "Would you like a glimpse into some of the homes of this far-away land? If so, imagine yourself with me at the close of our Tuesday afternoon Bible-class. The Bible-woman and the wife of our native teacher were invited to come with me; and after a long ride through a poorer part of the city, we came to a long, low block of houses, more like sheds for cattle than homes for human beings. One room constituted the abode of each family. In one an aged man was kneeling before a little shrine containing a small idol. His sightless eyes took no note of the strangers, nor did he cease his 'vain repetitions' and counting of beads, till one of the two daughters whom we had come to visit, spoke to her father of our presence, and we began to sing a hymn.

"'Jesus loves me,' fell upon his ear for the first time, and I must confess that when the worn pilgrim and his two daughters tried at the last to join in the chorus, there was a deal more of *tremolo* in the music than is found written in the books. Tears stood on more faces than one while the Word was read, the words of the same loving Jesus of whom we had just sung; and as the promise was given to the pure in heart that they should '*see* God,' a prayer rose from my heart that even here the eyes of this blind man's understanding might be opened. With the little knowledge I yet have of the language, I could not say much to the three eager souls; but as well as I could, I tried to express to them the knowledge of God's desire for their salvation, His great love for them, and displeasure at the worship of idols. They promised to come to church, one at a time, to learn about 'the Jesus way,' but said they were so poor, they could not afford to put away their work on the Sabbath.

"At our next visiting-place, we found an aged woman, who is already an attendant at our church, but not yet admitted to baptism on account of her lack of proper understanding as to the keeping of the Sabbath. We cannot appreciate the great change that must come to this people in this respect, nor its difficulty, with all around them moving as on other days, and no means of improvement in their own homes. Many could not read religious books, should they possess them. The son of this woman was not well, and seemed to appreciate the tender invitation of the Master to bless. We sang 'Pass me not,' and several other familiar hymns, which touch the heart in any tongue. Last Sabbath both mother and son were at church—I think the first time he has been there. In some homes, chopsticks, cake, and tea were brought in. I thought of Paul, and ate, 'asking no questions.' The tea, minus sugar or milk, was very strong and very hot; but it would have wounded them to have had it refused. On my first visit to Japanese homes, I did not understand the stress that they put on this practice, and refused the tea; but I have concluded that I cannot afford to be outdone in politeness, even by the heathen. Afterwards, we gradually glided to the feast of better things, and sang some more sweet hymns. Just as tenderly they touch the heart under the Japanese roofs as in any homes in the dear old mother-country."

After eight months of this happy labour, Miss Higgins was suddenly struck with illness. About a month before she died, having suffered for several days from severe and unusual pain, she obtained medical advice, expecting that the symptoms only betokened temporary illness, and looking for immediate relief. But as she underwent a medical examination, it was at once seen that serious illness had come—serious, sudden, and, sooner or later, fatal. Said the medical man, "You must return to America as quickly as you can get there. You may recover, but it is doubtful." Like a knell these words fell upon her ears, betokening the cessation of all her much-loved work, but she never flinched. Looking up in the doctor's face, she replied, "I am in the Lord's hands; living or dying, I am His." So, bravely and confidently, she commenced her rapid descent into the valley of the shadow of death.

Next day she went to Tokio, to arrange for sailing to America, intending to return to Yokohama on the following morning to pack up in order for going. But when morning dawned she was unable to leave her room, and before three or four days had passed away it was easy to be seen that she would never live to reach America. Indeed, day by day the end drew near, and at last Miss Higgins became sure that she must die in Japan.

But Heaven is as near to Japan as to America. So, comfort came to the dying missionary, while those among whom she was located ministered to her with loving, patient hearts. That seemed the season when, if ever, the Tempter would have especial power; but she was calm and confident, reposing on the Rock of Ages. A friend said to her, "Do you regret now that you came to Japan?" She said, "It was the Lord's doings; I had nothing to say about it. *He* knew of the incipient disease in my system, although the physicians did not, and, knowing all that, He told me to come to Japan, so it must be right." As the pain grew more excruciating, the prayer for release would rise to her

JAPANESE STREET SCENE.

lips; but one day she said, "I am afraid if my home friends hear how much I want to go to heaven, and how willing I am to die here, they will think I have forgotten them. Be sure to tell them how much I love them. Do you know these words, 'There is no man that hath left house, or brethren, or sisters, or father, or mother, or wife, or children, or lands, for My sake and the Gospel's, but he shall receive a hundredfold now in this life, and in the world to come eternal life'? Oh! how this has been verified to me." Being fond of singing, it was no wonder that she should ask the watchers round her to sing. One day the lady who was sitting by her commenced singing the hymn wherein those lines occur:—

> "Jesus can make a dying bed
> Feel soft as downy pillows are;"

but broke down because of sorrow. Miss Higgins immediately took up the strain, and sung on—

> "Oh! would my Lord His servant meet,
> My soul would stretch her wings in haste,
> Fly fearless through death's iron gate,
> Nor feel the terrors as she passed."

In this happy frame of mind she continued until the summons came; and in about four weeks from the time when she first complained of indisposition, she passed to the inner courts of the Temple above, where there is nought but perfect service. Only eight short months had she been able to labour for Japan; but during that time she had endeared herself to all with whom she had come in contact. The funeral service was attended by many of the Japanese, who had ornamented the little mission chapel with flowers, and who joined, amid their tears, in singing at the grave the hymn, "We shall meet in the sweet bye-and-bye." And not they alone, for European sailors were there who had received her ministry of mercy in Yokohama hospital, as well as missionary friends, who received a new inspiration from the contemplation of their friend's life. There is no doubt but that other labourers will step forward and offer themselves for Japan, so that Miss Higgins will do far more by her death than she could have done by her life, in that beautiful land of the Orient.

MRS. HANNAH KILHAM,

MISSIONARY TO SIERRA LEONE; OF THE SOCIETY OF FRIENDS.

" Thy light, dear saint, put out in darkness, sleeps
Beneath the gulf o'er which the negro weeps
When borne to bondage; from the ships of slaves
His tears are wafted homeward on the waves.
Hidden, but not extinct, below the dark,
Deep ocean. When the latest spark
Of Nature's conflagration shall expire,
Thy light shall shine above the sinking pyre;
A ray among the innumerable rays
Which from the ransomed, round their Saviour, blaze,
When He makes up His jewels; and no gem
Is wanting in that glorious diadem."

JAMES MONTGOMERY.

HANNAH KILHAM — or rather Hannah Spurr, for that was her maiden name — was the daughter of respectable tradespeople in Sheffield, having been born there on August 12th, 1774. From the testimony of those who knew her, it seems that she was remarkable for the grace of early consecration and devotedness to works of faith and charity. James Montgomery, the poet, spoke in the highest terms of her Christian charity and zeal, writing a sonnet in her memory when the news of her death at sea arrived in England. He said: "She was one of the most actively and influentially benevolent persons with whom it was ever my privilege to be acquainted. For there was a singleness of eye and a sincerity of purpose, as well as a humility of deportment, in all she did on behalf of religion and humanity, which were the pledges of her heart being right with God, while it was kindly affectioned to her fellow-creatures of every kindred, colour, and clime." This remarkable woman spent her strength and service on behalf of the negroes of Liberia and Sierra Leone, making three voyages thither, in order to carry on the mission-work. In the last of these voyages she died, and her remains now sleep beneath " the deep blue sea," until that " sea shall give up its dead."

Mrs. Spurr, Hannah's mother, appears to have been a devotedly pious woman; and although early taken from her family, there is no doubt that Hannah learnt much from her of the way of life. It is recorded of Hannah that from the age of ten years she was noted for her seriousness, amiability, and talents. At ten years of age, she regularly attended evening prayers in the parish church, leaving her playfellows or her work in order to do this. She also devoted her pocket-money to the relief of the poor, keeping a list of names, that she might relieve each needy case in turn. She also kept a diary of her good and bad deeds, recording each in opposite columns; but she soon relinquished this practice, because the bad deeds preponderated. These serious traits of mind and life followed her while at boarding-school; and when, on returning home, she was thrown into somewhat gay society, she voluntarily gave it up, as being detrimental to her soul's interests. When about twenty-two years of age, she joined the Society of Methodists. Indeed, from her childhood she had been permitted to listen to John Wesley and others who laboured with him; but now she took up her cross, and attached herself to the "despised saints." At twenty-four years of age she was married to Alexander Kilham, a travelling minister among the Methodists. He engaged prominently in the separation known as the division into "Old" and "New Connexion" Methodists, and was distinguished for his unceasing labours in the cause of the Gospel. They were married in April, 1798, but the union was of very short duration, for in December of the same year Mrs. Kilham was left a widow, with the charge of a child of his by a first wife. Mr. Kilham's removal was almost sudden, only being preceded by three or four days' illness, during which no danger was apprehended. This bereavement had the effect of deepening Mrs. Kilham's humility and devotedness, so that she gave herself up to the work of Sunday-school teaching with much ardour. A little girl was born some three months after Mr. Kilham's death, who became the subject of the deepest solicitude to the sorrowing widow; but the child was early called away to rejoin its father in the skies. From thenceforth Mrs. Kilham became, like Dorcas of old, known for her good works; while from engaging in home mission and Sunday-school work, her sympathies deepened and widened, until they sought an outlet in foreign lands, and among the degraded negroes of West Africa. Before this work was undertaken, however, Mrs. Kilham had joined the Society of Friends; indeed, it was known to their intimate associates that Mr. Kilham had intended taking this step before his death. His widow, therefore, carried out her conscientious convictions, by joining that body, in 1803.

About the year 1805, Mrs. Kilham opened a girls' boarding-school in Sheffield, and continued in this occupation till about 1821. She was very fitted for this profession, having received what was esteemed a liberal education, for a girl, in her youth. The composition and tone of her letters, and the style of her diary, exhibit a literary faculty not very common among women of that day, unless specially gifted. While engaged as schoolmistress, she was accustomed to set apart a certain percentage of profits for the circulation of tracts and Gospel books among children and young persons. In those days of semi-darkness, such a ministry must have been twice blessed, hallowed alike to the giver and receivers. She also engaged actively in work of different benevolent societies in Sheffield, and gained much affection in her house-to-house visitation. Among these societies we may name the Society for Bettering the Condition of the Poor in Sheffield, the Girls' Lancastrian School, the Society for Visiting and Relieving Aged Females, and the Sheffield Bible Association. In all these works of faith and labours of love, she was greatly blessed, and doubtless received unconsciously a training for the more extended work to which she was called in after-life.

In 1807 her mind was powerfully impressed with the conviction that she might and *ought* to further the cause of missions in Sierra Leone, by preparing a grammar and other school-books for the use of the children in the Friends' Mission-schools there. In 1819 her step-daughter, Sarah, departed to Russia, as teacher in some girls' schools in St. Petersburg; and painful though the separation was on both sides, the step seemed to clear the way for the enterprise which Mrs. Kilham had had laid upon her heart for some time, viz., that of going out to Sierra Leone as school missionary. Just at this juncture she went to London, to consult with some friends as to the advisability of removing to Sierra Leone, when they suggested that it would be preferable for her to remain in England a little while longer, and employ the time in learning the language from some natives of that part of Africa. About this time two young Africans arrived in this country, who were somewhat intelligent and willing to learn. They both spoke the Jaloof language—the one Mrs. Kilham wished to learn—and one of them the Mandingo, in addition. The Society of Friends' Mission placed these young men at Tottenham, under the care of a young man who engaged to teach them; and Mrs. Kilham remained in London several months, learning their languages from them, with a view to future service. She also studied Arabic, with the design of translating passages of Scripture into that tongue for distribution among the Arabs on the West

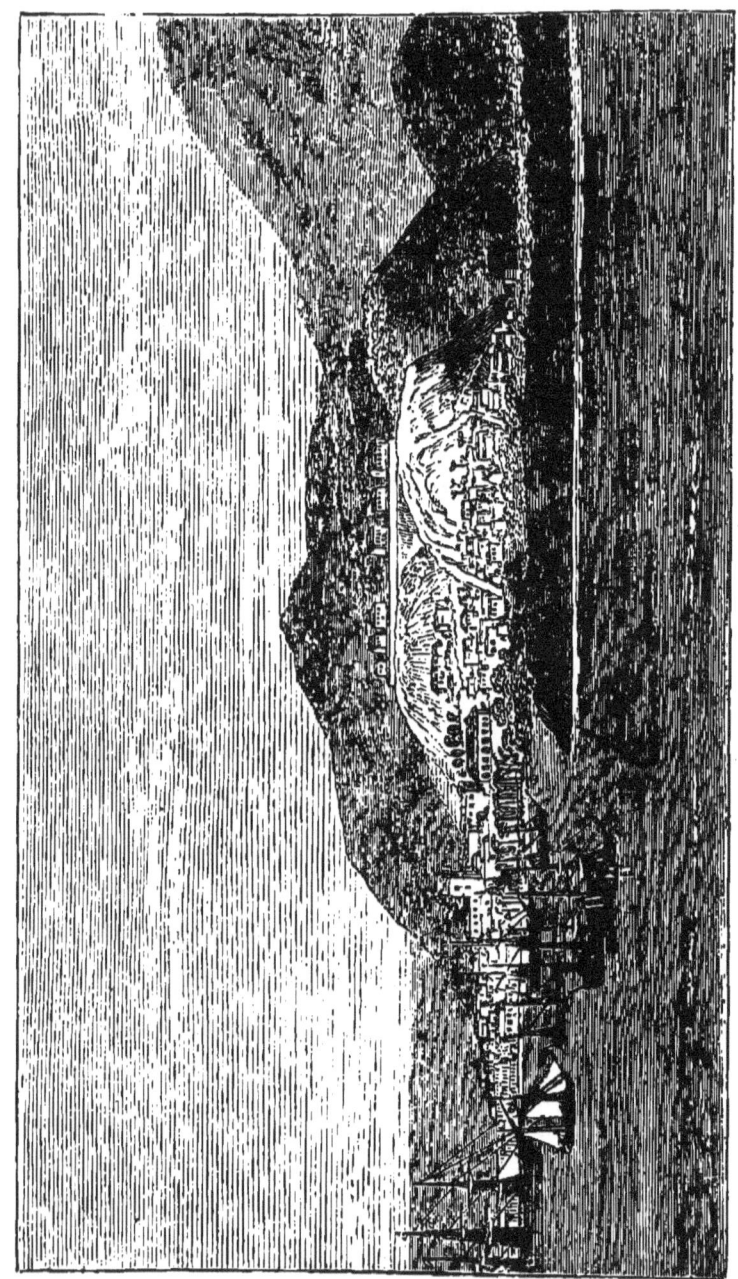

VIEW OF SIERRA LEONE.

Coast. Finally, she gave up school, although this was a decided loss, seeing that it was prospering largely, and during the interval between this step and her departure, undertook a visit to Ireland in 1823, on behalf of the British and Irish Ladies' Society, a society which had for its main object the relief of Ireland's destitute poor. Upon her return from Ireland, the Friends' Committee desired her to go out to Africa as a school missionary, so as to put into practical use the lessons and translations she had been preparing. Beside her, they appointed Ann Thompson to assist in teaching, and John Thompson and Richard Smith to work generally in the mission, as well as to promote a knowledge of agriculture. This little party was accompanied by the two young natives from whom Mrs. Kilham had learnt the languages, Sandanee, and Mahmadee. They embarked at Gravesend, on the 26th of October, 1823, in the ship *James*, bound for the Gambia. She kept a diary on the voyage out, and one sentence written there at this time seems to give the key-note to her life: "Obedience, obedience, entire dedication, this is what I desire may be the pursuit of my life, without choosing my own path, or seeking to avoid what is difficult and opposed to my nature." The way had been strikingly opened by the offer of the Governor of St. Mary's to provide a house for the missionaries; and on arriving there, they acknowledged that if they had had the providing of a place for themselves, they could not have gained more commodious premises. There was ample room for three separate schools—boys', girls', and young infants'. With reference to her translations, Mrs. Kilham writes: "Yesterday, Dongo Kerry, who is learning to read English, came to pay us a visit, wishing to hear something read in his own language. I read to him a few sentences. On hearing the first, he exclaimed: 'Ah, that's Jaloof!' and so repeatedly, evidently understanding them. A short narrative was then read, which pleased him very much; and he repeated several sentences in this and other narratives which were read, and by his actions and expressions evidently understood them. Afterwards I read to him the first section of the Scripture lessons, when he exclaimed: 'Great and good! Great and good!'" Evidently, the translations and lessons prepared with so much pains and labour in England, were destined to bear fruit now.

Very soon, schools were established for girls, boys, recaptured slaves, known as "king's boys," and women. That the women needed friendly interposition as well as teaching, is but too evident from her journal. She says: "I was asked, a few days since, to go and see a poor woman who was much hurt by some blows received from her husband. When I was in the hut of the poor sufferer, I was informed that her injuries arose from the brutal treatment of the man calling himself her husband, and who, by violent blows, had crushed some of her bones. Another husband, being dissatisfied with his wife, had ordered her legs to be broken, and the poor creature had died in consequence of his cruelty." Surely, Mrs. Kilham in her "woman's work for women," found abundant need and abundant scope.

She commenced and carried on her work of visitation among the schools already established, travelling from place to place, and recording in her journal whatever seemed most noticeable or interesting. Thus, she writes: "In this school there are about eighty or ninety scholars. The two girls who serve the mistress—one as housemaid, and the other as monitor—were inhumanly confined in a cask on board the slaver, to conceal them." "A little girl I saw in the school this morning had lost one arm, and on inquiry of the cause, was told it was lost in the fight in recapturing a slave-ship, and that the slaves had often been much wounded, and some of them killed, in these combats." "I have inquired of several of the people in this colony respecting the manner of their capture, and find it mostly thus: that when their towns were burnt, by an agreement between the slave-dealer and the king, they were seized as they escaped the flames. Sometimes, in time of war, the higher ranks are sold; but chiefly those who are already slaves are sold from one to another, and often pass through many hands ere they reach the coast." "The women do the field work; and we were told that, on returning from a hard day's work, it was their habit to fall down on their knees before their husbands, and thank them for their employment."

Having accomplished the work committed to her, Mrs. Kilham, with the two Thompsons, brother and sister, returned home to report to the Committee of the Friends. On the voyage home, John Thompson died, and within a few weeks after their arrival in England, the survivors heard of the death of Richard Smith, the single one of the party who had remained behind in Sierra Leone. His death was a great blow to the mission, and it appeared doubtful if the way would be opened up again for Mrs. Kilham to visit Africa; but she held herself at the call of duty, willing always to go anywhere, or do anything, to serve the cause of the Master. Indeed, at one time, she anticipated going out to Russia, or China, on missionary errands.

That Sierra Leone was the post of danger, may be inferred from an entry in her diary: "Affecting accounts are received by the Church Missionary Society of continued mortality among their missionaries at Sierra Leone. G. Nylander has finished his course. Five others have lately died, even though it has been mostly the dry season; and four are returning home to recruit." For some time she laboured in the evangelisation of St. Giles; and then the way opened up for a second visit to Africa. She accordingly sailed for "the dark Continent" in October, 1827, on a second visit of enquiry and labour. This time, some of the Church Missionary Society's agents accompanied her. They reached Free Town in December, and on the very day after landing Mrs. Kilham commenced her labours, by visiting the Eastern School. She says: "The engagements I had in view in Sierra Leone were, first, the obtaining of an outline of the principal languages spoken by the liberated Africans and others in the colony, so as by taking down in writing in an easy and distinct orthography the numerals and some of the leading words, to identify, as far as may be practicable, the dialects of the different tribes; to form an idea of the number of distinct languages spoken in Sierra Leone; and to con-

FREE TOWN.

sider what prospect there might be of proceeding to reduce those of most importance to a written form; also to prepare such an outline for elementary instruction in each language as might introduce the pupils in the liberated African schools to a better knowledge of English than they at present possess." She records that some of the poor little liberated slave-children, after being rescued from the hands of the slavers, were so reduced as to appear like walking skeletons. Indeed, nothing but the representation of death could equal the worn and wretchedly emaciated appearance presented by some on their liberation. In this starving condition they would frequently seize upon poultry and other kinds of food, as opportunity offered, and devour it ravenously, half raw. It was a task of no small difficulty to bring these children back by careful treatment to a proper condition of body, and then to train and inform the mind. Yet the mission, established in Sierra Leone by the Friends, succeeded in doing this to a large degree for the once enslaved but now freed negroes.

In 1828, having accomplished her second mission to a great extent, and being seized upon by fever, Mrs. Kilham returned to England. Soon after this home-coming, while awaiting the direction of Providence respecting other openings for work, she writes, in reference to the special training which missionaries need: "It is necessary that young missionaries should have a time of trial, under oversight, before they leave England. I am much impressed with the belief that a very sedentary and studious life is not favourable as a preparation for missionary enterprise. There should be more occupation for both body and mind as to exertion for others. The habit is too much that of ease and quietness for the subsequent difficulties of a missionary station. If they could be practised in carpenter's work, surgery, gardening, printing, book-binding, &c., it would be very valuable to them. Missionaries would, I think, have more effectual success if they could present a little community of farmers, spinners, weavers, joiners, and teach schools, and give religious instruction at the same time."

In the autumn of 1830, Mrs. Kilham sailed a third time for Africa, on what proved to be her last visit. It is remarkable that she had a great natural dread of the water, so that to cross the stormy ocean on this errand five times, was indeed a crucifying of the flesh. Nothing but the constraining love of Christ could have energised her for the task. On this visit she established a school at Charlotte, for negro girls. She had good-sized premises, including two school-houses, one of which was used as a meeting-room. Before, however, she could commence the work of instruction proper, she was compelled to clothe them, for they were all perfectly destitute of the commonest necessaries of clothing. But when this difficulty was conquered, she commenced the daily work of instruction, aided by a young, inexperienced teacher, who herself knew but little English. The work she carried on was threefold: she had first to provide for twenty-seven girls as to board, lodging, and clothing, beside herself and the teachers; then she had to teach them the rudiments of knowledge; and lastly, she had to instruct them in the "way of life." This work was carried on amidst much discouragement, and many opposing influences. Near the school-house was the gaol; and here the poor Africans who were immured received brutal treatment, so much so that her spirit was moved within her on several occasions, and she interceded for mercy on behalf of the poor wretches. She particularly records the case of one poor slave woman, who was compelled by the brutal gaoler to carry an excessive load of stone upon her head a distance of four miles, receiving the while, cruel stripes from the under-gaoler. Added to this, Mrs. Kilham had little intercourse with Europeans; and her spirit felt exceedingly depressed at times in this strange land. Still she persevered, and her school grew. From a newly-arrived slave-ship she received twenty additional fugitives; most of these poor girls were depressed, exhausted, and emaciated, as well as densely ignorant and brutalised in mind. An extract from her diary in reference to the African slave trade will serve to show that it was then the same horrible traffic in human life that it is now. Livingstone, Stanley, Moffat, and other African explorers unite in giving it this diabolical character. She says: "The Kossoo girls give affecting details of the wretched state of their country from almost perpetual wars for the purpose of making them slaves; so that they can seldom retire to rest at night and feel secure from an alarm. One of our children, about seven years old, has several scars on her limbs, of which she gives the following account. Her father and mother fled from the slave-dealer, and her mother, from carrying her, was hindered from moving so quickly as without her she could have

HEADDRESSES OF NATIVE WOMEN.

done. The father caught the child away from her, and threw it upon a fire, saying it was better for the child to die than for all to be made slaves. The mother could not bear this, but ran back and took up her child. The father ran on, and the mother proceeded as fast as she could with her poor burnt child until she got to a place where she thought she could stop securely to dress the little creature's wounds; but in doing this she was taken, and our poor little Towah saw neither father nor mother any more. . . . . Ninga's father would not leave his children, but brought them all four away in his flight.

Ninga says the pursuers killed her father, and she does not know to what place her mother and her two younger sisters were taken. The children say they sometimes flee in great numbers from one town to another, and hope to rest for a night; but while they sleep their restless enemy pursues them, and again all is distress and commotion. One of the girls goes silently by the brook, and weeps over the devastation caused in her home and family."

In the midst of her interesting labours among these poor, down-trodden, liberated slave children, ill-health came upon her with stealthy yet giant grasp. Part of this was to be attributed to lack of nourishing food, and part to the constant wearing anxiety which such a work engendered. She tells us that the flour was so stale that it had to be cleared of the insects generated in it before bread could be made of it, and that she was obliged to rest her head upon one hand while writing with the other. Still, increased opportunities of usefulness were opened up to her. For instance, on the relinquishment of the Church Missionary Society's schools at Bathurst, she took over fifty-six girls into her own school; an act of faith on her part, seeing that she did it without consultation with the Society; while her frame was already over-taxed. Still she said: "If I forego this opportunity, how can I ever forget their supplicating looks, and the expression of bitter grief on their countenances at being separated from those they desire to cleave to."

But the end was drawing near. This devoted servant of God was soon to lay down her work. Early in 1832, Mrs. Kilham went to Liberia, on a visit to the schools, leaving the house and schools at Sierra Leone in the charge of the matron and teachers. At that period the Friends contemplated carrying on two schools—one for boys, and another for girls, in England, for the liberated African children; and Mrs. Kilham's visit had reference chiefly to this matter. After accomplishing her mission, she set sail again for Sierra Leone; but the vessel had only been at sea two days when a severe storm arose, so that the captain put back to Liberia. On the following day Mrs. Kilham was taken ill of fever, and her enfeebled frame could not withstand its ravages. She speedily sunk into the arms of death, and was buried in the boundless ocean. There she sleeps, until "the trumpet shall sound;" but her work shall survive throughout eternity. Her record is on high, engraven in the book of God. "The lone blue sea" hath her remains; the billows dash over them in their restless motion, but the peace of "the better land — of the Father's house"—has long been her portion. Doubtless in the great Day of Judgment, many of Sierra Leone's enslaved children will joyfully hail Hannah Kilham as their spiritual mother.

MRS. MARY HOPE.

MRS. MARY HOPE,

Wife of the Rev. William Hope,

MISSIONARY TO KUNNUNKULUM, INDIA; OF THE CHURCH MISSIONARY SOCIETY.

"Have ye not seen the smiling
  On some beloved face,
As if heavenly sounds were wiling
  The soul from her earthly place ?
The distant sound, and sweet,
Of the Master's coming feet.

"We may clasp the dear one faster,
  And plead for a little while ;
But who can resist the Master?
  And we know by that brightening smile
That the step we may not hear
Is surely drawing near."

MISS MARY TOWNSEND was born in Exeter, September 15th, 1848, of parents who were both known and beloved for earnestness in all Christian work. Her paternal uncle was the Rev. Henry Townsend, well known for his missionary labours in Africa; and from the records of after-years, it seems probable that his devotion was the means of first turning her ideas and aspirations toward the mission-field. She appears to have been a child of tender and thoughtful mind; but the period of her confirmation seems to have ushered in a season of great spiritual blessing and consecration of life. She received her training at an educational establishment for young ladies at Blackheath; and there her influence for good was much felt by those associated with her. Speaking of this time, her old governess says : "I loved Mary dearly; she was one of my bright stars in rather a cloudy period of my life; but I blessed God for clouds and all, when I heard that she attributed her decision for the Lord's service to her residence at Blackheath." An old schoolfellow thus refers to her Christian character: "Never have I, before or since, come across such a Christian companion, or one who has exerted such power for good over me. When a girl, before she ever thought of marriage, she told me she intended, if possible, to join her uncle (the Rev. Henry Townsend, of Abeokuta) abroad, some day, to aid in his missionary work. To be a missionary was the one great desire of her life."

As young womanhood dawned upon her, this desire approached fulfilment, for she became engaged to the Rev. William Hope, of the Church Missionary Society, and prepared to be associated with him as a helpmeet, both in his life, and in his work for India. An extract from a letter, written by herself at this time, will show how she looked upon the prospect: "Oh, I do pray that nothing may step in to draw me away from looking to Christ, who must be our all in all! I have also prayed earnestly that I may not enter upon any undertaking without first asking God's holy will. I do trust that this step I am taking may prove a great blessing to myself and others. The precious promises you mentioned are most cheering and comforting." They were, shortly after, married.

Towards the end of 1868, she commenced her mission labours at Kunnunkulum, a large town in the northern part of the kingdom of Cochin, on the Malabar coast. This town was largely inhabited by Syrian Christians (or Christians of St. Thomas, as they are sometimes called); but, as it appeared, these people were decided opponents of the truth. In one of her early letters home, Mrs. Hope thus describes the mission-station : "This is such a very pretty place; the bungalow is situated on a hill, and the view of the town is very charming. I am sure you would quite enjoy it if you could only see it; but you must consider that it is a native town, not an English town. We are the only English people resident here; but I am quite sure we shall both be very happy, as there is a great work before us. The people have been sadly neglected, as there has been no resident missionary here for any length of time for many years. We have a beautiful little church, built quite close to our house, in the Early English style. We also have a very nice little harmonium, which I play every Sunday. The people like it very much; but they have no idea of singing. When the people go to church they cover their heads with a muslin cloth. You never see a man and his wife walk together—they always come separately—that is their custom. There is one very remarkable feature among these people—they are very fond of their children. My ayah and I have called to see some of them at their own houses; they have been much pleased to see me, and always want me to come in and sit down. Sometimes there is hardly any room, they have such small places; but they will put a mat down, and will think a great deal of my coming." In a later letter she thus writes of the difficulties of the work: "This place is rather trying to labour in, as there are many ways of opposition shown. I do not mean the opposition from the heathen, but from people who are connected with us. The mischief has been done in former years. The Syrians have much influence over the heathen, and it is they who raise such opposition. We have both agreed to leave them to themselves, and turn our attention to the heathen. I firmly believe that the reason our numbers are so small is to be traced to the bad influence of a corrupt church." Mrs. Hope set about opening a girls' school, but the difficulties were very great, as several years had elapsed since a resident missionary's wife had been there. It seemed almost impossible to establish a school again, but she persevered, and finally opened one with about fifteen scholars. The school-house was in a somewhat dilapidated condition, and Mrs. Hope was desirous of having another school-room built. After some obstacles had been removed, this was done, towards the end of 1869. Writing of her school, she says: "We have begun Sunday-school, instead of an afternoon-service, as we think it will be much better for the children, and then we must try to get the adults to come, some of whom are very ignorant. I do want to do what I can for these poor girls; and there are many living at out-stations, who are very ignorant, and cannot do anything but cook their rice. They have not a second idea. The only way we have of improving our Christians is to train up the children, and make them more intelligent and useful in after-years."

Mrs. Hope also endeavoured, unceasingly, to win over and influence the women for good, rightly judging that Christianity must bless the *mothers*, before the *homes* would manifest any improvement. In her own interesting way, she describes one of her mothers' meetings, the letter being dated April, 1870: "You will be much pleased to hear that I had a meeting of all the women, young and old, and their baby-children, yesterday; but it is very different to a meeting of the same character in England. My dear husband, and one of our agents, spoke to them, and we had a little singing and prayer. After tea we had a little refreshment. I gave them tea, rice, bread, and plantains. The two latter they enjoyed very much, but did not relish the tea, as they are not accustomed to drink it. I said it was very opposite to English women, as they very much enjoyed *tea*. We felt it would be a pleasant way to bring them together; but, of course, we shall not be able to do it very often, as we have a monthly prayer-meeting, to which the men come, and they have a little refreshment also. The women and men never come together; so we did not like the women entirely excluded." At this juncture, Mrs. Hope's correspondence is very full and interesting, telling of converts being won to the Saviour, of baptisms, of severe persecutions being overruled for good, of deliverances being wrought out, sometimes unexpectedly, for the young converts who were falsely accused, and of the fruition of their

GROUP OF HINDOO WOMEN.

bright hopes. Beside having the daily care of the girls' school, she kept all the mission accounts, for she was an excellent accountant and woman of business. Then little ones came, to fill the mission-house with sweetness, and her hands with loving work; but through it all her interest in the mission never flagged. She thus writes of the difficulty of providing funds for the repair of the Mission Church : " We have been very busy with the church roof, and it is finished now; every year it has to be fresh thatched, as the wood-work of the roof is not strong enough to bear tiles, and we have not money to repair it; so we shall have to let it remain in this way until we can get the needful funds. It will cost a great deal of money to do it properly. The Society is very careful of its money, as it expects the converts to begin on the self-supporting principle, but that will not do with infant missions. Our mission has gone through many changes, but we trust we may be spared to stay here, and see it more firmly established than before, though I am sure we shall have a great deal of trouble from without to contend with."

In December, 1872, some changes in the missions occurred, which indicated their removal. It was accordingly settled that they were to leave Kunnunkulum in January, 1873, then to take two months' rest and change in the Shevaroy Hills, and finally to settle down in Mavelicara, in the beginning of March. This was a year, not only of changes, but of deep affliction, as it was the year in which were first manifested the symptoms of that fatal disease which eventually brought her useful life to a close. After their removal to the Hills, a course of treatment was adopted which it was hoped would ward off the disease, but in vain. Mrs. Hope, writing to her friends, in March, spoke of her first weakness, with hopefulness, and believing in her own speedy recovery, directed them to send their letters addressed to Mavelicara, Quilon, South India. How little did she imagine that she would never see the Cochin, or Travancore, people again! Her mission to the heathen was ended. Her final testimony to them had been given at Kunnunkulum. Going down to Madras, medical advice was sought, and it was then discovered that there was a large cavity in the left lung. This was—
"The little rift within the lute,
Which, by-and-bye, would make the music mute."

On this account the doctor advised a stay at Coonoor, in the Neilgherry Hills, which was accomplished. Coonoor is a lovely place, and the sanatorium of Madras. In the hot season many people go there to reside for health's sake, as in England they do at the seaside. The views on these hills are lovely. All kinds of flowers abound —roses, geraniums, fuchsias, myrtles, and most English flowers. There are also many kinds of English fruit-trees; apple, pear, and peach trees abound. In this beautiful climate Mrs. Hope's health seemed to improve for a season, and she was able to enjoy the beautiful scenery of the Hills. It was her earnest desire that she should be raised up, as will be seen in a little note sent to a friend about this date; but life and death were subordinate to the Master's will, and she was content to leave it so. She says: "I feel I would like to write just a few lines, to tell you how loving our Heavenly Father has been in strengthening me a little. May He still continue to watch over me, and give me more strength, if it be His will, for the sake of my darling husband and children. I wish we were near you all; but I am sure you are praying for us. We have many praying friends here. Miss Gell, sister of the Bishop of Madras, is so kind in coming to see me, and in bringing me many little things to comfort me. Jesus is very precious." The Bishop of Madras, and his sister, appear to have treated Mrs. Hope with almost parental kindness; and her letters frequently bear testimony as to the affection which they had inspired in her. In September of the same year, they were back again at Madras, before the rainy season set in on the Hills, as damp of every kind was to be avoided. As usual, they still experienced much kindness from the Bishop and other Christian friends; but Mrs. Hope plaintively says: "We seem wanderers from place to place, having no settled home; but I do trust that nothing will happen to send us away from Madras, till the time comes to go to England." For it had become almost a settled point that a return to her native air must be tried, if recovery were to be gained. She says, in December of this year: "I am feeling a little stronger, and after such intense weakness, it is a great cause of thankfulness; but I am not sanguine enough to think that I shall ever be fit for much active duty, unless my native country does wonders for me. I feel, however, quite content to abide our Heavenly Father's will, for He will do what seemeth to Him good. My dear husband is in active service; he has charge of a large district, with the General Hospital to visit. He preaches five sermons a week, and sometimes he returns in the evening very exhausted; but he has great comfort in his work, having realised blessings in his ministry, especially in some cases in the Hospital." On Christmas Day she writes very touchingly, for it was her last Christmas upon earth : "We have just passed our Christmas Day—very quietly, but happily. We thought of you all, and spoke of where we were last Christmas Day, where we are now, and where would God direct us next year. We all hoped it might be in dear old Exeter." On the 13th April, 1874, Mrs. Hope, together with her husband and children, sailed from Madras in the *Khedive* for Southampton. During the first part of her voyage she rallied considerably, and hope revived. The improvement was short-lived, however, and succeeded by greater weakness. By the time they reached Gibraltar, another improvement manifested itself, and all around her united in hoping that she would, after all, be spared to see the faces of her dear ones at home. But on that same night, changes for the worse came on, and stamped their hopes as futile. From that date she steadily declined in strength; but as the body grew weaker, the soul put on fresh vigour, so that even in death she came off victorious.

Her patience and resignation were very striking, during the whole of her illness. She never murmured, and frequently said she had no fear of death. The only trouble which manifested itself was the thought that her young children might not know her in heaven. "We are told," she said, "that we shall meet as families in heaven; but my dear children will not know me there." She requested a lady who was kindly ministering to her, to read her some of Miss Charlotte Elliott's hymns. The poem entitled "The Daily Lesson," was read to her; and as it spoke somewhat sadly of the trial of being useless, bidden to sit still while the heart was eager to be up and doing, she observed: "Oh! that is exactly my case; I have felt that more than anything—so much to be done, and I am so active naturally. I have fretted more about this than about anything. For long I could not bear to lie still and do nothing—to be set aside." One day when the stewardess came into the cabin, Mrs Hope called her to her bedside, and said, after thanking her for the kindness which she had constantly shown: "Have you faith in Christ? There is only one Saviour, you know, and I want you to be a disciple of Jesus. You have been very good to me, and very kind when I have been sick; but I want you to come to heaven." The way in which she thanked the doctor, and the ladies who kindly and tenderly assisted her husband in watching by her, was very touching. One of these ladies says in a recent letter: "Her wonderful sweetness and resignation, her gentleness, and patience, touched us all, and taught a silent lesson more powerful than speech. It was quite impossible to sit there, and watch her day by day, unmurmuring and hopeful, and not to feel how strong must be the love that supported her, and how true and real the promises in which she trusted. Her thankfulness for mere momentary relief, and her gratitude to those who tried to help her were very touching. The day at Malta she seemed easier, and anxious to talk. She told me about the commencement of her illness, and her life in India, adding: "We were miles away from help, from nurse, or doctor, or medicines; we knew that no assistance could be had for a long interval of time, even in case of urgent need; but we got on very well—we trusted. I think we really seemed to live by faith." After this, her three little children were brought to her, for her to take leave of them; and when this was done, she calmly and patiently waited for the Saviour's call. That call came early on the morning of the 16th of May, 1874, about four days before reaching Southampton, in the Bay of Biscay. She was not permitted to see her friends again on earth, and without one murmur she resigned her long-cherished hopes, and looked on to the great meeting-time, when there will be no more parting. Her remains were not committed to the silent deep, but were, through the kindness of the captain, put in a shell on board, and landed at Southampton, and from thence taken on to Exeter, her native place. What a sad home-coming! And yet there was mercy in the sadness, for they were permitted to follow their loved and lost one to her last, long home, "in sure and certain hope that the separation was not for ever."

On the news of Mrs. Hope's death reaching India, letters of sympathy and sorrow came back from all who knew and loved her there. Foremost among these expressions were Christian letters from the Bishop of Madras, and his respected sister, Miss Gell. They had both ministered most lovingly to Mrs. Hope while in India, and now they strove to heal the fresh wound caused to her bereaved partner by her death. The native Christians, too, wrote in their simple affectionate style, giving utterance to their deep sorrow that their dearly beloved teacher was no more. The Christians of Kunnunkulum had manifested their affection during Mrs. Hope's short residence at Coonoor, by sending two of their number to *see* her, and to report on her condition. They took this long journey entirely at their own cost, out of pure love. When it is remembered how reluctant the Malayalim people are to leave their native land, and especially to travel over mountain districts, some idea may be realised of the sincere affection which the poor people bore for their teachers. The evident sincerity of the writers must be our excuse for quoting from one or two of their letters. A native school-master at Kunnunkulum wrote thus: "Most respected and dear sir, I beg your pardon in apologising for my long silence, caused chiefly by the sad bereavement of our respected and dear madam. Since we heard of her departure I did not know how to write of consolation under so heavy an affliction. Although it is painful either to talk or think of her removal, yet let us rejoice that she is in the enjoyment of everlasting happiness, and look forward to that happier world where we shall meet together, not to part again. She is now in the society of angels and saints: how beautiful and shining is her present garment. O how sweetly she sings, and praises the Almighty! I remember how sweet and high was her voice when she sang in the church. O how sweeter it is now we cannot imagine. We know human consolations are weak, under such circumstances, and therefore may God Himself comfort your honour amid all your sorrows." The native scripture-reader at Kunnunkulum wrote thus: "When we heard about the death of madam, we wept from the unbearable grief. I am in great confusion about the children: what shall we do? I humbly beg master to give up his sorrowful condition, and to live brave and in consolation. I am very sorry, as I am quite unable to get any more kind letters from my dear madam. But I am sure that I shall see her in heaven; and I must humbly beg master not to forget me till he leaves this world. I write to master with my tears. I wish to hear that master will come back to India, and I pray the Almighty for that purpose continually."

Thus ends the record of a life which, though brief on earth and uneventful, as compared with many, yet left fruits which will last throughout eternity. Although cut short, her life was not "thrown away;" it was full of bright, earnest, patient, loving work for the Master; and *His* Word is—" Whoso loseth his life for my sake shall find it." Mrs. Hope has now entered into *the rest,* and the *thousandfold* " *recompense of the reward.*"

"Life is the hallowed sphere
Of sacred duties to our fellow-men,
The precious and appointed season, when
    Sweet deeds of love the mourner's heart may cheer;
The hour of patient and unwearied toil,
When seed of heaven is sown in earth's dark soil.

"Ours is this work below:
Our lips may breathe the message of the cross,
Which soothes the sinner's anguish and remorse,
    Irradiates with joy the grief-worn brow,
Flings hope's bright sunshine on the pilgrim's road,
And plants in man's cold heart sweet trust in God.

"How glorious is life
Thus consecrated; and how poor appears,
    Beside the Christian's struggles, toils, and tears,
The earthly warrior's sacrifice or strife!
Beautiful are the efforts faith employs
To fill this earth with heaven's immortal joys."

FINIS.

www.ingramcontent.com/pod-product-compliance
Lightning Source LLC
Chambersburg PA
CBHW032109230426
43672CB00009B/1688